Handbook for Academic Authors

Handbook
for
Academic Authors

Third Edition

BETH LUEY
Arizona State University

CAMBRIDGE
UNIVERSITY PRESS

Published by the Press Syndicate of the University of Cambridge
The Pitt Building, Trumpington Street, Cambridge CB2 1RP
40 West 20th Street, New York, NY 10011-4211, USA
10 Stamford Road, Oakleigh, Melbourne 3166, Australia

First published 1987
Second edition 1990
Reprinted 1991, 1992, 1994
Third edition 1995

Printed in the United States of America

Library of Congress Cataloging-in-Publication Data
Luey, Beth.
Handbook for academic authors / Beth Luey. – 3rd ed.
p. cm.
Includes bibliographical references and index.
ISBN 0-521-49549-0. – ISBN 0-521-49892-9 (pbk.)
1. Authorship. 2. Authors and publishers. I. Title.
PN146.L84 1995
808'.02 – dc20 95-7148

A catalog record for this book is available from the British Library.

ISBN 0-521-49549-0 hardback
ISBN 0-521-49892-9 paperback

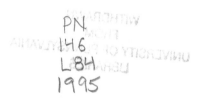

For Mike and Nora, again

Contents

Contents

Contents

Illustrations

Preface

In 1980, after ten years as an editor of scholarly books and textbooks, I began teaching scholarly editing and publishing. I soon learned that my faculty colleagues regarded me as a window onto a mysterious and often frustrating publishing world. They asked my advice on questions ranging from semicolons to royalties, from en dashes to remainders. At the same time, they informed me of a number of publishers' practices – many admirable, some reprehensible – that I had never encountered.

As a teacher, I met daily with students who were curious about aspects of publishing that I had avoided. I have little artistic ability, for example, and had always regarded book design as magic. That explanation was clearly inadequate for bright, curious graduate students. My expertise in the dollars-and-cents area of publishing was equally sad; to correct my deficiencies, I even went so far as to take an accounting course so that I could use the proper terms in explicating the financial arcana.

In 1982 I began to worry that my theoretical knowledge, though apparently sound, was untested. Besides, I had some ideas for books that needed to be written. I formed a small publishing company and, with the assistance of my husband on legal and financial matters, learned firsthand the realities of what I was teaching. There is no better way to learn the economics of publishing than to invest your own money. Nor is there any better motivation to improve your marketing skills than to have your closets taken over by unsold books.

Having been editor, indexer, publisher, production manager, marketing manager, and shipping clerk, I decided it was time to try being an author. The result is this book. I have tried to test my advice by following it, and so far it has worked. I have also discovered that I am not immune to authorial paranoia and irrationality. Although Colin Day, my editor at Cambridge, diligently kept me informed of the manuscript's progress, I was periodically convinced that it had been sucked into a black hole. And although the copy editing was tactful, the green deletion of every little comma nevertheless caused a twinge of psychic pain. I have added empathy to my professional skills.

Finally, a word about this book and Cambridge University Press. Relations between author and publisher are always complex. They are doubly so when the book is about publishing. The book is not an official Cambridge guide for authors. It describes the general range of publishing practices, not all of which the Press follows. I sent a prospectus to a dozen presses. I submitted the completed manuscript to Cambridge and received a contract four months later. Only after acceptance did they offer generous assistance and suggestions. More than a half-dozen people in the New York and Cambridge offices commented in detail on the manuscript, but at no time did anyone attempt to dictate content. I incorporated their suggestions happily – when I agreed with them. But the ideas and opinions in this book are my own.

I am grateful to many employers, colleagues, and friends in scholarly publishing who have shared their ideas, pleasures, and frustrations, especially Margot Barbour, John Bergez, Georges Borchardt, Louise Craft, Fred Hetzel, Naomi Pascal, Elizabeth Shaw, and Phyllis Steckler. My colleagues at Arizona State University have helped me understand authors' problems and puzzlements. I must especially thank Brian Gratton, who not only commented extensively on several chapters but also convinced me to learn to use a computer so that I could finish the book promptly. I have edited books for more than a hundred authors, and I have learned something from each of them. I must thank my students, who have taught me a great deal. Finally, Cambridge University Press – personified in Colin Day, Rhona Johnson, Brigitte Lehner, and Christopher Scarles – has been prompt, courteous, helpful, and enthusiastic: an exemplary publisher.

Preface to the Second Edition

Soon after the first edition of this book appeared, it became clear that publishing practices were changing so rapidly that I needed to begin thinking about a new edition. The most significant change has been in the expanded use of computers for composition and desktop typesetting. A clear majority of academic authors write with computers, and the practice of typesetting from authors' disks has moved beyond the experimental stage. This edition therefore has a new chapter, Chapter 10 [Chapter 11, in the third edition], about using the computer and about electronic publishing: databases, CD-ROMs, and the like.

Another change has occurred in the structure of the publishing industry, which has become increasingly global. Commercial scholarly publishing has a greater presence in the United States because of the expansion of British and European houses into the U.S. market both through the opening of new offices and by the acquisition of U.S. firms. Although the long-term implications of internationalization remain unclear, it seems important to provide more information about commercial scholarly publishing and about the practices of transatlantic publishers. You will find most of this information in Chapter 4, but it appears throughout the book wherever it is relevant.

My own experience has expanded over the past three years to include editing the journal *Book Research Quarterly*, retitled *Publishing Research Quarterly* in 1991. As a result I have expanded Chapter 2 to add what I have learned. I am also working on a book about grants for publication, and I have provided an introduction to that subject in Chapter 5 and in the appendix. I have updated the bibliography and incorporated some of the suggestions made by reviewers of the first edition, to whom I am grateful.

Preface to the Third Edition

The five years since the second edition of this book appeared have witnessed economic and technological changes in scholarly publishing and in the academic world. The nation's economic recovery has not been reflected in the budgets of colleges and universities. The anticipated improvement in the market for Ph.D.'s has not occurred, and academic jobs remain scarce. Library book budgets have shrunk, reducing the sales of scholarly publishers. University press budgets have suffered along with those of academic departments, and presses are more than ever tightening their belts and seeking new markets.

There are some brighter spots, however. Personal computers have made it easier for authors to prepare manuscripts and cheaper for publishers to manufacture them. Electronic networks and CD-ROM technology have created new products and more efficient distribution methods. The technology is young, and neither publishers nor authors are entirely comfortable with it, but it is promising. For example, although university presses are not putting their books online, you will find their catalogues on the Internet.

For the academic author, these changes mean that publication is more important than ever, more difficult than it has been, and likely to take new forms. In this edition, I have tried to help authors adjust to this new climate by providing current information on both the state of new technologies and their meaning to authors. I have revised Chapter 12 to reflect the changing costs associated with reduced print runs.

Most important, I have added a chapter on writing for general readers. I did so not only because scholarly publishers are eagerly expanding into this market, but because the understanding of scholarship that such books generate may be the best way to maintain and extend public support of education and research.

Chapter 1

The Publishing Partnership

> I promise to do all I can to make you a great publisher even as
> I expect you to do all you can to make me a great author.
>   Robert Frost to Alfred Harcourt

Faculty members are always writing or talking about writing and of necessity are always thinking about publishing. Each has an article nearly finished, about to be started, or stuck somewhere in the middle. Many have a book manuscript under way or under consideration at a press. And some are complaining, half-sincerely, about the tedium of reading galleys. Although writing and publishing are discrete processes, they are interdependent. Why write if no one will publish? And what is there to publish if no one writes?

Despite this obvious interdependence, academic authors and publishers of scholarly books and journals do not always understand each other very well, and they sometimes find it difficult to coexist peacefully. Publishers and journal editors lose sight of the tremendous pressure to publish that is exerted on scholars, particularly young, untenured scholars. Authors, for their part, are guilty of not understanding either how publishing works or how to use the system to their advantage.

Publishers' ignorance of a scholar's plight, although somewhat dysfunctional, does serve a purpose. The editor considering a manuscript who remains conscious at every moment that the fate of another human being is at stake may not make the best decision. Especially in this period of nearly nonexistent academic jobs and often unrealistic administrative demands for "productivity," failure to publish early and often may force a scholar to resort to driving a cab or even enrolling in law school. But the editor who too generously takes that into account and publishes too many marginal manuscripts may also end up driving a cab. Authors' ignorance of publishing, however, is both self-imposed and self-destructive. It is not difficult to learn how the world of scholarly publishing works, and it is foolish not to make the effort. Once you understand what publishers want from authors, it is easy enough to provide it and thereby improve your chances of publication. That is what this book is designed to help you do.

Publishing What You Write: How to Use This Book

In an ideal world, people would write only when they had something important to say. Discovery or inspiration would be the driving force. In the real world, though, this is only one of several worthy motives. Academic authors do write for the pure joy of communicating ideas, but they also write for tenure, money, and fame.

Let us assume for the moment that you are writing because you want to get tenure, be promoted, or get a raise. Perhaps you want to publish so that you can find another teaching job at a more hospitable institution. In these cases, depending on your field, you are going to have to write articles for scholarly journals and possibly a book or two for scholarly presses. Because university administrators believe that the refereeing procedures of these journals and presses guarantee the scholarly value of the works they publish, they accept such publication as evidence of the author's scholarly accomplishments. Chapter 2 explains how to find an appropriate journal for your work and how to speed up the refereeing process; it also offers some suggestions about effective article writing and about revising talks and speeches for publication. Chapter 3 is devoted to the problems of revising a dissertation for book or journal publication. Chapter 4 describes the various sorts of book publishers and tells how to decide which publisher would be best for your book. It also suggests ways to make acceptance more likely. Chapter 5 tells how to work with a publisher, including an explanation of how to read your contract and a discussion of how to seek grants for publication costs. In Chapter 6, I offer advice on editing multiauthor books and compiling anthologies.

Perhaps you are not concerned about tenure or promotion but do want to make some money. In that case, skip the journals and monographs and get to work on a textbook. (Either that or shift to romance fiction or diet books.) Journals do not pay authors, and few scholarly books generate significant royalties. Writing textbooks, however, can be profitable. As you will learn, the money is not quick or easy. Writing a textbook usually will not help you get tenure, because deans and other administrators mistakenly exclude textbook writing from scholarly activity. Although writing a textbook does not require original research, it does demand a comprehensive knowledge of the field and an original, well thought out perspective on it. Chapters 7 and 8 will help you write a textbook, find a publisher, and see the project through to completion.

If it is fame that you seek, you need to write a book that nonacademics will read, that will be reviewed in newspapers and popular magazines, and that will be stocked in respectable numbers in bookstores. This is not as easy as it sounds and requires authors to involve themselves in the publishing process in new ways. And although writing books for general readers is more profitable than writing monographs, it is typically less lucrative than writing textbooks. Chapter 9 discusses the writing, publishing, and economics of trade books.

Chapter 10 explains the mechanics of authorship, regardless of whether you are writing a journal article, monograph, textbook, or trade book: how to prepare a typescript, obtain permission to quote and to reproduce illustrations, proofread, and index a book. Chapter 11 provides help in using computers to prepare a manuscript so that your disks can be used for typesetting, explains how to create camera-ready copy, and introduces electronic publishing.

Because money is so often a bone of contention, I have summarized the economics of book publishing in Chapter 12. There you will find an explanation of why books cost so much and where the money goes.

Finally, the bibliography, which is briefly annotated, lists books on writing, guides to journals in various fields, style guides, and further information on most topics covered in the book. It is organized topically, following the order of the text.

Publishing can lead to security, status, wealth, and (occasionally) fame; surely it is worth the effort to learn a bit about it. This book is an introduction to scholarly publishing. The serious writer needs several other books as well.

The Scholar's Bookshelf

Anyone who writes should own *The Elements of Style* by William Strunk Jr. and E. B. White. This brief paperback solves the most common difficulties of grammar and diction and offers sound, memorable advice on clear writing. I read it once a year without fail. (Full information about this and all other works mentioned in this book is provided in the bibliography.)

You must also own a good dictionary. Although the Merriam-Webster dictionaries (the third edition of the unabridged or the latest collegiate edition) are the most generally accepted, I prefer the *American Heritage Dictionary* because it provides good usage notes and has a more pleasing layout. Other popular dictionaries are the *Oxford American Dictionary* and the *Random House Dictionary*. If you plan to write a book, you must own *The Chicago Manual of Style*. Nearly every book publisher relies on it, and it is the authority for many fields on note and bibliography style. It also tells you how to proofread and index your book. It is fairly expensive, but it is worth buying. In 1993 it went into its fourteenth edition, and the references in this book are to that edition. If you deal with British publishers or journals, Judith Butcher's *Copy-Editing: The Cambridge Handbook* will be helpful. The writer about to revise a dissertation will find *The Thesis and the Book*, edited by Eleanor Harman and Ian Montagnes, helpful. It is available in paperback.

If you become interested in the world of academic publishing, you may want to subscribe to the *Journal of Scholarly Publishing* (formerly *Scholarly Publishing*), a quarterly journal of interest to authors and editors, published by the University of Toronto Press, and to *Publishing Research Quarterly* (formerly *Book Research Quarterly*), published by Transaction Publishers. If you do not subscribe, make sure your library does and take time to browse through the journals occasionally. *The American Scholar* includes at least one article a year on some aspect of book publishing.

The Publishing Partnership

While authors are worrying about getting their books published, editors are out busily acquiring manuscripts. It is the same process viewed from different angles. The reputations of authors and publishers ride on the same books. When a book is well reviewed or even wins a prestigious award, both author and publisher share the glory. The book that succeeds commercially puts money into both the publisher's coffers and the author's pocket. When a book fails – critically, financially, or aesthetically – author and publisher share the disappointment. Why, then, is there conflict between partners?

Ignorance is one source of conflict. The author who does not understand the refereeing process, who does not read the contract, and who does not learn to proofread is bound to be unhappy with how long it takes to get a book accepted, to feel cheated on discovering that most publishers do not provide an index, and to become outraged when a reviewer points out typos.

Illusions about money are another source of friction. An author whose book is priced at $40.00 and whose royalty is 10 percent figures "$4.00 per book, and they're printing 1,500, so I should get $6,000." Unfortunately, the royalty may be paid on net receipts (20 to 40 percent less than gross), at least 100 copies will be given away free for reviews and publicity, and not all the other copies will be sold. When the first royalty check arrives and the author gets, say, $1,500 – knowing that the first year is probably the best – disappointment sets in. With disappointment comes suspicion. Where does the rest of the money go, anyway? Authors who do not know what it costs to produce a book and who do not understand prices and discounts are apt to think mistakenly that presses are getting rich from their labors. They are not. University presses do make money on some titles but rarely more than the authors do. Successful trade books do make money, but authors should not be misled by the six-figure advances paid to a handful of bestselling authors. For most serious nonfiction books, royalties are respectable but far from extravagant. Textbooks, too, should make money for both author and publisher, with the amount depending on the number of students who enroll in the relevant courses, the book's share of the market, and the book's longevity. Throughout this book, I explain the financial implications of various policies, and Chapter 12 discusses the economics of scholarly publishing in some detail. I hope that this will reduce one source of mistrust.

Editorial changes can lead to disputes. Most writers have worked hard on their manuscripts, and many resent any attempt to alter their words and punctuation. They view the editor's suggestions as attempts to take over their books, and they see editorial queries as questioning their authority. The editor, however, is trying to correct errors, clarify meaning, and eliminate clumsy constructions in order to make the author's book better. I hope that the sections in Chapters 5, 8, and 9 on working with your editor will help you to develop happy and productive relationships with those who labor to improve your writing.

Some authors also fear that their publishers are not doing

enough to sell their books. The level of marketing effort, and the types of marketing activity undertaken, will depend on the nature of your book and the publisher's estimate of the size of the audience. Chapters 5 and 9 explain the marketing strategies of scholarly and trade publishers and suggest ways authors can cooperate in reaching the largest possible market.

Much of the conflict between authors and publishers is rooted in the very interdependence that also makes them partners. Authors resent having their professional stature and even their livelihoods rest in the hands of nonacademics. And just as faculty members often comment on how great teaching would be if it weren't for the students, publishers occasionally long for the day when books would magically appear without authors. With a little understanding, however, the two sides can get along quite nicely.

This book is, in a sense, an effort at making peace as well as informing. The writer who understands publishers will be more successful in dealing with them and will make the publisher's life much easier. Writers may view my effort as one-sided, since all the instruction is directed at them. Throughout the book, though, I have set a high standard of behavior for publishers and have suggested ways authors can hold publishers to these standards. For most authors, publishing is rewarding and even fun. Needless to say, the same is true for most editors, or they would be in a better-paid field. I hope that this book will make publishing easier for both authors and publishers and that it will reduce the friction that often seems inevitable.

Chapter 2

Journal Articles

He put his hand into the well-known nook under the pillow: only, it did not get so far. What he touched was, according to his account, a mouth, with teeth, and with hair about it, and, he declares, not the mouth of a human being. . . . "Gayton, I believe that alchemist man knows it was I who got his paper rejected."

M. R. James, "Casting the Runes"

Journals are the vehicle most frequently used by academic authors for disseminating the results of their research. In some fields, particularly in the natural and physical sciences, book writing is rare. A biochemist may publish hundreds of journal articles and never think of writing a book. Journals are also the least professionalized of the publishing media. In the humanities and social sciences, journals are often edited on the side by academics with regular teaching and research assignments and without professional staff.[1] (This is less common in the physical and natural sciences.) The advent of personal computers, relatively inexpensive phototypesetting,

[1] Should you ever become a journal editor, you will want to consult an excellent handbook: Lois DeBakey, *The Scientific Journal: Editorial Policies and Practices: Guidelines for Editors, Reviewers, and Authors* (St. Louis: Mosby, 1976). Although written primarily for those in the medical sciences, it contains thoughtful discussions of issues facing all journal editors, as well as excellent practical advice on organizing an editorial office. On the nuts and bolts, including financial questions, you will find help in *Journal Publishing: Principles and Practice,* by Gillian Page, Robert Campbell, and Jack Meadows (Boston: Butterworth, 1987).

and desktop publishing has led to the creation of numerous small, specialized journals run out of faculty offices. Electronic journals that are "printed" only on one's computer screen are also beginning to appear; these are even easier to start and cheaper to distribute.

The growth of specialized journals since the 1960s has expanded opportunities for publication. At the same time, the end of the academic hiring boom of that decade and the stabilization of the size of the academic community have decreased the number of submissions received by many journals. This adds up to improved possibilities for getting good articles published, even if they are on very specialized topics. To take full advantage of these opportunities, authors need to write well, select carefully the journals to which they submit their work, prepare their manuscripts properly, and communicate well with journal editors.

Writing Well

Good academic writing is clear and succinct. (To use myself as an example, I first wrote that sentence: "For the purposes of academic writing, writing well is writing clearly and succinctly." I read it, saw that it was neither clear nor succinct, and rewrote it. One key to being a good academic writer is having the patience to reread and revise.) If you can move beyond clarity to grace and elegance, you are to be congratulated. Editors will happily settle for clarity, however.

Many fields have formal conventions about article writing: All articles are organized in the same way, with subsections covering specified topics (e.g., title, abstract, introduction, method, results, discussion, references). Because disciplines vary, you should familiarize yourself with the conventions of the field in which you are publishing. If this is the field in which you have done most of your research, you probably have absorbed such conventions subliminally. You will have to make a special effort, though, if you are writing in an area outside your usual territory (e.g., a historian venturing into a medical journal or a lawyer writing for a psychology journal). The bibliography of this book includes the official style manuals for a variety of disciplines. If your discipline has a generally accepted style manual, you should own and use the current edition. The bibliography also includes several general guides to writing, guides to writing for specific fields, and dictionaries.

Intelligent readers are impressed by ideas and clear expression, not by elaborate constructions and excess words. If your writing is obscure, vague, and verbose, readers will translate what you have written into plain English and wonder why you did not write it that way in the first place. There are two possible answers, neither of which is flattering. First, perhaps you did not know how. More damning, perhaps you realized that reduced to plain English your idea did not make sense or was so obvious that it wasn't worth saying. Good writing saves the reader's time and your reputation.

Beyond the basic advice on writing offered by Strunk and White in *The Elements of Style,* I can offer a few suggestions that may help you avoid errors common in academic writing.[2] A frequent error is the use of jargon. It is easy to forget that the lingua franca of your discipline frequently departs from standard English. However, it is rarely necessary to use a word that is not in the dictionary. This does not mean that you should avoid technical language, for a technical term often expresses an idea most economically and will be understood by your readers. In writing for specialized journals you need not worry about whether a layperson will understand a given term, because no layperson will read it. To determine whether you are using technical expressions appropriately or whether you are simply resorting to jargon, ask yourself if you are using the plainest word that will say precisely what you mean. Do not use technical words merely to impress. It sometimes can be helpful to define technical terms precisely, within your

---

[2] If English is not your native language, you will find assistance in Gregory A. Barnes, *Communication Skills for the Foreign-Born Professional* (Philadelphia: ISI Press, 1982).

article, to ensure that you are using them properly and that your readers will understand exactly what you mean. Technical terms can take on a life of their own if not used carefully.

Bureaucratic language is a form of jargon that provokes the special ire of editors and careful readers. Do not use *finalize, monies,* or *debrief* when you mean *finish, money, or question.* (Reading Edwin Newman's books, listed in the bibliography, should cure you of this tendency.) Equally to be avoided is trendy language, which rapidly becomes overused and then dated. "Excellence," "the best and the brightest," and "the right stuff" all fell victim to this phenomenon, but even words that have not been used in book titles are vulnerable. (I once deleted "the agony and the ecstasy" from a technical report for the Department of Defense.) Some of these – though not all – were perfectly good words at one time, but overuse has worn them out. If you feel you must choose between being stuffy and being trendy (a false dilemma), choose stuffy.

Also avoid cuteness, especially in titles. Your title, of course, should be brief and should tell the reader what your article is about. Occasionally a title can be used to attract attention but usually not in a scholarly journal. If a title is not clear, your article may be indexed incorrectly, so that it goes unread and uncited.

Another frequent fault in academic writing is the repetition of certain words, notably qualifying adverbs and abstract nouns. *Rather, quite,* and *somewhat* can usually be omitted without sacrificing meaning. Similarly, you should rewrite sentences to avoid the use of such phrases as "friendly by nature," "in terms of," "on a weekly basis," "generous in character," and "for the purpose of."

Even if you are deaf to the beauty of language, you can be accurate. Check and recheck all quotations. A literary scholar once quoted Macbeth's hags on the heath as chanting, "Double bubble toil and trouble." The failure of referees to catch such mistakes should not be taken as license to butcher the Bard – or anyone else. Also, be accurate and complete in the citations you provide in notes and bibliographies. Any of the style manuals in the bibliography – including, of course, *The Chicago Manual of Style* – will assist you in this task. Some journals and a few book publishers routinely check citations, but you should not rely on this. The reader who cannot find an article using your citation has good reason to doubt your reliability.

In sum, you can write well by being clear, direct, precise, and accurate. If you can accomplish this apparently modest goal – and if you have something new and important to say – you will be on your way to publication.

Selecting a Journal

Few journals tolerate multiple submissions. In fact, some regard this as a sin so serious that they report it to the author's department chair. Because you can send your work to only one journal at a time, you should choose carefully. The best way to decide where to submit an article is to look through the journals you read regularly. As long as you are writing in the mainstream of your own discipline, one of these journals will probably be the place to start. If, however, you have ventured into new territory, you will have to do some exploring. Investigate journals cited in your manuscript first. Many field-specific guides to journals are published (see bibliography), and you should consult them. This rooting around will produce a list of journals that cover your subject area. The guides will often provide further information, such as maximum length of articles, usual time for review, preferred style, percentage of submissions accepted, and time between accceptance and publication. Because journals frequently change editors and addresses, however, and because policies change, you should always consult the latest issue of the journal to verify its current location, staff, and editorial policy.

Most journal editors do not welcome query letters, so it is up to you to decide whether a journal is appropriate or not. If a journal regularly publishes articles in your field and of the same length and scope as yours, then it is appropriate. Do not, for example, submit a bibliographical review to a journal that never includes such reviews, even if it does include other sorts of articles in the same field. When you have a list of journals, look at the current issue of each. Many journals include a description of editorial requirements; all provide an address to write to if such information is not published. You may have to eliminate some journals from your list because your article is too long or too short or because your article is illustrated and they do not accept artwork. Perusing a few issues may also disclose an ideological or theoretical bias that renders the journal unsuitable. You may decide to eliminate others because they seem sloppily produced or edited. Take a look at the date of the current issue to see whether the journal is hopelessly behind schedule.

If, contrary to the norm, the journal's note to contributors or directory listing indicates that the editor does expect a query letter, compose a brief one that includes the subject of your article, why you believe it is suitable for the journal, and why it is worth publishing. Also include a physical description (length, illustrated or not, how many notes, and so forth). If your manuscript is on a computer disk, say so. You may send such query letters simultaneously to as many journals as you like; the single-submission rule applies only to the full manuscript.

In deciding where to submit, you first may want to figure out whether to choose a less prestigious journal that you think will probably accept your article and publish it quickly or to begin by trying for one of the big names. This decision will depend on your own impression of how administrators evaluate publications, on how much of a hurry you are in, and of course on how much you yourself value publication in a major journal. Do not automatically assume that a lesser journal represents your best bet. Journals are quirky, and you may find your work rejected in the minor leagues and accepted in the majors. However, remember that more prestigious journals may take longer to get your work into print because of backlogs of accepted articles. They may also demand more extensive revisions than lesser journals. Whenever possible, choose a refereed journal – that is, a journal whose submissions are reviewed by outside readers in addition to the editor. Most universities distinguish between articles in refereed and nonrefereed journals when awarding tenure and raises, but many do not distinguish among refereed journals. You can find this out from your colleagues and chair.

Your colleagues are also a good source of information on how prompt a journal is about refereeing, how quickly articles are put into print, and how well promises are kept. You should take much of this information with a grain or two of salt, since horror stories abound. (For truly terrifying and entertaining accounts of how bad things can get, see the articles by Robert C. Maddox and Jack B. Ridley listed in the bibliography.) If you get consistent accounts of mistreatment by a journal, put it low on your list.

You also may want to ask one or two colleagues to read your article before you send it off. You probably know who is likely to be helpful in providing suggestions on content, organization, and writing. If you do this, however, be prepared for criticism and accept it graciously. If you just want a pat on the back or uncritical encouragement, read the article to your dog.

After reading the manuscript, your colleagues may suggest a journal that you had not thought of. Do not take the suggestion without checking the journal yourself for appropriateness and editorial requirements.

Another way to get criticism of your work is to present the paper at a national or regional meeting or at a less formal colloquium. Some writers regard such public presentation as insurance against plagiarism by referees. Such dishonesty is too rare, however, to make this a genuine concern. The real value lies in the opportunity to receive criticism and suggestions.

Some authors achieve lengthy publication lists by recycling their research. They change the emphasis slightly, alter the length, rephrase, add a section or two, and submit two or three articles instead of one. Although journal editors and subscribers may initially be unaware that they are being victimized in this way, eventually word gets out. Both editors and colleagues read more than one journal. Although this practice is legal, it is ethically questionable and wastes the time of editors, referees, and readers. In the medical sciences, it can have serious consequences for patients. A researcher doing a meta-analysis (a synthesis of several studies on, for example, nonsurgical treatment of a specific cancer) may unknowingly be counting the results of a single study more than once, if its authors have published it more than once. This duplication will alter the statistical results and may mislead practitioners into thinking that a treatment is more (or less) effective than it really is.

On the rare occasion when republication of material is appropriate – for example, if the first appearance was a brief note in a journal with very limited circulation, or in another language – you should nevertheless tell the editor the circumstances of the first publication. Enclosing a copy of the original article or manuscript will enable the editor to verify the differences and make an informed decision.

A variant on duplicate publication is "salami publishing," in which each bit of research is divided into the thinnest possible slices (sometimes referred to as "LPUs," for "least publishable units"), with each slice submitted as a separate article. This is marginally more ethical than duplicate submission, but it is equally wasteful. Nor is it clear that it does the slicer much good. In any serious review of a scholar's work (for tenure, promotion, or major grants), reviewers look at all of the applicant's work as a body. If there is only one ounce of salami there, slicing it thin doesn't make it any weightier. One significant article in a major journal almost always benefits a researcher's career more than four or five trivial pieces scattered in lesser publications.

Another way that lengthy bibliographies are built is by overstating the number of authors. In the humanities, where single authorship is the rule, this rarely happens. But when scientists work in research teams, each team (or sometimes each department or institution) sets rules for who may be considered an author. (In a few cases, more than a hundred authors have been listed for a single article.) Some professional societies are trying to establish standard definitions of authorship, but so far none has been widely adopted. Most standards revolve around two issues: knowledge and responsibility. To be listed as an author, one should have direct knowledge of the conduct and results of the entire study and should be willing to take responsibility for its conduct, data, and conclusions. In the absence of accepted standards, each author must follow the guidelines of institution and conscience.

Preparing the Manuscript

The general rules for preparing an article manuscript for publication are very simple: type neatly on 20-lb, white 8½- by 11-inch bond (not erasable bond) paper, double-space (text, notes, and bibliography), and leave ample margins on all four sides (at least 1 inch). If you use a computer, print the article on a laser or letter-quality printer if possible, but at least make sure that the print is dark enough to photocopy well. It is usually all right to send a photocopy if it is of good quality and on ordinary paper. Carbon copies are not acceptable. Some people argue that sending the original assures the editor that you are not submitting the article elsewhere. The fallacy of this argument is obvious, particularly in the era of computer-generated "multiple originals."

Beyond these commonsense requirements, be sure to follow the instructions provided by the journal to which you are submitting the paper. Specifically, if the journal's format includes notes in a particular place and in a particular style, comply with these conventions. Conforming to a given footnote style can be a nuisance if journals in your field do not agree on which style to use. Using a computer, however, it is not that difficult to change from one footnote style to another; some word-processing programs have the basic styles built in. If the editor wants two copies of your manuscript, send two copies. If the journal publishes abstracts, prepare one. If quotations must be in English, provide translations. If the journal follows the style book of the Modern Language Association, American Psychological Association, Council of Biology Editors, or some other professional organization, or if it has its own style sheet, get the style guide and follow it. (See the bibliography for a list of style guides.)

Proofread the manuscript carefully (see Chapter 10) and correct it neatly. Make sure you have a printed copy of your own, even if the manuscript is also on a computer disk. If you send your manuscript on a disk, keep a backup disk as well as hard copy.

Unless you are told otherwise, be sure to provide a title page with your name, address, and article title. Repeat only the title on the first page of the text. Do not put your name on each page, because this makes it difficult to implement blind reviewing, in which referees are not told the author's identity. Mail the manuscript flat, not folded, and enclose a self-addressed envelope of appropriate size with return postage. Send it first class. If you want reassurance that the manuscript arrived safely, send it by certified mail with a return receipt or enclose a self-addressed, stamped postcard. Journals should automatically acknowledge receipt of submissions, but not all of them do. When submitting articles to journals outside the United States, enclose International Reply Coupons for return postage. They can be purchased at the post office.

A brief cover letter is adequate unless you have something specific to tell the editor. For example, if you have sent photocopies of artwork, you might want to let the editor know that you have the originals and will obtain permission to use them. (On illustrations and permissions, see Chapter 10.) Let the editor know if your manuscript is on disk. Some journals are able to use authors' disks, and a few even give precedence to such manuscripts in scheduling. Some require that you provide disks and even specify acceptable word-processing programs.

Refereeing

On refereed journals, experts review submissions; for nonrefereed journals, the judgment of the editor or the editorial staff suffices. Thus, editors of nonrefereed journals can make decisions faster, but publication in these journals does not offer the prestige or the assistance provided by the refereeing process. The notion that refereeing provides a service to a would-be contributor may be alien to the author busily collecting rejections or requests for revision. Nevertheless, it is a service. Referees can save an author from mistakes of fact, poor logic, ignorance of sources, and other embarrassments. Their purpose is not merely to screen out bad articles but also to recognize good ones and help move articles from the unacceptable category into the acceptable. Although you should not expect referees to correct minor details or rewrite bad prose, they will often give general advice on further sources or weaknesses in your argument whose correction would make your work publishable. Certainly not all criticism is constructive, but much of it is. As an academic writer, you are likely to wear the hats of both referee and author during your career. To perform both jobs well, you should try to keep in mind what it is like to be under the other hat.

Most articles are read first by an editor who determines whether they are appropriate for the journal and good enough to be sent to a referee. "Good enough" may mean sufficiently original and interesting, adequately researched and documented, clearly written, or all of these. Articles that survive this initial scrutiny are then sent to at least one referee, who is either a member of the editorial board or a specialist unaffiliated with the journal except as an occasional reviewer. Journal editors may ask referees specific questions about the article or ask them to fill out a form; some ask for a "grade" in addition to comments and recommendations. More often, however, the referee is asked merely whether the article should be published in the journal and why or why not. The major scientific and medical journals have an even more elaborate refereeing process that may include review by a statistician or other technical experts in addition to review by outside referees.

Referees have a great responsibility, and no one who is not willing to take the job seriously should agree to review an article. A referee must be competent in the field (and that includes being familiar with current research), able to judge other people's work objectively, willing to spend the time it takes to evaluate the article and make useful suggestions, and committed to doing all of this under a deadline. As a contributor, you expect this of referees. When you yourself are asked to be a referee, make sure you meet your own standards.

Because most people who write articles also judge other authors' work, you may need some more advice about what to do when wearing the referee's hat. As you read an article, you will be asking yourself a number of questions: Is the topic worth investigating? Is the author's research sound? Have the relevant sources been tapped? Is the thesis clearly and convincingly argued? Does the evidence support the thesis? Is the article adequately documented? Is the writing clear and succinct? Did I learn anything from reading this? One question you should not ask yourself is, Is this the way I would have written the article? The least fair, least useful reviews result from asking this question. One reason research is fun and exciting is that no two people approach a question in the same way. Perhaps you would have done it differently, and perhaps your way would have been better, but that is not the issue. You have been asked to evaluate an article as written, on its own terms. Do so.

Remember, too, that the manuscript you have been sent is a privileged communication. You must not cite it or use it in any way. You should not show it to others or discuss its contents. If you feel that a colleague or graduate student might be a better referee, ask the editor's permission before passing it on. Communicate with the author only through the editor.

It is possible – and in some fields even probable – that a second journal will send the same article to the same referee that the first journal used. If you are asked to referee an article that you have previously advised be rejected, you should behave in a civilized, ethical manner. It is not acceptable to blight anonymously and eternally another person's career. The solution least prejudicial to the author, yet helpful to the editor, is to decline without reason and suggest another referee. There is an exception to this rule: an article that you felt was inappropriate for journal A but all right for journal B. It is of course reasonable to referee an article for journal B that you recommended for publication to journal A but that its editor nevertheless declined. (Do not be outraged if this happens. The journal editor or another referee may have disagreed, or perhaps the author declined to make changes required by the editor.)

Now, back to the author's hat. While one or more referees are reading your manuscript, what are you doing? Not sitting at home chewing your nails, I hope. You already have a second journal in mind for your article in case the first one rejects it. (In an article offering suggestions on journal writing, Richard Penaskovic recommends using the term *returned* rather than *rejected*. You, too, may find this comforting.) You are launched on a new project. But you have not forgotten about your article. On your calendar, about three months after the date you submitted your article, you have written a note reminding yourself to send the editor a polite note: "On 5 September I sent you my article on the lost continent of Atlantis. When may I expect a response?" Mark a date three or four weeks ahead for another inquiry if you have not received an answer by then. If you still have no answer five months after your initial submission, telephone. Then, if the response is inadequate, write to the editor, withdrawing your article from consideration, and send it elsewhere. (You need not wait for the physical return of your manuscript.) For articles in the sciences, or in any case where timely publication is vital because of the article's subject, this timetable should be speeded up considerably.

Good News, Bad News

When a journal accepts your article, the editor may publish it as is or ask for revisions. If revisions are required, make sure you understand exactly what is wanted. For example, if the article is to be shortened, by how much? If you are to shorten the article, yet include additional material, how is this miracle to be accomplished? Find out when the revised manuscript is due. Make sure, too, that the article will definitely be published if you make the revisions. Sometimes an editor hedges, and you may not want to revise extensively to someone's specifications if the article may still be rejected despite your additional efforts. At a minimum, seek the editor's assurance that if the article is to be re-reviewed, the same referees will be consulted.

If you have quoted extensively from other people's work or if you are reprinting tables or illustrations from other sources, you must get written permission from the copyright holder. Do this the minute the article is accepted. Chapter 10 provides information on acquiring such permission.

You may be asked to review a copy editor's work on your article, or you may merely receive proof to be read (see Chapter 10 for instructions). In either case, read carefully. If you have an edited manuscript, you may still make changes and ask for clarification of editorial changes you do not like or understand. In proof, you must restrict yourself to changes that are absolutely necessary unless the editor permits more extensive alterations. Return manuscript and proofs on time.

Although it is certainly better to have an article accepted, you should not be disheartened by two or three rejections. The rejections in fact may have nothing to do with the quality of your work. That particular journal may have a backlog of articles in the same field, or the editor may feel that your article is – in the publisher's vague jargon – "not quite right for us." It may easily be "quite right" for another journal. If your article is returned, try to answer the referees' objections (if they are valid) and then send the article on to another journal. When articles are returned without comment, write a polite letter to the editor asking whether you might see some of the referees' criticism. You may not get a response, but it can't hurt to ask. Also, be sure to incorporate any new information or citations that have appeared while your work was under consideration. Even if you do not change a word of the article, make a fresh photocopy if the copy you sent to the first journal comes back dogeared and shopworn. There is no reason to make your second-choice journal aware of its status.

Some journal editors make a special effort to be helpful to authors who submit their work. They will send referees' comments and their own suggestions and sometimes even recommend other journals that might be more appropriate. Unfortunately, most editors do not have the time to do this. When you are given such generous help, write a note to thank the editor. Perhaps your next encounter with the journal will have a happier ending.

Revising Oral Presentations

Many journal articles begin as talks presented at professional meetings. Not every oral presentation can become an article. For example, a report on work in progress is not ready for publication, and a paper that is part of a panel may not survive out of context. Many conference papers, however, can be revised for publication.

Before undertaking revision, check with the conference sponsors. Some groups publish proceedings of their meetings, and they may want to include your paper. Others ask that you give their own journal the right of first refusal. You should, of course, honor those expectations.

There are many differences between oral and written presentations. If you have ever sat through someone's reading of an article (after a banquet, in the worst case), you have some clues to the differences viewed from that angle. The talk was probably too long, too dense to follow easily, and devoid of enlivening spontaneous remarks. Reading an article instead of presenting a paper is a mistake. But submitting an unrevised talk to a journal is also a mistake. Shifting from the oral form to the written requires some work.

The most important consideration when revising a talk for publication is the audience for the article. The audience for your oral presentation may have been only a handful of specialists; perhaps it was a roomful of amateur enthusiasts. In any case, it is not the same group as the one your article will reach. Revise with your readers in mind, and alter the level of detail, the background information, the tone, the tables and illustrations, and the documentation accordingly.

In some cases, revision will require substantive changes. It is always wise to incorporate changes based on your audience's reaction. Any doubts, misunderstandings, or questions your hearers expressed will occur to readers as well, and you should deal with those problems when you revise. If your talk was a brief summary of your work, you will probably want to flesh it out with examples and details when you prepare it for publication. The article may also offer opportunities to review background and earlier work, to discuss possible limitations or qualifications of your conclusions, and to expand on opportunities for further research. If, by contrast, your talk was discursive and chatty, you will have to tighten it up.

A speech generally contains references to the occasion of its presentation. In an article, an initial note can tell the reader where and when the material was first presented; references within the text should be eliminated. The obvious ones are easy to omit ("It is a pleasure to be here in Punxsutawney on Groundhog Day"), but be on the lookout for subtler references, such as those that refer to the nature of the audience, the interests of the group, or an earlier paper or other event at the conference. These, too, must be omitted or altered. Similarly, references to time should be adjusted.

If you have used visual aids, these must be adapted for publication. This is not simply a matter of preparing your slides in a different medium. Readers of journal articles have more time to look at tables or graphs and to relate them to the text. Speakers who have selected or compiled their tables somewhat hastily must make up for those lapses as they revise. Make sure that the table actually says what you have claimed, that it is accurate and succinct, and that you have documented the sources. If you have simply copied a table, graph, or drawing from someone else's work, you will have to get permission for publication.

Also make sure that the illustrations are really needed. Speakers often use slides and overhead transparencies to liven things up and to keep the audience's attention. In the written incarnation, however, illustrations should be kept only if they are vital to the argument.

An article requires more rigorous documentation than a speech, which does not come with footnotes. In a speech you may get away with something like "As Lomonosov has pointed out. . . ." In an article you must add first name, article title, journal name, date, volume, and page number. You must also check to see that you have quoted accurately. Speakers occasionally indulge in such statements as "Someone once claimed that" or "At a conference I attended a few years ago, a speaker argued that. . . ." Some of these quotations, I suspect, are fictional. In any case, they must be omitted or documented when revising for publication.

The tone of an article is generally more formal than that of a talk. You may wish to shift from the first or second person to the third, in addition to removing or formalizing jokes, anecdotes, and other casual features. You may have to find an appropriate punctuation mark or phrase to substitute for the raised eyebrow, hard stare, or eloquent gesture that you relied on when speaking.

When you are writing, you may want to provide more structure for your argument, and the medium of print allows you to use headings and subheadings. Some speakers display or circulate outlines of their talks, and these can be transformed into headings.

Although some speakers expend as much effort on an oral presentation as on a written one, they are the exceptions. Most academics regard such presentations as trial runs. Journal editors have learned this, and they do not look favorably upon unrevised speeches. On the other hand, a speech that has been presented to a critical audience and then properly revised has received a sort of preliminary referee's report and can be a valuable contribution.

Money

Scholarly journals rarely pay contributors or referees. At most, authors receive a few extra copies of the journal or some offprints. Some journals – generally those in disciplines such as literature where amateurs frequently venture – even charge submission fees that you must pay before they will consider your article. These fees are meant to defray the cost of mailing articles to referees and to discourage frivolous submissions. In the physical and life sciences it is accepted practice to bill authors a "page charge" for publishing their work. This does not mean that enclosing a check with your manuscript guarantees publication. Rather, once the article is accepted on its merits, through the usual review procedure, you are informed that you must pay x dollars (anywhere from $10 to $100) per page. (In fact, some journals that impose page charges may waive them, but they generally limit the number of free articles per issue. This means that your article will probably be published, but not for quite a while.) Journals in the physical sciences have charged these fees since about 1930, and they are common in the natural and medical sciences. Some journals in other fields are considering their adoption as well. Because there is a good deal of misunderstanding about them, they merit some discussion.

It costs money to publish a journal. Staff must be paid, as must typesetters and printers. Paper and ink cost money. The postal service charges for delivering mail. Journals are housed in buildings that charge rent, and they use utilities that charge fees. Typewriters, computers, and copying machines cost money.

All of this must come from some combination of five main sources: subscriptions, advertising fees, page charges, offprint charges, and contributions from a university or a professional association (e.g., cash or subsidized rent). Subscriptions and advertising fees go hand in hand: The more subscriptions you have, the more advertising you can get and the more you can charge for it. This is why popular magazines can pay their contributors: More readers mean more advertisers paying more money, so even if the charge per subscription is not particularly high, the magazine is profitable. A specialized journal cannot do much to increase the number of subscribers (especially when academic hiring and library budgets are declining) or to increase a university or an association subsidy. Although some journals could attract more advertising than they do, there are definite limits on what they can charge. Some journals, for ethical reasons, limit the sorts of advertising they accept or accept none at all; some have too few subscribers to appeal to advertisers. So that leaves only three sources of money to meet rising costs: subscription rates, offprint fees, and page charges. Page charges cover 23 to 70 percent of the costs of journals that impose them.[3] A journal without page charges must ask readers to pay higher subscription rates and must charge contributors more for offprints. If you belong to a professional organization that publishes a journal or if you subscribe to a journal, you are helping to underwrite publication. Paying a page charge is just another form of subsidy.

Some journals that do not ordinarily impose page charges may charge for publishing photographs (especially in color) or complex tables. These fees are meant not to discourage the use of such material but to cover the additional cost of preparing and reproducing it.

[3] Marjorie Scal, "The Page Charge," *Scholarly Publishing* 3, no. 1 (October 1971): 64.

If you work in a field where page charges are common, you should be prepared to pay them. Universities sometimes provide funds for this purpose. If your research is supported by grants from a government agency or a private foundation, you should write publication costs into the proposal. They are legitimate costs, and your research is of little value if you cannot tell others about it. Page charges are most common in the natural and physical sciences, and writing in these fields is usually far more concise than in the humanities and social sciences. No causal relationship between these two facts has been established, but it is a promising subject for research.

Electronic Journals

When an author has prepared a manuscript electronically, and when the potential readers have computers, it may be possible to save a great deal of time and some money by skipping the paper-and-ink stage of publishing altogether. This is the rationale for electronic journals – journals that exist on paper only if the reader prints them out from a computer terminal.

An electronic journal can work as an advanced electronic bulletin board, with writers sending their work directly to the members of a network. This is certainly quick, but it provides no quality control – no editor and no referees. The usefulness of such materials to readers is consequently limited, and the value of these publications to authors at the time of tenure decisions is doubtful. However, for speedy communication – perhaps with the goal of acquiring broad-based criticism and information – such journals are useful.

Alternatively, electronic journals can be edited and refereed. In this case, the electronic manuscript goes directly to an editor, via a modem or a network. The editor sends it electronically to referees, who return it electronically with comments. The editor can reject the manuscript electronically (there are no data on whether this is more or less traumatic than traditional rejection), send requests for revision, or accept the manuscript. When the manuscript is ready for publication, it is sent out to subscribers on a network, either free or for a subscription fee.

The main advantage of electronic journals is the saving of time that is possible because both mailing time and the production stages of typesetting, proofreading, printing, and binding are eliminated. Also, the whole idea of an "issue" can be dispensed with: articles can be published as they are accepted, without waiting for enough articles to accumulate to put together an issue. This makes electronic journals especially attractive in fields where practitioners such as doctors need timely information on new treatments. The costs of traditional production are also eliminated, but there are certainly costs involved in sending material via a modem over phone lines. These phone transmission costs impose the main limitation of electronic journals: Most cannot afford to transmit articles longer than roughly fifteen hundred words. Nor is it yet possible to include high-quality graphics. An additional significant drawback is that readership is limited to those who have computers, network connections, or modems. This may exclude students and those who live in less prosperous nations.

There are some ways around the nonfinancial difficulties of electronic journals. For example, if the electronic journal is regarded as an adjunct to traditional publication, the articles or their abstracts can be transmitted to subscribers electronically, without graphics, at the same time that they are sent to the typesetter. This gives readers quick access to articles of interest, with the illustrations (and, in the case of abstract-only electronic journals, full text) to follow later. Book reviews are another good candidate for electronic publication. They are short, and getting them out quickly is desirable.

The bibliography includes some guides to electronic journals. These guides become obsolete very quickly, but they are a good place to start. The less formal journals are on the Internet, and numerous travel guides to the electronic information highway are available (some are listed in the bibliography).

Book Reviews

Most academics enjoy reviewing books in their fields. It is a way to make sure that you keep up with the current literature or, to put it bluntly, that you actually read the things you mean to read. You will not be paid for your review, but you do get a free book. Reviewing is also a relatively quick and painless way to publish. Although book reviews do not count with tenure committees nearly so much as refereed articles do, they are worth something. They also offer you a chance to express your opinion on subjects of interest to you.

If you want to review books for a journal, write to the editor or to the book review editor, if such a person is listed on the masthead. You should state your interest in reviewing, the fields in which you wish to review, and your qualifications. Many journals are eager to expand their stable of reviewers. Do not, however, submit unsolicited reviews. The editor has probably already assigned the book to another reviewer, and yours will not be published.

A book review is supposed to help readers decide whether to invest their time and money in a book. For that reason, the review should be primarily an evaluation, rather than a summary or abstract. Certainly, you will have to tell what the book is about, but that is only the beginning. Your evaluation can include comparisons with similar books when appropriate, but lengthy comparisons should be reserved for survey articles whose purpose is to review several current works on a subject. Similarly, although your opinion of the book is the heart of the review, you should reserve lengthy expositions of your own ideas for review essays of the sort found in the *New York Review of Books*. The reader of scholarly journals generally expects a review focused on the volume in question.

You may find it useful to think about how a book review compares with a referee's report. An obvious difference is that a review is signed. A more important difference is the audience. When you referee, you are writing for the editor, who must decide whether to publish, and for the author, to whom you are offering suggestions for revision. When you review, you are writing for potential readers who want to know what the book is about, whether it presents information and ideas not available elsewhere, and whether it is well written and accurate. When you referee work in progress, your comments on grammar and usage or suggestions that another document be consulted are useful. When you review a bound book that will not be altered, your reader will be interested in minor flaws only if they are so numerous that they detract from the work. Nitpicking to demonstrate your own superior knowledge is neither necessary nor appreciated. Finally, a referee's report is informal, whereas a review is written for publication. You will want to take more pains with your writing, and you must adhere to the journal's specifications about length.

Refereeing and reviewing do share some important features. Both require that you meet deadlines. If you cannot review a book on time, decline. Both also require that you be objective. You should not attempt to review a book whose author you loathe or whose approach is anathema. Your review would not be credible and would be a disservice to yourself and the reader. If you find that in all fairness you cannot recommend a book, say so matter of factly and explain why. As in refereeing, vitriol and ad hominem arguments are out of order.

Chapter 3

Revising a Dissertation

> There are men that will make you books, and turn 'em loose into the world, with as much dispatch as they would do a dish of fritters.
>
> Miguel de Cervantes

Many junior faculty members feeling pressure to publish see their dissertations as the most likely place to start. At first glance, this seems to be sound reasoning. After all, the research is done, your work has been thoroughly reviewed and approved by experts, and you are the world's leading authority in the field. Why not just change the title page and ship it off to a university press, sit back, and wait for the inevitable acceptance, glowing reviews, and swift tenure and promotion?

Not so fast. Thirty or forty years ago it was often possible to do that. University presses were expanding and prospering, and it was not difficult for new Ph.D.'s to get their dissertations published, perhaps with minor revisions. Today, however, presses' resources are much more restricted, and the publication of unrevised dissertations is rarely a wise use of their time or money. Also, students in many fields are turning to narrow topics that are intrinsically less worthy of publication as books. (Besides, dissertations are now easily available on microfilm or in photocopy.) On the whole, this change has been for the better. Most unrevised dissertations are not worth publishing, and the quality of scholarly books

31

has improved as presses have become more selective. However, some department chairs and deans date from the era of easy publication and do not always understand the problems younger faculty now face.

The Differences between a Thesis and a Book

Why isn't your thesis a book just waiting to be published? A thesis differs from a book in many of the same ways a graduate student differs from a faculty member. You may have noticed that as soon as you got your degree your status rose inexplicably. No longer an ignorant youth, excluded from department meetings and (if you were lucky) paid a salary in four digits, you are suddenly a scholar and colleague, with (if you are lucky) a five-digit salary. Instead of spending your life convincing people that you know something, you are in front of a classroom filled with students who think you know everything. Whereas you used to be the trembling candidate quaking before a committee, you are now sitting sternly and confidently on the other side of the table. The change seems to be instant and magical: yesterday a frog, today a prince or princess. In fact, of course, a lot of work went into the transformation.

A thesis is much like a graduate student: It has a limited purpose and a small audience; it is often insecure and defensive, justifying itself with excessive documentation; it is too narrowly focused; and it has not yet developed a style of its own. Henri Peyre lists "the most common faults" of the dissertation as "excessive length, repetitiousness, exasperating slowness of pace, monotonous synopses of novels, of plays, or of earlier critical works" and then says that dissertations are too defensive, dogmatic, and inaccessible, containing too many footnotes and too much jargon.[1] Among "the dissertation's deadly sins," Robert Plant Armstrong

[1] Henri Peyre, "Random Notes on a Misunderstanding," in *The Thesis and the Book*, Eleanor Harman and Ian Montagnes, eds. (Toronto: University of Toronto Press, 1976), p. 13.

counts "amateurism, redundancy, trivialization, specializa-tionalism, reductionism, and arrogance."[2]

Before you abandon your dissertation in shame and de-spair, please remember that not all dissertations are this bad. But before deciding whether yours is one that can be saved, you should understand the aspects of the dissertation that must be evaluated before any attempt at revision.

Purpose. The purpose of a dissertation is to demonstrate your research and writing ability. You must show that you have read and taken into account all the relevant work done by others, and you must anticipate objections that your com-mittee may raise. This leads to the repetition, slowness, mo-notony, defensiveness, and other faults enumerated by Peyre and Armstrong. A book's purpose is to communicate ideas. There is no need to rehash common knowledge or attack straw men. There is a need to organize relevant material in a way that supports a coherent, original argument in an inter-esting, attractive manner.

Audience. A dissertation is directed to a committee whose job is to educate you. You can assume they know your field, no matter how narrow. They must read your dissertation, no matter how boring it is, because that is what they are paid to do. People who read books, however, pay for the privilege. Your book must attract their attention and hold it. And their backgrounds are more varied than those of your committee members, so you must assume less depth of knowledge.

Author. Dissertations are written by students who must convince their readers that they have done their homework. Books are written by scholars whose readers assume they are intelligent, well educated, and well read. Even though you are the same person, your new status imposes new responsi-bilities and extends new privileges.

[2] Robert Plant Armstrong, "The Dissertation's Deadly Sins," in *The Thesis and the Book*, Eleanor Harman and Ian Montagnes, eds. (Toronto: University of Toronto Press, 1976), p. 28.

Scope.   A thesis is narrowly focused. The subject is rarely set in a broader context, but lavish attention is paid to sources, methodology, and theory. A book must provide a context for its subject and should not rehearse the history of previous scholarship. It should stand on its own.

Tone and style.   A thesis sounds like a demonstration of knowledge. Students tend to write in the passive voice, and the reader senses an enormous effort at objectivity. A dissertation is mannered and often full of jargon. Its superstructure shows through (Here's what I'm going to say. . . . Look! I'm saying it. . . . Here's what I just said). A book is a more open, honest communication. The degree of formality is a matter of choice, and the work should demonstrate that a human being did the thinking and writing.

Documentation.   Because the dissertation is a display of acquired knowledge, it bulges with quotations and footnotes. The bibliography is meant to show that no conceivable source has been neglected. In a book, quotation is used appropriately and for limited purposes, footnoting is simplified and reduced, and all items in the bibliography are relevant.

As you decide what to do with your dissertation, keep these distinctions in mind. Perhaps you were fortunate enough to have an advisor who teaches students to write books instead of dissertations. If so, you can probably revise easily. But most people are not so lucky.

Deciding What to Do

You can do three things with a dissertation: Forget about it, turn it into a book, or extract one or more articles from it. In many cases, the wisest course is to put the thesis on the shelf and leave it there. Many dissertations are designed and executed as straightforward, single-purpose exercises. Once they have served their purpose, they have no further value. This is a hard fact to accept, particularly if the dissertation has cost you a lot of time, effort, and anguish. For that reason, almost everyone who has written about revising theses offers the same advice: Don't do anything with your dissertation right away. Set it aside for several months and go back to it only when you think you may be able to regard it more objectively.

Some writers figure that, instead of letting their work lie fallow in this waiting period, they should send it off to a publisher. Usually, the press of the university that granted the doctorate is approached; often the student's advisor sends a letter of endorsement. As a courtesy, the press will at least look at the manuscript and will perhaps send it to a reader. This is a terrible waste of the press's time and money and an unwarranted imposition. Probably not one dissertation in a hundred submitted in this way is accepted. What's more, it is a mistake from the author's point of view. If you are like most people, when you reexamine your dissertation in a year's time you will be at least mildly embarrassed. You will see mistakes, gaps, and ill-chosen rhetoric. You will want to change things. If you have sent your thesis to a press in its original form, you will have alienated one prospective publisher unnecessarily. If the press has sent it to a reader, there will be at least one person at professional meetings whose eyes you will want to avoid – and you won't even know who it is. Do not submit your dissertation anywhere until you have let it rest for at least six months and then reread it. If your rereading discloses perfection and publishability, then send it off to a publisher.

One very common result of rereading one's dissertation is to relive all the agony that went into the original work. If you were one of those who suffered great pain in writing a thesis, it is probably best not to do anything with the dissertation. Ask yourself whether you can face it again, and if your honest answer is no or maybe, just let it go. You should also abandon the dissertation if you are simply tired of it. Revision is rarely quick or easy, and if the subject bores you and you are eager to get on with something else, do so. You will gain nothing from bringing an already stale mind to a mound of overworked material. Someday you may regain your interest, and that will be the time to return to the project.

Another signal to leave the thesis unrevised is the feeling that you know it is not publishable but you don't know how to fix it. If you still cannot fix it after reading this chapter and some of the items in the bibliography, set the dissertation aside for another year or two. Then, when you have done some other writing and have more confidence in your judgment, you may want to try again.

If rereading your dissertation revives your interest in the subject and does not cause nightmares, then you are ready to decide whether the work is worth revising. First, and most important, does your thesis have something new and important to say to a significant number of people? It may be buried in formalities and jargon, and it may be only a small part of the dissertation, but if there is something in there worth communicating, then revision is probably justified. As William C. Dowling says, "The genuine book is an elaboration of a single significant idea, and the warmed-over dissertation isn't."[3] If there is no such idea – if the originality amounts to mere refocusing or embroidery or technique – then reworking will waste your time. One test is to try to write a one-paragraph summary of the major idea in clear, ordinary, non-specialist English. Do not discuss sources, data, or structure of argument. Just tell us what you have to say that we do not already know – and that we will find interesting. If you cannot do this, put the dissertation back on the shelf.

If there is an idea there, how much needs to be said about it – twenty pages or two hundred? In other words, do you have an article to write, or a book? Once the dissertation hardware is removed – the review of the literature, the excessive quotation, the chapter that turned out to be irrelevant but was left in to show that you tried – what will be left? Perhaps you have two or three ideas to express. If so, are they related logically so that they can be joined together in a

---

[3] William C. Dowling, "Avoiding the Warmed-Over Dissertation," in *The Thesis and the Book*, Eleanor Harman and Ian Montagnes, eds. (Toronto: University of Toronto Press, 1976), p. 49.

book? Or do you have two or three articles to write? Another possibility is that the really important concept that came out of the dissertation was actually of minor significance in the thesis itself. When this is the case, you are really starting all over again.

The Thesis–Book Continuum

A number of excellent articles have been written on how to revise a dissertation. The most practical is the series by Olive Holmes that first appeared in *Scholarly Publishing* and was reprinted in *The Thesis and the Book*.[4] This chapter agrees generally with Holmes's advice. A more extreme view is taken by Dowling, who in the same volume advocates taking the single idea that emerges from your dissertation and starting all over. This process no doubt produces better books, but most authors prefer revision to complete rewriting. It is much more difficult to rethink the organization and structure of your work than it is simply to take out the pruning shears (and, where necessary, the hatchet) to reshape what you have.

There is no single moment during revision when your dissertation becomes a book. The two items are rather on a continuum (see Figure 1), and it is possible to stop at various places en route to "book" and declare your revision complete. The first step in using this idea is to place your dissertation accurately on the continuum. If it is a typical dissertation, it is at or near the left end of the scale in most respects. If you are a more sensitive writer and have had good advice, your thesis may show some features closer to the middle. If you are a very good writer who chose a broad, generally interesting topic and got very good advice, your dissertation may be very close to the right of the chart, although specific

4 Olive Holmes, "Thesis to Book: What to Get Rid Of" and "Thesis to Book: What to Do with What Is Left," in *The Thesis and the Book*, Eleanor Harman and Ian Montagnes, eds. (Toronto: University of Toronto Press, 1976), pp. 52–85.

items like footnotes and bibliography may be all the way back at the left. See where your own work falls in respect to each item listed at the left of the figure.

Next you must decide where you want to end up. Do you want to achieve a first-rate book that would register all the way at the right of the scale? Do you want merely to disguise the dissertation's origins? Or do you want to create something in between? Then take a good look at what you must do to get from here to there.

There are two cases where doing the minimum is easily justified. On the one hand, you may have a very well written thesis on an interesting topic, placed in a context that makes it accessible to a broader academic audience. Because it is a thesis, however, you have fitted it out with the appropriate trappings: excessive headings, quotations, footnotes, and lists; an exhaustive literature review and bibliography; and perhaps an overly visible outline. You can easily reduce or eliminate these elements and come up with a publishable manuscript. On the other hand, the value of your thesis may lie solely in its presentation of important new information. The audience will be small, but their need for what you have to say is great and possibly urgent. The publisher will decide whether to accept your manuscript almost entirely on the basis of its content, with only minimal expectations for literary merit. In this case, again, it makes sense to clean up the details and put your thesis in the mail. Both these examples, as different as they are, are candidates for piecemeal cosmetic cover-up. You will end up with a manuscript that has lots of crossing-out and occasional changes, to be retyped for submission.

When we move on to "limited remodeling," we are talking about some rewriting. Instead of merely removing jargon and academic clichés, you must tighten up your language, making it more precise, descriptive, and lively. You should define terms for a more general audience. You must remove blatant "directional signals" and repetition that had provided transitions and replace them with less obvious structural elements. In addition to removing redundant quotations, you must reduce those that remain and paraphrase where appropriate. The basic organization and argument of the thesis will remain, but the length will be reduced and the writing will be more straightforward. You will, in a sense, go inside the writing instead of just fixing up the surface.

The changes described so far are reasonably self-contained and can be made without much rethinking. Structural changes, however, involve reshaping the dissertation. You must add the setting or context that will make your work accessible and attractive to people outside your immediate specialization, though not necessarily to the general reader. You must reorganize to avoid repetition and the need for traffic signs. And all of this is in addition to the cosmetic and limited remodeling work already described. As in fixing up your house, even if you knock out walls and replaster, you still have to paint. Making structural changes is a qualitative jump from merely revising. You will not just be crossing out and making minor alterations; you will be rewriting whole sections and chapters. Although you will not be starting from scratch, you will have to look at your material in a fresh way, to imagine it in a new form. If you do not think you can do this, do a limited remodeling and call it quits.

The "complete overhaul" approaches Dowling's notion of extracting the significant idea from your dissertation and starting afresh. He tells you to rewrite completely, "realigning your original insights with your major point, getting rid of smothering documentation and digressive or irrelevant material, and (one hopes) gracefully subordinating the particular to the general."[5] The result of this labor, according to Dowling, is a rough draft. Clearly this course is not for everyone, but it is good advice if your topic is worth the effort and you feel up to making it.

To summarize, if you think you should turn your dissertation into a book, let it sit for a while and then make an honest appraisal of its merits and your ability and desire to work on it. Decide how much you want to revise. Reread Strunk and

[5] Dowling, "Avoiding," p. 51.

THESIS	Cosmetic cover-up	Limited remodeling	Complete overhaul	BOOK
Narrowly focused				Broadly focused
Minimal context				Substantial context
Impersonal, passive tone				Personal, direct tone
Mannered, discursive style; jargon	delete jargon	tighten language		Personal, easy style
Attracting reader immaterial	attract reader in introduction			Writing tells story
Visible superstructure		delete blatant transitions	rework to minimize structure	Organization: subtle to invisible
Extensive repetition	delete summaries	delete obvious repetition	delete borderline repetition	
Exhaustive literature review	delete least relevant literature		delete borderline literature	

THESIS				BOOK
Explicit, detailed methodology	summarize methodology	include methodology in appendix	include methodology in preface	Methodology not included
Multiple headings	reduce number of headings			
Extensive quotations	reduce number of quotations	abridge quotations		
Multiple plot summaries	reduce number of plot summaries		include only vital plot summaries	
Multiple lists	delete nonessential lists	rework to include lists in text		
Multiple tables	delete nonessential tables	simplify tables		
Exhaustive footnotes	delete nonessential footnotes	convert to endnotes		
Exhaustive bibliography	delete nonessential citations			Selective bibliography

THESIS ⟶ **BOOK**

White, *The Elements of Style,* before beginning. It will clear your head and keep your language clean. Review the section on writing well in Chapter 2 of this book. Read Chapter 4 on finding a publisher, both for inspiration and to get an early start, and the sections in Chapters 10 and 11 on preparing a manuscript.

Mining for Articles

If you find a number of significant ideas in your dissertation but conclude that they are best treated separately, then you should consider writing an article or two. Chapter 2 goes into the art of writing for journals in more detail, but a few points need to be made specifically about articles that begin in dissertations.

The first thing to consider is whether you really need to wait until the dissertation is complete before publishing anything from it. In the natural and physical sciences, many dissertation-related research projects generate brief journal articles while they are under way. Writers in the behavioral sciences and humanities should consider whether some of their work might be published in process as well. Certainly, prospective employers are impressed by those who publish in graduate school. In addition, publication may put you in touch with people whose work will be helpful to you (although the journals outside the sciences are generally so slow that this is unlikely). In any event, if discrete parts of your research can be written up for journal publication, you should develop these as articles. Doing this will help you to see your work more clearly and should make your final writing of the dissertation easier. It is unlikely that having such articles published will reduce the possibility of book publication, should you decide to try that when the dissertation is finished. In fact, an article in a well-read journal may attract the attention of a diligent book editor and bring you an invitation to submit your work.

What sorts of material are candidates for journal articles?

Preliminary surveys, case studies, a methodological or technical innovation, new biographical material, a manuscript find, a bibliographic note – anything that stands on its own. You may even discover, in the end, that the material does not belong in the dissertation, yet it is new and interesting and can be written up with little extra effort. The amount of effort is important. After all, you are supposed to be writing your dissertation. Nevertheless, at this stage in your career, a publication – no matter how brief – is worth a week or two. If you have such material and cannot spare the time now, set it aside for the weeks when the dissertation is being typed or the summer before you take a job.

When the dissertation is finished, it can generate articles of a very different sort. For example, your dissertation, once stripped of the literature review, methodology, excessive annotation, and the like, may boil down to a single interesting point that can be stated, illustrated, and proved in twenty or thirty pages. That is something to turn into an article. Unfortunately, you usually cannot just take the dissertation and hack it into shape. You should probably start writing from scratch.

It is also possible that, with minor revision, a chapter can be turned into an article. Case studies, biographical studies, textual studies, and the like are good candidates. Sometimes a bit of extra research is needed to round out the article.

Perhaps nothing in your dissertation can easily be transformed into a publishable article. You may still have material that could be the basis of some good new work that could be completed differently. For example, the case study you did of an unmarried male high school dropout may not be earth-shaking, but suppose it were compared with broader studies of unmarried male high school dropouts, or with a similar case study of an unmarried female high school dropout or a married male high school dropout. Perhaps you unearthed some correspondence that was mostly irrelevant to the dissertation but of interest nevertheless. Sometimes a bit of statistical analysis that you did not include in the dissertation can be combined with published findings to show a relationship that is worth pointing out. In other words, do not regard the search for articles as a mere red-pencil effort. Look at the dissertation as a source of ideas as well as words.[6]

To return to the mining metaphor, however, be sure to recognize when the seam is exhausted. A dissertation was never meant to be the lode from which a lifetime's treasure is dug.

---

[6] For more ideas on inspiration for articles, see Richard Penaskovic, "Facing Up to the Publication Gun," *Scholarly Publishing* 16, no. 2 (January 1985): 136–40.

Chapter 4

Finding a Publisher for the Scholarly Book

It circulated for five years, through the halls of fifteen publishers, and finally ended up with Vanguard Press, which, as you can see, is rather deep into the alphabet.

Patrick Dennis, on *Auntie Mame*

Types of Book Publishers

Scholarly books are issued by five types of publishers: university presses, profit-making scholarly publishers, trade publishers, university centers and learned societies, and vanity presses. These publishers differ in their refereeing procedures, to some extent in the kinds of works they publish, in their approaches to marketing, and in the contractual arrangements they make with authors. Despite some overlap, they serve different purposes, and authors should understand the differences before deciding where to seek publication.

University Presses

University presses are the main outlet for book-length scholarly work. They are nonprofit publishers. Although some large presses are self-supporting and not subsidized, most university presses have their costs underwritten to varying extents by the sponsoring institutions and sometimes in part by private foundations or government agencies. Some have general endowments or endowments for books in certain fields. There are about eighty university presses in the United States and Canada that belong to the Association of American University Presses; a few other university presses are not full members of the AAUP.

The purpose of a university press is to disseminate knowledge by publishing books and journals. In its search for the best in new scholarship, a press encourages research and writing. Some presses initiate scholarly projects such as reference books and new editions of the Bible or of classic literary and historical works. University presses also seek to extend the audience for scholarship by acquiring and promoting works that make current research accessible to a general, popular audience. In addition to traditional monographs, therefore, university presses may publish poetry, fiction, translations, children's books, anthologies, and cookbooks. Increasingly, they are publishing works of scholarship addressed to nonspecialists. Many university presses, especially those at public institutions, publish books on their state or region for both scholars and general readers. These may include works of history, literature, anthropology, botany, zoology, and political science.

University presses also vary greatly in size: Some publish fewer than ten books a year, while others publish around five hundred. Some specialize in a few academic fields, while others publish in nearly every subject.

Like any other part of a university, a press's noble aims must be carried out in the less lofty realms of limited budgets, limited space, and limited staffs. A press has many publics to please: the university administration, sometimes the state legislature, the faculty, its authors, librarians, bookstore owners, and its readers. It is a complex organization that often seems mysterious to would-be authors. Because its purpose is to find, recruit, and publish the works of promising scholars, however, a press's staff is generally happy to meet with faculty to discuss how they work and what they are looking for. Although I will not go so far as to urge you to take an editor to lunch, I do suggest that you attend the press's open house, invite an editor to meet with your department's faculty and graduate students, and generally take advantage of the staff's expertise and interest. Even if you do not want to publish with your own university's press, or if it is not active in your field, the staff can be helpful and informative.

Academics hold many misconceptions about university presses. The first is that presses do not need to make a profit and thus do not concern themselves with the salability of a book. This is not true. Most university presses may run in the red – at least on some titles – but they mustn't drown in the ink. They must be responsible publishers, using limited resources wisely, and they must on balance earn more than they spend. Since they cannot offset their inevitable losses on some titles with the profits from romance novels, celebrity biographies, and other "commercial properties," they must be very careful about how they use their funds. No university press will turn down a book simply because it will not be a best-seller, but costs and salability are always important considerations. The lifetime sale a university press expects may be as few as five hundred copies. However, every university press must publish some books that will sell considerably more than this. Many university press books could be published equally well by commercial (trade) houses, and on such titles presses must offer competitive terms to authors.

Another misconception is that a university press exists to publish books by the faculty of its own university. Again, not true. Although most presses encourage home faculty to submit manuscripts and do try to publish their work when it is worthwhile, all manuscripts are subject to the same reasonably impartial refereeing process. Works from outside the university are treated the same way as are those from within. Because this misconception is so widely held, many authors avoid their home presses for fear that colleagues will regard the publication of their manuscript as a favor. If you are publishing for prestige or promotion, and if your colleagues are unsophisticated about publishing, you may want to avoid your home press. In fact, you need not fear (or hope) that your home university press will accept your book just because you are on the faculty. Besides, publishing locally may guarantee more intense, prompt attention and enable you to be on the spot throughout the consideration and production of your book. Even if your home press does not publish in your field, its editors should be willing to give you advice on which presses do.

Another misconception about university presses is that they are stuffy, unimaginative, and uninterested in promoting their books. Some are stuffy, and some do not make much effort at promotion. Most, however, are staffed by bright, innovative people who want their books to be bought and read. Again, you should consider your own interests. If a book is of limited salability, it will not help if the publisher emblazons the title on the flank of an elephant and parades it down Fifth Avenue. You should choose a publisher whose strength is in the area where you need the most help.

University presses generally pay royalties, though not always. The decision is based on expected sales and profitability. Some even offer advances, at least on an author's second book and on books that other publishers are competing for. No one, however, should count on making a lot of money from a scholarly monograph. (Chapter 12 illustrates the monetary return to an author and a publisher from a typical monograph.) Some university presses have even begun to request subventions. This controversial practice is discussed in Chapter 5.

The main difference between a university press and a commercial scholarly publisher (other than profitability) is the process used to select manuscripts. University presses use a rather elaborate system involving in-house reading, expert referees, and a faculty review board. This procedure has two main advantages for the author. First, you get expert opinions and the opportunity to revise your work, anticipating adverse comments and reviews of the finished book. Second, it reassures colleagues, administrators, and search committees that your book is truly worthy of publication, having met the standards of impartial reviewers. The disadvantage is the amount of time it takes. A manuscript of average length will take from one to eight weeks for in-house review (depending on how busy the staff is, how thorough the review is, and whether cost estimates are required), a month or two per outside reader (usually at least two readers, occasionally as many as five), a week or two for recommendations to the faculty committee, and two weeks to two months waiting for the faculty committee to meet. Add in mailing time, and you're up to a minimum of three months. If a summer intervenes, you're up to a minimum of five or six. And that allows no time for reviewers' tardiness. Occasionally review takes more than a year. Later in the chapter I will suggest ways to minimize this period of agony.

University presses are also distinguished by greater emphasis on substantive editing and copy editing and (often) by higher standards of design and production (e.g., better paper and sturdier bindings).

The people who work at university presses are known by a number of titles. Each press has a director who has overall responsibility for the operations of the press, but from there down you will find little consistency in nomenclature. The person who goes out looking for books and evaluates incoming manuscripts may be an acquiring editor, a sponsoring editor, a senior editor, a humanities (or economics or biology) editor, or just plain editor. An editor in chief or editorial director may oversee the work of the acquiring editors and possibly the manuscript editors as well. Manuscript editors – who go over manuscripts line by line correcting spelling and grammatical errors, improving the flow of ideas, and suggesting other changes – are also called copy editors, line editors, and sometimes editors, associate editors, or assistant editors. The senior copy editor may be called the managing editor.

Outside the editorial department, production of your book will be handled by a designer and a production editor (who often coordinates free-lance manuscript editing as well), production manager, production director, or production assistant. Marketing is headed by a manager or director, sometimes with assistants for advertising, direct mail, and promotion. A rights and permissions or subsidiary rights manager may be in charge of selling paperback, translation, serial, book club, and other rights. The business office employs numerous people, sometimes including the enticingly titled fulfillment manager, whose job is not to make authors feel good but to get the books out of the warehouse and into the hands of customers.

Throughout this book I have tried to be as specific as possible when designating the person you should write or call on various matters. However, since presses are organized differently, this is very difficult. Generally, the acquiring editor is the person to regard as your connection with the rest of the staff, but in a small press, the manuscript editor may fill this function. As a result, I will sometimes refer simply to "the editor."

Commercial Scholarly Publishers

The commercial scholarly or "professional" publisher publishes books for scholars in certain disciplines or for specific professional groups, such as practitioners in the behavioral, medical, physical, and life sciences, in business, or in engineering. They often publish books in series. Academic Press, Jossey-Bass, Greenwood, and Addison-Wesley are good examples, as are some of the European publishers, such as Elsevier, Methuen, and Springer Verlag. Many of these European publishers have editorial offices in the United States as well as in Europe. Commercial scholarly publishers compete with university presses for some books, so it is important to understand the differences between the two groups.

The selection processes of these publishers are similar to those of university presses, except that they do not have faculty committees. Referees' reports are considered by individual editors and editorial committees instead. Their decisions can therefore be more prompt, although this is not always the case.

The quality of editing and production among commercial scholarly publishers varies greatly. Some expend a great deal of effort on editing, while some do only the most cursory correction of punctuation. Some routinely win industry prizes for design and production, while others use camera-ready copy produced by the author. One complaint more frequently lodged against some commercial scholarly publishers than against university presses is that production time (the activities between the completion of the editing and the appearance of the book) is excessive. This may occur because a publisher has a small staff and a large backlog of manuscripts or because of cash-flow problems. (These problems are not unknown among university presses, either.) On the other hand, some small, new publishers have such technologically advanced equipment and flexible procedures that they can produce books in record time. Overall there is greater variation in quality among for-profit publishers than among university presses. This means simply that authors must do more research and ask harder questions when selecting a for-profit publisher.

Scholarly and professional publishers market their books through well-developed mailing lists, exhibits at professional meetings, and advertisements in relevant journals. Their marketing focuses on well-defined target groups, not the general reader. The European publishers are experienced in selling books outside the United States and are therefore especially attractive to authors whose books have an overseas market, as many books in the sciences do. Because they need to make a profit and are not subsidized, they often price their books higher than a university press might, particularly for highly specialized books and those for professionals used to paying high prices, such as doctors and lawyers. They are also more likely to pay royalties.

Consider commercial scholarly and professional publishers if they are active in your field, particularly for books of a practical or an applied nature. Their efficiency in decision making may also be useful if you are facing publication pressures for tenure or promotion.

Trade Publishers

Academic authors may wish to work with a trade publisher. General trade publishers issue nonfiction that is of interest to the general public. If you have written a book that will appeal to a broader audience than do most monographs, because of either its subject or your approach, you may want to try your luck with such a trade house. The relevant publishers are most of the giants (HarperCollins, Simon & Schuster, and so forth) as well as some smaller trade houses or subsidiary imprints (e.g., Beacon Press and Basic Books).

Trade publishers' reviewing procedures vary, but their decisions are usually more prompt than those of university presses. However, an unsolicited manuscript will often get short shrift from a trade house. It simply may be added to a stack of manuscripts to be read when and if someone has the time. Unless you can get some sort of introduction to an editor, or make sure through correspondence that your manuscript is expected and desired, submission to a trade publisher may not be a good idea.

Prestigious trade houses generally carry the same clout with college administrators as does a university press. The dean may be less impressed by run-of-the-mill publishers. If you are worried about promotion or tenure, check out the attitudes of the powers that be.

In marketing, trade publishers are likely to place magazine advertisements, and they employ salespeople to visit bookstores and libraries. They view bookstores as the main outlets for their publications. They are good at reaching the general public but do not generally target specific audiences. Large university presses with experience in marketing general interest or professional books are just as effective at marketing such books as are the trade houses. Smaller university presses generally do not do as well, because they lack the experience, the contacts, and the budget. However, if a smaller press views your book as a potential best-seller (on a university press scale), it may go all out and make an exceptional marketing effort. This is particularly true of books with great local or regional sales potential.

Trade publishers pay royalties and sometimes offer cash advances. An "advance against royalties" is simply payment to the author of a specified amount that the publisher subsequently deducts from royalties. It is not money in addition to royalties. Only a handful of academic authors receive six-figure advances, but even a small advance may help defray research expenses. The amount depends on what the publisher expects the book to earn, and the timing will depend on your reputation and how badly the publisher wants the book. An established author with a salable idea may get an advance or a partial advance on the basis of an outline and a sample chapter. More commonly, the advance is paid on delivery of the completed manuscript. If you get an advance for an incomplete manuscript and do not finish the job (or do not finish it to the publisher's satisfaction), the publisher may ask you to return the advance, as your contract will state. In fact, however, publishers usually insist on this only if the amount is large, but it is unwise to count on their sympathy. If the publisher misjudges your book's marketability and does not sell enough copies to pay off your advance, that is the publisher's problem; you cannot be asked to return the advance for that reason.

You should approach a general trade publisher only if you honestly believe that your work is of interest to those outside academia. Otherwise, you are wasting both your time and the publisher's. Chapter 9 discusses trade books in more detail.

University Centers and Learned Societies

Often, university-affiliated institutes and centers publish books in their special fields, although sometimes their publishing is limited to research they sponsored. This is a good way to publish your book for a small, specialized audience. The production varies in elaborateness from a photocopied typescript in a spiral binding to paperbacks typeset with a laser printer to regular typeset, casebound, jacketed books. Some series are refereed; others are not. Some of these groups have distribution arrangements with university presses. Some pay royalties. You should not neglect these organizations, particularly for specialized works. The most reputable ones will impress a dean as much as a university press will.

To get information about a center or institute, ask about its publishing program, refereeing procedures, and recent publications. The best way to evaluate a university center series is to find out how colleagues in your field regard it. Are the books reviewed in the best journals? Does the series have a few well-known authors? Just ask around.

Similarly, some learned societies, museums, and libraries publish monograph series that are suitable for a manuscript that will sell too few copies to interest a university press. These are all respectable, and many are extremely prestigious. They range in scope from international scientific organizations to state and local historical societies. Go to the library to see what sorts of things they are doing and write to the society for information.

Vanity Presses, Self-publishing, and Cooperatives

Vanity presses, sometimes called subsidy publishers, charge you money to publish your book. If you are willing to pay, they are willing to publish. No editorial or expert judgment enters the picture. For this reason, publication by a vanity press carries no prestige and no clout with tenure committees. Nor does it bring riches, since you are paying all the production costs plus a profit to the publisher. Your book will not be reviewed in reputable publications. If you just want to see your work printed and bound and can afford to pay handsomely for it, there's no harm done. But there's no side benefit, either.

How do you spot a vanity press? Anyone who advertises,

"Writers! Publish your book in no time flat!!!" is a vanity publisher, and vanity presses are not listed in *Literary Market Place*, the annual listing of publishing houses and other literary services. If you do not detect the nature of the press earlier, it will certainly be clear in the contract.

Some publishers sit on the border between genuine scholarly publishing and vanity publishing. They claim to offer peer reviewing, but in fact their review procedures are nominal and their editorial committees are rubber stamps. They require camera-ready copy and author subventions on virtually every title they publish. If you are in doubt about a publisher, either steer clear or ask hard questions. For example, what percentage of the manuscripts submitted to them do they publish? Will you receive referees' reports? On what financial assumptions are subventions based (see Chapter 5)? Also ask your department chair and dean whether publication by that press will count in your favor.

Self-publishing and publishing cooperatives are cheaper than vanity presses, but like vanity presses they offer no prestige and provide no independent review of the quality of your work. They are designed for people who are convinced they have written a best-seller and do not want to cut a publisher in on the profits. (In all fairness, it is true that a few have proved right on this score and have made a lot of money.) Again, in the unlikely case that you simply want your work in type and bound, these options will do just fine. Chapters 6 and 11 offer advice on the mechanics of self-publishing.

Choosing a Publisher

The most important issue in choosing a publisher is whether the press publishes in your field. No matter how good your philosophy manuscript is, a press that has not published philosophy for a decade is a bad bet. Make a list of ten or twenty recent books in your field and look up the publishers. Also look through *Literary Market Place* and the *Directory* of the Association of American University Presses. If you have written an economics book, then a publisher that produces a series in economics or that lists a staff member whose title is "economics editor" is a likely prospect. The Association of American University Presses *Directory* includes a chart that lists subjects and the presses active in them. Talk to publishers' representatives at academic meetings and conventions. They will not have time then to look at a manuscript, but they can let you know whether the press is likely to be interested. Look at publishers' catalogues and at *Publishers' Trade List Annual*, found in the reference section of your library, which provides lists of books in print organized by publisher. See which publishing houses are advertising in the journals you read, and evaluate the quality of their recent selections. Then compile a list of a dozen likely publishers from those who are currently active in your subject.

The next task – and it is a very important one – is to compose a letter and supporting documents to send to prospective publishers (this is sometimes called a prospectus). The letter, one or two pages long, should provide a brief summary of your manuscript, the audiences to whom you expect it to appeal, and what is unique, important, and exciting about it. It should be written for an intelligent, critical, well-read lay reader (that's what a publisher is). This is a work of salesmanship and advocacy; the goal is to convince the editor to ask to see your manuscript. It should be honest and straightforward, but this is not the occasion to express lingering doubts or deep-seated misgivings. If a well-known scholar in your field, one of the press's authors, or an expert at the press's sponsoring university knows the manuscript, suggest that the press consult him or her. *Spare no effort in writing this letter.* If it is muddled, boring, semiliterate, or just thrown together, the publisher may not even look at your manuscript, let alone publish it.

In addition to the letter, you should send the table of contents, lists (or just numbers) of tables and illustrations, a brief summary or narrative outline (sometimes the introduction will serve), a sample chapter, and a curriculum vitae if yours is impressive. The curriculum vitae is optional; skip it if you are unpublished and unknown. If you do not include it, however, use your letter to provide vital information such as where you did your graduate work. Do not send more than this unless you are asked.

Send the letter and documentation to the publishers on your list. In a field such as history, you may have a dozen prospects; in the sciences, perhaps half a dozen. Address your materials to a person, not a title. Get the appropriate name from a current directory – either the director or the acquisitions (or executive) editor in your field. If your book would be part of a series, and if you know the series editor, you can send the prospectus directly to that person rather than to a member of the press's staff. Type each letter individually or use a word processor; never send a photocopied form letter. (Curricula vitae, tables of contents, and so forth can be photocopies.) You want to show that you would be a model author, so write carefully, type neatly, and proofread thoroughly.

It is not legitimate to submit a complete manuscript to more than one publisher at a time (unless both presses are aware of the dual submission and agree to it), but it is perfectly all right to solicit interest from several presses simultaneously. At this stage, presses are generally not investing money in readers' reports, and they do not expect exclusive consideration.

Letters of introduction or endorsement can be useful when trying to interest publishers in your work. If a scholar who has published with the press or who is well known in your field writes such a letter, the acquiring editor will pay attention. For such a letter to be useful, however, the writer must be both familiar with your manuscript and able to endorse it sincerely. A vague letter saying only that you are an awfully nice person who has undoubtedly done a good job will do more harm than good.

Once you have gotten responses indicating interest in your manuscript, you need to decide where to send it first. You can judge publishers by the quality of what they publish and how well they market their products, so look closely at recent books they have done. Are they well designed and readable? Are they well manufactured? Are they books that you would like to see on a shelf next to yours? Have you received mailings or seen advertisements for their books?

Ask people who have published with various presses about their experiences. Was the refereeing handled promptly and fairly? Did editing begin soon after acceptance? Were they pleased with the quality of the editing? Would they submit their next manuscript to the same publisher or go elsewhere? Ask more than one author per press, since authors and experiences vary. Weight the responses according to your needs. For example, if you know you are a sloppy writer, you want a publisher who will take the time to do a thorough job of copy editing.

Another consideration may be the press's ability to market your book abroad. Some scientific and technical books can be sold in considerable quantities in Europe and Asia without being translated. A study of German history or society may be a good candidate for translation into German. If your book has such prospects, be sure to select a press that has the ability to promote your book effectively in the relevant markets. Ask the acquiring editor how the press would handle this opportunity. In such cases, international commercial publishers may have a clear advantage.

After considering these factors, list the interested presses in the order of your preference and send your manuscript to the first one on the list. Ask the acquiring editor whether the press would like two copies of the manuscript. (This permits simultaneous review by either two referees or a referee and an in-house editor.) Do not tell the other publishers that you are sending it elsewhere first; knowing that a rival rejected your manuscript may color their decision.

Agents and Editorial Consultants

Academic writers often wonder whether literary agents can help place their manuscripts. Usually the answer is no. Literary agents receive a fee of 10 or 15 percent of the author's royalties. Since the royalties on most scholarly monographs barely keep their authors in computer disks, there is little reason for an agent to take them on. Textbook companies do not usually deal with agents either. The only time an agent is likely to be interested and useful is when you have written a trade book, one for a general audience that should be published by a commercial house. An agent who agrees with your assessment of the manuscript's potential may accept you as a client, particularly if you have published other books, and having an agent will certainly help you persuade trade houses to look at the manuscript. Chapter 9 provides more information about literary agents.

Editorial consultants, sometimes called author's editors, work directly with authors rather than exclusively for publishers. Some institutions, particularly hospitals and research institutes, employ such editors to work with staff authors. Most author's editors, though, are free-lancers. They offer services ranging from manuscript evaluation (usually for a fixed fee) to copy editing (usually at an hourly rate). They can be helpful to first-time authors, revisers of dissertations, writers for whom English is a second language, or authors of manuscripts that present unusual problems. They can also help when a manuscript has been turned down two or three times and the author is unsure about how to revise. However, they vary greatly in their qualifications and experience. Many people who have never worked for a publisher and who in fact have little editorial experience of any kind put themselves forward as editors. If you decide to seek the help of an independent editor, find someone who has had at least three years of editorial experience with a university press (on staff or as a free-lance editor) and who has worked in your field. There are many such people. Ask an editor at a nearby university press to recommend someone if you need help and be willing to pay for the author's editor's services. You should be aware, too, that your publisher will still copyedit your manuscript, even if your own editor has done an excellent job.

Sometimes publishers will accept a manuscript contingent upon the author's hiring an author's editor to revise it. Presses do this when they believe that a manuscript's content is valuable but that the writing and organization need more editorial work than they are willing to contribute. This may be costly, but if it is the only way of securing acceptance it will be worth the expense. Ask the publisher to suggest two or three editors and call each one. Ask how soon they could get to your manuscript and what their fees are. (They will not be able to give you a firm estimate of total cost without seeing the manuscript.) Hire the one with whom you feel most comfortable. Make sure the publisher sends your editor the referees' reports and in-house editorial evaluations, as well as the name of an editor at the press to consult during the work.

Submitting the Manuscript

Before submitting your manuscript to a publisher, you must get it into the proper physical form. Chapter 10 explains the correct preparation of typescripts, and Chapter 11 adds instructions for electronic manuscripts.

When you do submit your manuscript, you need to give the publisher some important information. First, you should explain that others have expressed interest in the manuscript and that you are therefore hoping for a prompt response. It never hurts to let them know they have competition. Second, if you want to suggest possible readers or warn them away from readers you expect would be hostile, now is the time. You should be honest about this. Do not recommend your dissertation advisor, best friend, or sister-in-law. Do recommend the best-qualified people in the field, particularly if they are known to be fair and open-minded. Publishers may not use your suggestions, but if the same names come up when they ask others, they will. Give complete names, current addresses, and phone numbers. Valid reasons for asking that they not use specific readers include personal animosity (I once nearly sent a manuscript to the disgruntled ex-husband of the author's current wife), professional rivalry (you're up for tenure and he wants your job), or ideological animosity (you've written a Freudian interpretation of Eliot, and the referee thinks Freud was a fraud). Third, if there is anything peculiar about the manuscript that may raise eyebrows, mention and explain it. This shows that you are aware of the issue and prevents it from becoming a surprise stumbling block. Such oddities might range from an unusual notation system through the use of nonstandard editions to your denial of the law of gravity. Finally, if the publisher has sent forms to be filled out or has requested information, fill out the forms or answer the questions. Close the letter with a request that they let you know when you may expect a decision.

Keep at least one copy of the manuscript for yourself, even if you have it on disk. *Never send the only copy of a manuscript anywhere.* Publishers are not responsible for things getting lost in the mail, and although postal insurance may cover photocopying, it will not cover retyping – let alone rewriting. Send the manuscript first class and certified or by a commercial delivery service. Certification makes a package easier to trace. Wrap the manuscript carefully and seal it well in a sturdy box or a padded book-mailing bag.

Refereeing

University presses and other scholarly publishers base their publishing decisions largely on the opinions of consulting scholars, and trade houses often consult outside experts. Although the following discussion refers mainly to university presses, it applies as well to other publishers.

When a publisher receives a manuscript, an editor reads it to see whether it seems suitable for the press, to judge the quality of the writing and the amount of editing likely to be required, and to decide what sort of expert reader is needed. A manuscript may be rejected on the basis of this reading, usually because it will not fit into the press's publishing program. (The submission of a prospectus, recommended earlier, may enable the editor to make this decision before seeing the whole manuscript, thus saving you some time and pain.) A manuscript that requires more extensive editing than the press is prepared to do may also receive an early rejection.

Some presses work up a financial analysis of the book. They estimate production costs and likely sales and see what the likely investment and return will be. Other presses wait until they have made a tentative or firm positive decision before doing this analysis. A financial analysis can result in rejection, particularly if your book is full of tables or illustrations and is likely to have very limited sales. That is one reason to alert the publisher to these features – and to your willingness to reduce the number of tables – in your initial letter of inquiry.

If the manuscript survives the in-house reading and financial analysis, it is sent to a specialist in the field, known as a reader or referee. The selection of the first referee often determines the press's final decision: A convincing, well-stated argument for rejection usually carries the day. A positive review will generally lead to a second reading. (Some presses will ask for two copies of your manuscript and send it to two readers at once.) If the readers disagree, the press will either seek a third opinion (sometimes including an evaluation of the two conflicting reports) or else resolve the matter by making its own evaluation of the two reports. Excessive, undocumented praise or condemnation is suspect. A publisher wants a careful, rational reading rather than a gut reaction.

Publishers often ask readers to fill out questionnaires. Figure 2 is a list of questions often found on such forms. If you can be sufficiently detached, try to give the answers you would expect from a reader of your manuscript. This may help you to anticipate criticism and revise your work accordingly.

Whether your work is accepted or rejected, you can expect to get at least excerpts or paraphrases from the readers' reports. You will not be told the name of the reader unless the report was positive and the reader has given permission. Nor

1 Originality and value: Is the manuscript a contribution to the field? Is it original? Is it important? Did you learn something from reading it?

2 Scholarship: Is the scholarship sound? Was the research well planned? Was it well executed? Have any major sources been neglected? Is the documentation adequate? Are the notes and bibliography in an appropriate, usable format? Is the information the manuscript provides, to the best of your knowledge, accurate?

3 Purpose: What is the purpose of the book? How well does the author accomplish this purpose?

4 Market: Is this work vital to specialists in the field? Does it have any value as a textbook? Will it be of interest to readers outside the immediate field?

5 Competing works: Are there any other books published on this subject? How does this work compare with them? What does it add to their coverage of the subject?

6 Style: Is the manuscript clearly written and readable? Is the length appropriate? Did you find the style appealing?

7 Organization: Is the book well organized? Is there any repetition? Is the argument easy to follow?

8 Special features: If the manuscript contains tables, figures, or other illustrations, are they adequate? Are they necessary? Are they easy to understand?

9 Do you have any suggestions for improving the manuscript?

10 Do you recommend that the manuscript be published?

Figure 2. Typical questions for manuscript readers.

should you insist on getting the entire report. Contrary to popular opinion, editors are basically kindhearted people. If criticism seems excessively harsh, undiplomatic, or irrelevant, they may withhold it. They will usually send anything they think may be helpful to you. If you do not understand a comment, feel free to ask for clarification.

Please note that rarely, if ever, does it do any good to protest a rejection. Read the comments as calmly and objectively as possible, make any changes you think are appropriate, and send the manuscript off to the next publisher on your list. Rejections are never heartening, but they can be useful if you get good advice. You should not be unduly discouraged until the number of rejections hits two digits. Think of rejections as criticism or advice and do not take them personally. It is hard to detach yourself from something to which you have devoted so much time, but make the effort. You can learn from the experience if you view it objectively. And always remember that few books are published by the first or second publisher that looks at them; one publisher's meat is another's poison.

Getting a Prompt Answer

Whether your work is going to be rejected or accepted, you want a prompt decision. Screening prospective publishers to make sure they are active in your field, sending out prospectuses, and carefully choosing where to submit first will help prevent time-consuming, unnecessary rejections. Once you have submitted your manuscript to a publisher, the best way to prevent delays is to speak up. If you have not heard from a press within three months, write a polite letter asking when you may expect a decision. If your letter is not answered within two weeks, write again or call. You may be told, "We expect to reach a decision by June 15." If June 20 arrives with no word, write or call. Keep after them. Do not be obnoxious, just firm. A polite letter or moderately worded phone call will do. But do not be afraid to be persistent. No publisher will reject your manuscript just because you are assertive. Threats, nagging, and tears, however, are counterproductive.

If things do get out of hand – your letters go unanswered, your phone calls are not returned, and months slip by – take firm action. Set a date by which you expect a response and inform the publisher. If you do not hear by then, write a letter withdrawing the manuscript from consideration and send it elsewhere. Send postage and ask that the manuscript be returned. If you like, you can write a letter of complaint to the president of the university. This will not get your manuscript accepted, but it will get a response and may prevent future abuse of authors.

Authors have been known to submit a manuscript, hear nothing for a year, and then meekly accept a form rejection letter. Don't do it! Be reasonable in your demands, but expect responsive, responsible behavior in return.

Revisions

A publisher may accept your manuscript but ask that you make certain revisions. Sometimes you will not get a contract until the revisions are made. If you do get a contract, it will have a clause about the acceptability of the final manuscript. Make sure that you and the acquiring editor agree on precisely what sort of revision is required. "Please shorten the manuscript" is inadequate; get the number of pages to be cut, or a percentage, and specific suggestions for cutting. "Fix up your notation system" requires elaboration: Exactly how should the notes be done? What style guide should you follow? "Clean up the tables" should be accompanied by a sample of the proper format. If you are asked to revise according to the suggestions of a referee, make a list of the expected changes as you understand them and ask your editor to confirm its accuracy and completeness. This is especially important if acceptance of the manuscript is contingent on revision, but it is worth doing even if the changes are merely suggested. Agree in writing on a realistic date for completion of the revisions.

You may find some of the requested revisions to be unacceptable. You may feel that they threaten the integrity of your work, that they are ill advised or irresponsible. If so, explain your objections. Both your needs and the publisher's can probably be accommodated. If not, you may have to find another publisher. The only guideline here is to make sure that the fuss you raise is commensurate with the importance of the issue. It is not worth going to the mat over footnote style or whether the book will have five illustrations or eight. Do insist that your ideas and argument remain intact.

If your publisher has not asked for revisions, but you feel some are needed, discuss this with the acquiring editor. Explain what changes you have in mind and how long it will take you to make them. The manuscript editor will want to postpone work until your changes are complete.

When you revise, follow the recommendations in Chapter 10 about retyping. Although manuscripts need not be letter perfect (unless they are being typeset from your disks), acceptance of your work is not a license for sloppiness.

Chapter 5

Working with Your Publisher

I have dealt with a good many publishers, and while I have found some few of them arrogant, discourteous, oppressive, and generally abominable in both personal and business intercourse, I desire to record my testimony that as a class they are courteous and honorable gentlemen; fair and liberal in views, intentions, and actions, and pleasant and intelligent in mind and intercourse.

Frederick B. Perkins

When a publisher accepts your book, you are beginning a relationship that will last for years. You will both be happier if you understand clearly what the publisher expects and what you can reasonably expect of the publisher. The basic responsibilities of both author and publisher are set out in the publishing contract, and you must read and understand that document. You should also know how to work with the press's staff throughout the various stages of editing and production. Finally, you should think about how you can help the publisher promote your book.

The Contract

You will receive a contract when a publisher decides to publish your book. Most publishers send two copies, both signed, with the request that you sign and return one copy. Others will send a draft contract for your review. Even in the former case, you should *never sign a contract until you have read and understood it*. Nor, in the former case, should you conclude, as many authors do, that the contract is non-negotiable, that you must simply take it or leave it. Within limits, contract provisions can be altered, and you should not hesitate to discuss your concerns with the publisher. This is now easier than it once was, since contracts are more often written in plain English rather than in legal jargon. They are less mysterious, and it is easier to see how their provisions affect you.

This section explains what you can expect from a contract with a publisher. Although it will help you to interpret the terms of a contract offered to you, it is not meant as a substitute for a lawyer's advice. If your book has unusual complications, if it has movie or TV possibilities, or if you are simply uneasy about the whole process, find a lawyer who specializes in the law of intellectual property (copyright and patents) or communications law. Your state bar association or a law school faculty member can provide a referral. The sections that follow describe the main elements of a publishing contract and some typical provisions. Publishing contracts, of course, may vary in format and organization; see *One Book/ Five Ways*, listed in the bibliography, for examples.

Timing

A publisher may offer you a contract at any time from receipt of your prospectus to acceptance of the finished, revised manuscript. A first-time author is unlikely to be offered a contract for a mere prospectus, although this does happen occasionally. Established authors may get contracts on the basis of a prospectus alone, although publishers usually want to see a chapter or two. As scholarly publishers have become more aggressive and competitive in acquiring books, the advance contract has become more common.

Publishers feel safe in offering contracts for unwritten books because all publishing contracts contain an escape clause. They usually say something like, "The author agrees to deliver to the publisher a manuscript acceptable in form, style, and content." In other words, even though you have a contract, your manuscript is still subject to internal editorial review, review by expert referees, and – in the case of a university press – approval by the press's faculty board. This clause is very broad and, as a result, has been the subject of litigation between trade publishers and authors. It is not a license for publishers to change their minds arbitrarily but a way for them to ensure that the product they ultimately acquire is of the quality they expected when they made the offer. Imagine the publisher as someone who has bought a house on the basis of an architect's plans. A buyer who approves plans for a house with four bedrooms, three baths, and 3,000 square feet of livable space will not happily pay for and take possession of one with three bedrooms, one bath, and 2,000 square feet. This clause allows the publisher to demand revisions, additions, excisions, and so forth. If such clauses did not exist, it is unlikely that any but best-selling authors would ever receive contracts for unfinished books.

A contract for an unfinished book – just like a contract for a finished one – binds the author to sending the completed manuscript to that publisher and bars negotiations with other publishers. In that sense, it is unequal: The author has no escape clause. However, an advance contract does offer certain advantages for you. It permits early and continuing collaboration, so that you get an editor's advice as you are writing, perhaps avoiding massive revision. It may include a cash advance, which always comes in handy. It may be helpful in securing tenure, promotion, or research grants. By relieving you of the worry of finding a publisher, it may enable you to work better. As a practical consideration, an advance contract reached at an early stage may make it easier to produce the book from your computer disks. Finally, although the contract does have an escape clause, it is an expression of the publisher's commitment to your book. Some university presses do not offer advance contracts without approval from their faculty boards; clearly such a contract is a serious undertaking. Others make the offer more casually. In either case, however, I believe that publishers put more effort into helping an author revise a manuscript that is not quite satisfactory if it is under contract than they do if they are seeing it for the first time.

Advance contracts do carry some disadvantages. The publisher you would most like to work with may not offer a contract while another does. Then you will have to accept the security of your second choice if you want a contract in hand. Contracts always specify a delivery date, and if you do not manage deadlines well, this can be a source of unwanted pressure and anxiety. Publishers are almost always willing to allow extra time, but contracts are sometimes canceled when a manuscript is long overdue. (This is particularly true of books that are marketable because of timeliness, such as those to be published in connection with a centennial or other commemorative event.) Contracts also generally specify maximum or minimum length, as well as a maximum number of tables, illustrations, or maps. If you have not yet started the book, or are not very far along, it may be difficult to evaluate the reasonableness of these limits. Again, no publisher will back out of a contract because a manuscript has one extra table, but if you promise a 300-page manuscript and deliver 700 pages, you may be in trouble.

I think the best time to sign a contract is when you know with a fair degree of certainty both what the book is going to be like and when you can finish it – and when the contract is offered by a publisher you think you will be happy with. Be wary of offers from presses that you know little about and that have seen little of your work. The possibilities of misunderstanding, conflict, and disappointment are too great.

Purpose

The purpose of a publishing contract is to transfer some of your rights as an author to the publisher in exchange for publication and, generally, payment. When you write a book you own it, just as you own any other sort of property. And what you own is not merely the manuscript as a physical object (which, indeed, you can sell or give away separately) but the right to copy it, distribute it, translate it, film it – to exploit it in a great variety of ways. As an individual, you are not in a very good position to take advantage of your book's potential, so you reach an agreement with a publisher to develop it.

Your rights to the book will last fifty years past your death, according to current U.S. and British copyright law, a period during which your publisher may also become defunct or possibly be reincarnated as a subsidiary of a video games and fast food conglomerate. A well-drawn contract will protect your interests, and those of your heirs, far into the future, when no person now living will be around to recall what happened.

A contract, even when written in the stuffiest legal prose, is a living document. Before it is signed, it is the subject of negotiation, of give and take, of bargaining. After the contract is signed, its full possibilities become vivid. What looked like a boilerplate clause about translation rights comes to life when a French publisher wants to issue a French edition. Perhaps the provision for a paperback edition that you ignored as unlikely suddenly becomes crucial ten years later when your book unpredictably becomes a standard text in undergraduate courses. The provisions for electronic rights become reality when a chapter of your book is included in a CD-ROM. A contract is designed to provide for all contingencies, no matter how remote. As you read it, make sure you understand what each clause means and what it implies for possible future events.

To make sure that you and the publisher work together amicably and efficiently throughout the book's publication and subsequent life, the contract spells out the rights and responsibilities of both publisher and author. It provides remedies for each party should the other fail to meet some requirement. The purpose is not to enable the publisher to steal the profits, make you do all the work, or weasel out at the last minute. Nor should the contract allow you to receive royalties when the publisher is losing vast sums on your book, to avoid doing jobs that are best done by the author, or to run off to another publisher in the middle of production.

To some extent, as noted, the terms of a contract are negotiable. Negotiations should be undertaken in a calm and objective frame of mind. Avoid paranoia. Explain why you want to change something and be prepared to offer a concession in return. This chapter will help you know what is usual and reasonable, giving you a realistic view of which contract provisions matter most, which you can expect to alter, and how much change you can hope to negotiate.

Transfer of Copyright

As the author of your work, you own the copyright. Most publishing contracts require that the author transfer, or assign, the copyright to the publisher. This means that all rights that were yours become the publisher's. These include, but are not limited to, the right to publish the book in English and all other languages, to publish excerpts or condensations in magazines, and to adapt it for film or television. It is not legally necessary to transfer the copyright; you can instead grant only certain rights to the publisher and reserve the rest. For example, you might grant the publisher only the right to publish the book in a hardbound edition in the English language. Some specialized publishers do ask only for cloth and paper publishing rights because they assume that the books they publish have no further commercial possibilities, and they have no interest in pursuing the sale of translation, serial, and other rights. Most publishers, however, will not accept such a limited grant.

It is not generally to the author's advantage to retain rights because such an arrangement would require the author to sell all the other rights (paperback, translation, movie, and so forth) separately. Aside from the fact that few of these rights are valuable for most scholarly books, authors are rarely equipped to negotiate with paperback houses, foreign publishers, and movie moguls. Publishers can do this better, and the share they take of the profits is generally well earned. Authors of best-sellers, along with their agents, may try to reserve various rights, but even they rarely succeed. For best-sellers, much of the publisher's profit comes from the sale of foreign, paperback, serial, movie, or TV rights rather than from sales of the hardback book. They are unlikely to give up these profits.

By transferring the copyright, you do not give up your share of profits from nonbook rights. As we shall see, the contract spells out how the proceeds from the sale or licensing of each right are divided, and the percentages are negotiable.

Transfers of copyright are not eternal. They can be terminated in two ways. First, the contract may provide for termination after a specified period or if the publisher allows the book to go out of print (i.e., if the publisher no longer has copies available for sale and declines to reprint). Second, even if the contract does not mention termination, the copyright law allows authors (or their widows, widowers, children, or grandchildren) to terminate the transfer during the five years beginning thirty-five years after the date of the transfer and ending forty years after that date (for publication rights, the five-year period can begin either forty years after the date of the transfer or thirty-five years after first publication, whichever is earlier). After thirty-five or forty years, however, most of the damage is done, so including a termination clause in the contract is much to your benefit. Termination returns to you only the basic publication right plus any others not yet sold or licensed. For example, if your publisher has sold the Italian publishing rights, that contract continues in force for its full term, despite your termination of the assignment of copyright from which it was derived.

Specific Rights

The most basic right involved in a book contract is the right of publication, of offering copies to the public. The contract will grant the publisher the exclusive right to publish your work in book form; in return, the publisher will (usually) pay you a royalty, as I will explain shortly. Generally, contracts will include under this right book publication in all languages throughout the world. You must understand that by granting the publisher this exclusive right you are promising not to allow anyone else to publish your work as a book in any language anywhere in the world.

How publishers exploit this right will depend on their view of the book's market abroad and on their usual marketing arrangements. For example, a large Anglo-American press is in an excellent position to sell your book in English in the United States, Canada, the United Kingdom, Australia – throughout the English-speaking world. American publishers are likely to seek British co-publishers if they foresee the possibility of sales in the United Kingdom. To exploit a non-English market, presses sell translation rights. Some publishers are more diligent about such activities than others, and some books are more salable abroad than others. If you have ideas about translations, share them with your acquisitions editor or the subsidiary rights manager. More important, if a foreign press or scholar writes to you about translation rights, respond by explaining that the rights are held by your publisher and that you will pass on the inquiry. The proceeds from such sales will be divided between you and the publisher, as I will explain shortly.

Some contracts specify that the publisher will consult the author before selling foreign rights. If your book has potential for translation, and if you are knowledgeable about the publishers in the relevant countries, such a clause is valuable. Similarly, if you are fluent in a language, you may want to ask for the right to review and approve any translation into that language.

A closely related right that is sometimes listed separately is that of publishing the book in paperback. The paperback rights to best-sellers are generally sold (sometimes at auction) to paperback houses for large sums. With rare exceptions, however, publishers of scholarly books retain these rights and publish the paperback edition (if there is one) themselves. Authors are paid a royalty.

Rights other than publication and translation rights are sometimes called subsidiary rights. One group of such rights that the contract will specify is serial rights – the right to publish portions of your book in magazines, journals, or newspapers. "First serial" rights refer to such publication before the book appears; "second serial" rights apply to such publication after book publication. You need not worry if some of the material in your book, or even a whole chapter, has appeared in a journal, although you should certainly let the publisher know. Once you have signed a contract, however, you should not attempt to publish portions of your manuscript elsewhere without consulting the book publisher.

Serial rights can be important in generating income, especially if they are sold to a periodical with a large general circulation (e.g., *The New Yorker* or *Psychology Today*). More often their importance lies in their ability to generate sales by calling attention to the book, even if the direct payment by the periodical is small. As in the sale of foreign rights, proceeds of such sales are divided between author and publisher, and the contract may require the publisher to seek the author's consent before granting such rights.

The right to sell abridged, "digest," or condensed versions of your work may also be specified. Scholarly books are rarely of interest to *Reader's Digest*, but abridgments may be anthologized, and condensations of multivolume works are not unheard of, especially when such condensation makes them attractive as textbooks. You will probably want to ask for the right to review and approve abridgments and condensations; in fact, you may want to specify that you be asked first to do any condensation the publisher itself issues or licenses to another publisher.

Excerpts from scholarly works are sometimes published in

readers or anthologies, and your contract will mention such uses specifically. Usually the compiler will want to use a chapter of your book, although sometimes an abridged version is used. You are granting the publisher the right to review such requests, to specify the conditions under which the material can be used, and to set and collect a fee. You may also want to review such requests, and the contract will specify your share in the fee. Like you, the publisher will be concerned about the way your material is treated in the anthology; permission probably would be denied if your work was to be used as a bad example or if the abridgment distorted your argument. The publisher also will be concerned about the effect of the compilation on the commercial value of your work. For example, the inclusion of one chapter in an anthology might increase interest in your book and enhance sales, whereas publication of another chapter (say, the conclusion) might actually reduce sales of your book. Any requests you receive for reprinting part of your work in an anthology must be referred to the publisher. You or your publisher may also receive requests to include part of your book in an electronic database or other nonprint medium. These requests should be handled in the same way.

Similarly, the contract will specify that the publisher has the right to grant permission to quote from your work. "Permissions" are discussed briefly later in this chapter and at length in Chapter 10. When other writers want to publish portions of your work that fall somewhere between a few words and an anthology selection, they must ask permission. These requests are a real nuisance to deal with, and you should be delighted that your publisher is taking them on. If any fee is collected, it will be shared according to the contract provision.

Book club rights increase circulation and sales of your book. Although few scholarly books are candidates for the Literary Guild or Book-of-the-Month Club, some may interest more specialized groups. It is probably worth your while to look through the book club listings in *Literary Market Place* to see whether any group looks promising. If you find one or two, send the suggestion to your publisher. Authors generally receive less money per copy on books sold through book clubs (contracts generally share the proceeds of book club sales equally between author and publisher, but book clubs receive large discounts). Nevertheless, sales to book clubs permit publishers to take advantage of the economies of larger print runs (see Chapter 12), and they do enhance the visibility and sales of books.

The contract will also list specifically some rights that are more exotic – and less likely to be sold. Even though your monograph is unlikely to appear on "Masterpiece Theater" or to be animated by the Walt Disney Studios, read the provisions and check on the division of revenues.

Electronic rights are currently the subject of dispute between authors' groups and publishers. Some publishers are issuing contracts that require the author to assign all electronic rights; authors' groups argue that authors should retain such rights. The discussion is important because no one knows how extensive electronic exploitation will be, what forms it will take, or how much revenue these uses will generate. Publishers want to know that authors will not take a profitable use of their work elsewhere; authors want to ensure that they are not giving away something of value. There are no norms to follow in this area, so you will have to negotiate this on your own. If your contract does not specifically assign electronic rights to the publisher or contain a clause that says all rights not specifically assigned belong to the publisher, then you have retained these rights.

Despite the great variety of these rights, their transfer to the publisher involves only a few important ideas that you need to understand. First, the publisher will exploit only some of these rights directly, selling or licensing most of them to others. For example, an American publisher will sell to a French publisher the right to translate the book into French and sell it in the French market; grant a movie producer an option to produce a film version; and sell an excerpt to *Vanity Fair*. These arrangements may be exclusive or nonexclusive (perhaps *Elle* will buy another excerpt, or two different anthologies might include the same chapter); indefinite or for a specific period (movie options expire and can then be sold to another would-be producer); and worldwide or geographically limited (Spanish-language rights throughout the world, for example, as opposed to English-language rights outside North America). Also, although few books can be fully exploited, every contract provides for all rights just in case. Do not ignore these provisions, even though they seem remote. Finally, even if you have assigned all rights to the publisher, you retain a financial and professional stake in them. Pass on all inquiries about translations, anthologies, and so forth, as well as any ideas you have about possible buyers of various rights, to your acquiring editor or to the manager of subsidiary rights.

The Publisher's Duties

As explained earlier, you assign the copyright of your book to a publisher in exchange for publication and payment. The publisher's most important obligation is to publish your book – that is, to edit, design, produce, and distribute it. The contract will make this clear, but it will not usually state how quickly the publisher must do all of this. You may ask that the publisher agree to publish the book within a certain time after you submit a complete, revised manuscript; two years would certainly be adequate. Most publishers would prefer not to include such a clause, and they often have good reasons. But if you are concerned about excessive delay, either because your book is on a current topic or because the press has a reputation for tardiness, you can ask. (Remember, however, that should the deadline pass, you would have to start all over again to find another publisher. This is unlikely to get the book out faster.)

The contract will require that the publisher copyright your book and make sure that it is published in conformity with copyright regulations. This is very simple for publishers to do. They need merely print the standard copyright notice in an appropriate place in the book. Most publishers will also file a form, send two copies of the work (for deposit in the Library of Congress), and pay a small fee to the U.S. Register of Copyrights. Although your rights are protected without registration (i.e., your failure to register the copyright does not make it legal for others to steal your work), you cannot sue for copyright infringement until the book is registered. Since registration is simple and inexpensive, most publishers consider it a wise precaution.

Upon publication of your book, the publisher will give you a specified number of free copies (usually five or ten). Most contracts also permit you to buy additional copies for your own use (not for resale) at a discount of 40 to 50 percent. Many also offer authors discounts on all the books they publish.

Royalties and Other Payments

The royalty system is a financial expression of the idea that the fates of author and publisher are inextricable. If a book succeeds, both parties share in the rewards. If it fails, neither party makes any money. Why, you may ask, is the author's share a measly 5 to 10 percent? Chapter 12 illustrates how that percentage compares with the publisher's profit and, in fact, demonstrates that it is usually a pretty fair share. For now, it is probably adequate to understand that the publisher does not get the other 90 to 95 percent; most of it goes to typesetters, printers, binders, paper manufacturers, whole-sale jobbers, and retail stores. The publisher's share must also pay salaries, rent, utilities, and other expenses.

Royalties, generally paid once a year, begin sometime after publication, depending on the publisher's accounting year. The check is preceded or accompanied by a statement of sales or revenues. The contract will spell out when royalties are to be paid and should give you permission to inspect the publisher's records insofar as they relate to your book.

Some contracts provide for an advance to be paid on royalties. As noted in Chapter 4, an advance is a cash payment made to the author on signing the contract, on delivering an acceptable manuscript, or at some other specified moment. It is not money paid in addition to royalties or instead of them; it is simply a sum paid in advance and subsequently deducted from the royalties the book has earned. Obviously, publishers will not offer advances of more than they expect a book to earn. Authors of scholarly monographs can expect only small advances, if any. Publishers may offer an advance to help you finish your book more quickly (e.g., money for a research trip), to help you pay for illustrations or other costs, or just to compete successfully with another publisher. You can ask for an advance, but do not expect a large sum. For example, suppose the publisher expects to sell 2,000 copies of your book (an optimistic estimate for many a monograph) at $30.00 a copy, paying you 6 percent of the retail price in royalties. The most you could expect to earn would be $3,600, and the publisher would probably balk at advancing more than half of that.

Royalty rates vary and are negotiable. They are calculated as a percentage either of retail price or of net sales (the publisher's revenues) of your book. It is easy to estimate royalties calculated on retail price: If a book sells for $30.00 and your royalty is 10 percent, you will receive $3.00 for each copy sold. When royalties are paid on net sales, the calculation is more difficult. Some books are sold directly to readers for the full $30.00; others are sold to retailers and wholesalers at discounts ranging from 20 to 40 percent or more (netting $24.00 to $18.00 or less). Your 10 percent, then, is $3.00, $2.40, or $1.80. Generally, royalties based on retail price will be paid at a lower percentage than those based on net price. As a rule of thumb, 10 percent of net is roughly equal to 6 or 7 percent of retail. The percentages are negotiable, though the base usually is not: Publishers prefer uniform accounting procedures. This means that if you are offered a royalty of 8 percent of net sales, you may succeed at bargaining for 9 or 10 percent of net, but you will not get 8 (or even 6) percent of retail.

Regardless of the base on which royalties are calculated,

the range of royalties begins at zero. Some publishers simply do not pay royalties on some books. Some pay royalties but only after a certain number of books (usually 500 or 1,000) have been sold; this practice has become increasingly common in recent years. Some offer an escalating royalty schedule: As sales reach certain specified levels, the percentage increases (say 5 percent for the first 2,500; 7.5 percent for the next 2,500; and 10 percent thereafter). Most offer one schedule for casebound (hardback) books and another for paperbacks. The top of the scale for scholarly books is probably 10 percent of retail; for textbooks, it is 15 percent. Feel free to bargain within the range, but do not expect to raise an offer by more than a percentage point or two.

One case in which it is appropriate to ask for higher royalties is that in which you do work that is traditionally the publisher's. If, for example, you enter the manuscript editor's changes and the typesetting codes onto your computer disks so that the book can be set directly from your disks, you are entitled to higher royalties than if you had merely provided a typescript. Some publishers automatically write this differential into their contracts, giving an extra percentage point or two to the harder-working author. Others might simply pay the author an amount based on the typesetting charges saved. Alternatively, the savings can be used to keep the price of the book down.

Most contracts list the types of transactions for which royalties are not paid. These include books given away free as a courtesy or for review, books that are returned by booksellers, and books sold at or below cost. The first category is obvious, but the others require a brief explanation. Unlike most retailers, booksellers have the privilege of returning merchandise that they cannot sell. Thus, what registers on the publisher's ledger as a sale in January may appear as a return in June. Since returned books are never actually sold, no royalties are paid on them. This may be reflected in your royalty statements, with an amount deducted from your second-year royalties for books that appeared to be sold – and on which royalties were paid – in the first year but that were subsequently returned. Trade publishers may also deduct a certain amount from royalties as a reserve against expected returns. Books may be sold below the publisher's manufacturing cost when they are "remaindered." If, after a few years, a book is selling very slowly or not at all, the publisher may offer it at a sale price. If it still does not sell, the publisher may sell the remaining copies to a company that pays very little and then sells them for somewhat more. (The obvious case is the giant coffee-table book on the bargain table for $4.95.) If the book is sold to the remainder house at a price below the publisher's cost, the author receives no royalty. After all, the royalty is a share in the book's success.

Many contracts provide that the publisher need not pay royalties when the total due is less than a specified amount or when fewer than a certain number of books are sold. This is done because of the bookkeeping costs involved. Generally the sum is held over until the next year, although sometimes it is not paid at all. This is a reasonable provision if the amount specified is reasonable – say, $25.00 or the sales needed to generate that amount in royalties. Sums beyond that should be paid out. After all, it doesn't cost that much to write a check.

Although royalty contracts are the most common, publishers sometimes pay authors a fee, either at one time or in installments (say, one-third on signing the contract, one-third on submitting the manuscript, and one-third on final acceptance). The advantage for the author is getting cash up front; the disadvantage is that in the end the author will get less than royalties would have provided if the book does well. The fee arrangement is most common for contributors to a collection of articles or essays, where it is a practical and generally fair way of doing business. However, a contract of this sort for a complete volume should provide for unanticipated success. For example, the author should get an additional payment if the book is reprinted, or a supplementary royalty schedule might kick in after a certain (large) number of copies have been sold.

In addition to royalties or fees, an author may receive payments from a publisher that represent the author's share of rights sold or licensed to others. The contract will state what percentage of the proceeds the author gets from the sale of such rights. The variations are endless, but 50 percent is common. For serial and movie rights, the author's share may rise to 75 or even 90 percent. These shares are paid either when the publisher collects them or in the annual royalty accounting.

In sum, the publisher's job is to publish your book, exploit its possibilities, and collect and share the proceeds of all sales. What is the author's job?

The Author's Duties

The contract will tell you when you have to deliver the completed manuscript (if you have not already done so) and in how many copies. It may specify a minimum or maximum length and the number of tables, maps, photographs, and other illustrations that will be expected. It may be very specific about the physical condition of the manuscript. Some publishers may require that you submit your manuscript on computer disks as well as in hard copy. This provision may be very specific about the software to be used and other details. Still other contracts will require that you submit "camera-ready copy" (pages that can be photographed as is, for printing). If you are unable or unwilling to do this kind of work, you must negotiate these provisions with the publisher. Chapter 11 discusses such provisions in more detail.

The contract will also enumerate the tasks you must do during production: reviewing the copy editing, proofreading, and preparing an index. Chapter 10 discusses these processes in detail. What you need to understand as you read the contract is the financial implications of these provisions.

The publishing contract specifies at what stages in the production process you will be allowed to make changes and how extensive those changes can be. In reviewing the edited manuscript, you are free to make changes quite liberally. In fact, you should regard this as the last opportunity to make changes. When you are reading proof, the number of changes you can make is greatly restricted. Some contracts permit no changes in proof beyond correcting the typesetter's errors. Others allow a small number, which is expressed as a percentage of the total typesetting cost. This is a very difficult number for authors to interpret. Say the contract provides that you will be charged for all changes that cost more than 5 percent of typesetting costs. If the typesetting bill is $3,000, then you will be allowed to chalk up $150 worth of changes without charge. Changes made to proof are done by labor-intensive hand methods and are far more expensive than the original typesetting, so that the $150 gets eaten up very quickly. In fact, 5 percent barely allows for normal human error. It would be very unusual for a publisher to allow the author more extensive free changes in proof. The only time this possibility would be worth raising is in the case where a book is very timely and last-minute changes in, say, election statistics are expected. In most cases, the best way to avoid disagreements and expense is to review the edited manuscript very carefully and make all your changes then.

If you are submitting your manuscript on disk and are responsible for entering editorial and authorial changes, this clause is rendered meaningless: The typesetter's bill will be reduced (or even eliminated if the publisher uses its own laser printer), and the cost of making changes falls on you anyway. What is important in these cases is that you not make changes without the publisher's knowledge. Although I have not yet seen an appropriate substitute clause, publishers should soon think of a way to limit the timing and extent of changes that does not relate to typesetting charges.

The standard contract provides for the author's reading of galley and page proof only. If you wish to see later stages of proof, you will have to negotiate such a provision with your publisher. This is necessary only in the case of an unusually complex or demanding work, such as a critical or documentary edition, and such a request is unlikely to be granted in other cases.

Another duty that may fall to the author is to provide artwork. This means that you must locate or create the art, get written permission to use it, provide acceptable copies, and pay reproduction charges and permissions fees. Chapter 10 provides detailed information on procuring illustrations. For now, you should understand that, except for some text-books, the contract places this responsibility clearly with you. In the case of a heavily illustrated book, you may be able to get the publisher to share the costs of acquiring art. Another possibility is to get the publisher to pay such costs out of royalties so that you do not have to come up with large amounts of cash. All these possibilities should be raised and negotiated.

Most contracts stipulate that the author must provide an index or pay to have it done. Chapter 10 provides advice on preparing indexes. At the contract stage, however, if you think you will want to hire a professional indexer, ask the publisher to find one and, if possible, advance the fee from your royalties.

The clause that imposes a duty on almost every academic author is the one that gives the author the responsibility for getting permission to reprint other people's work. This is an obvious task in the case of anthologies and for illustrated books, but it occurs in dealing with unillustrated monographs as well. Anytime you use someone else's tables, figures, or words at significant length, you must get written permission and, if requested, pay a fee. Chapter 10 provides guidelines, and your publisher may have some suggestions as well.

You may be asked to give the publisher the "right of first refusal" on your next book. This means you must submit it to the publisher first, to accept or not. Most publishers will give up this right if you ask them to do so. If the relationship works out well, you will come back anyway; and if it doesn't, they will not want a hostile author. Some contracts simply stipulate that you not publish any competing book as long as this one is in print. This provision is relevant mostly to textbook publishing.

Important Legal Considerations

In signing your contract, you represent that the work is your own, that it is not libelous, and that you have not promised it to anyone else. Sometimes you must agree to pay any expenses arising out of litigation involving claims of libel, copyright infringement, or plagiarism. These representations are a combination of ethical commitments that we all hope are universally understood and of legal considerations that require some explanation.

Of course, if we all obeyed the ethical canons of our professions automatically, they would not need to be written into contracts. Rather than moralize, let me remind you very simply that you have an obligation to credit others accurately and fully for their work. "Others" include colleagues whose work you have used, students who have assisted with research, and friends or informants who have provided information. "Work" includes words, ideas, drawings, memories, data – all the raw material of scholarship. All original work is built upon the contributions of others, and these contributions must be acknowledged. I must remind you also that what you write should be true – no falsified data, no fictional notes, no creative quotations. Also, do not sign more than one contract for the same book.

Using someone else's work without giving credit may go beyond plagiarism into copyright infringement. As a responsible author, you should understand the fundamentals of copyright law. Under U.S. copyright law, all works of an author – whether published or not – are protected from unauthorized use from the moment of creation until fifty years after the author's death. (There are some variations on this for older U.S. works because the current law went into effect in 1978.) "Works" include fiction, nonfiction, poetry, letters, tables, graphs, paintings, sculpture, drawings, photographs, music, and song lyrics. The law is designed to protect authors' rights, not to restrict unnecessarily the legitimate use of their works by others. Under the doctrine of fair use, you can quote a reasonable (though unspecified) amount from protected works without permission. If you wish to use more than that, you must get written permission from the copyright holder and, if asked, pay a fee. Although this may seem a nuisance when you are the quoter, you can appreciate its importance when you are a potential quotee. Chapter 10 provides a summary of when you need permission to quote and how to go about obtaining it. The bibliography lists books that provide more detailed information about copyright.

Libel is a legal problem that academic authors tend to ignore, believing that it is something only journalists have to worry about. Unfortunately, it is quite possible for a scholarly writer to libel someone. You commit libel when you write something about a living person that is both untrue and harmful. In libel law, harmful statements are those that damage a person's reputation, business or profession, or social life. They include statements or suggestions that someone is a criminal, communist, Nazi, or bankrupt, suffers from a loathsome or feared disease, or has behaved unethically. There are of course many other possibilities. Libelous statements need not be blatant. They can be as subtle as the classic entry in a ship's log: "Captain was sober today."

Libel law is complex and changing. For example, the standards applied vary depending on whether the subject is an ordinary person or a public official. Libel law is also much stricter outside the United States, most relevantly in the United Kingdom and Canada. If you are writing about controversial events or subjects, you need to be sure that what you say about living people could be proved in court. If you are not sure, you need to write very carefully. Though you need not resort to the journalist's "alleged perpetrator," you can avoid difficulty. For example, instead of claiming that "Alderman X accepted bribes from numerous contractors," you may need to write, "Good government groups have repeatedly charged Alderman X with accepting bribes, but he has denied the charges. He has been tried twice for bribery, but both trials ended with hung juries." You may also want to have a lawyer review your manuscript for libel. Your state bar association will refer you to lawyers experienced in the field.

Even scholars writing about events that occurred hundreds of years ago can commit libel by making careless accusations against fellow scholars. In commenting on the works of others, you should avoid hyperbole. If you consider a theory far-fetched, limit yourself to a reasoned assessment of the theory and do not call its originator a fool, an incompetent, or a lunatic. Do not accuse your colleagues of plagiarism, shoddy research, or unethical conduct unless you can prove the charges. And even if you think you can, is it really worth the expense and delay of a lawsuit? Litigation can keep your book in limbo for years and cost thousands of dollars. It is best to avoid the problem by careful research and writing.

Like copyright law, libel law is not meant to limit freedom of expression. It is designed to protect against unwarranted embarrassment and harm to one's professional or personal reputation. On the whole, compliance with the law benefits writing by making it more careful, accurate, and precise.

Signature

If there is anything in the contract that you do not understand, ask the publisher to explain it. If some provision is extremely important to you and is not spelled out, explain this to the publisher and ask for a rider on the contract or a letter of understanding. For example, you may wish to review translations, excerpts, or condensations for accuracy. When you understand everything in the contract and are satisfied with it, sign one copy and return it. Keep the other copy in a safe place.

Subventions

Many university presses receive subsidies from their sponsoring institutions and, often, from private foundations or government agencies. For a long time, some presses hesitated to seek outside money with strings attached, fearing a loss of control or integrity. For example, if a foundation or government agency offered a press $50,000 to publish books in economics, might the publisher not select more economics books than otherwise? Or even accept inferior works to avoid losing the gift? This hesitation has largely been overcome as the fears associated with limited-purpose grants have proved unfounded.

Author Subventions

A more controversial form of subsidy is the author subvention – a grant of money from the author to defray the costs of publication. "Aha!" you say. "That smacks of vanity publishing!" Yes, it does, and that is why it is so controversial among publishers. In fact, it is not the same thing, but the differences can become blurred. Remember that a vanity press will publish anything, as long as the author pays for it. The author's money is both necessary and sufficient for a positive editorial decision. University presses that request author subventions separate the decision to publish from the author's willingness to pay. If the manuscript does not meet their standards, they will not publish it, even if the author offers money. In other words, the subvention may be necessary, but it is not sufficient. Sometimes it isn't even necessary: The press may request a subvention but publish even if the money is not forthcoming.

Another difference is in the amount of money requested. A vanity press requires the author to pay all costs plus a profit to the publisher. A university press will ask only that the author share costs. According to a 1977 survey by John

Hazel Smith, the average subvention requested by university presses was between $2,000 and $5,000, with the range covering $1,000 or less through $15,000 (although it can go as high as $100,000 for art books).[1] (Despite overall inflation, these numbers probably have not changed much.)

Finally, university presses ask for subventions not to enhance their profits but to enable them to publish books that otherwise would not make economic sense. You may have written a book that will be of immense value to a few hundred people. If it is to be published in an edition of a few hundred copies at a reasonable price, a subvention will be needed. A book of wider appeal – with potential sales of, say, a thousand copies – that is expensive to produce because of elaborate tables, many photographs, or difficult typesetting may also require a subvention. Presses do not routinely request subventions, but many will ask for them when a good manuscript cannot otherwise pay its way.

Some publishers, in lieu of a cash subvention, ask for a commitment on the part of the author's university bookstore to purchase a certain number of copies, presumably for sale as textbooks. This seems to me more problematic than a cash subvention. If the book really is a textbook it should be published as such and should be used in courses other than the author's. Many universities require faculty members to get a dean's permission to use their own books as texts, to avoid abuse. Subventions can legitimately come from authors, their institutions, or foundations but not, I think, from students.

What should you do if a reputable press accepts your manuscript but asks for a subvention? You can, of course, refuse. They may agree to publish the book anyway, or you can go to another publisher. But if the publisher is the one you know you want to work with, if you are under pressure to publish quickly, or if you have been turned down by several other presses – and if you can come up with the money – you may well agree to pay the subvention.

[1] John Hazel Smith, "Subventions of Scholarly Publishing," *Scholarly Publishing* 9, no. 1 (October 1977): 19–29, provides details on amounts and conditions of subventions.

The subvention need not come from your own pocket. Some universities are willing to pay subventions for faculty members and have special funds for the purpose. Others are willing but have to label the grant something else – research assistance, faculty grants-in-aid, or some other blanket category. Still others cannot give money for faculty publication but can provide services, including production of artwork and photographs, proofreading, typing, preparation of an index, mailing of advertising flyers, and so forth. In specialized fields, a publisher may require you to provide camera-ready copy rather than typesetting the book (this practice is more common among commercial scholarly publishers and university research centers than among university presses). Your university may be willing to provide this service. Explore these alternatives with your publisher and your dean.

If you do agree to pay a subvention, there are four issues to raise before signing a contract. First, make sure the amount is reasonable. You can ask how it was computed, and look again at the range of subventions given earlier. If your manuscript is a fairly ordinary scholarly work – up to 500 manuscript pages, without many tables or illustrations, and using no foreign alphabets – anything over $5,000 is probably excessive. If it is illustrated, especially with color plates, if it has a lot of tables or requires complex typesetting, the amount requested may reasonably be much higher. Do not hesitate to bargain over the amount. Remember, the publisher does want your book.

Second, the contract should provide for royalties to return the subvention if the book miraculously sells enough copies to repay the publisher's investment. Publishers are not infallible, and their pessimism about sales may be excessive.

Third, ask the publisher to cooperate with you in seeking outside money. Publishers should be aware of funding sources in fields in which they are active, and they should be willing to spend some time looking for help. The next section provides an introduction to this process.

Finally, if your department or administration suggests that it regards the subvention as a form of vanity publishing, the press director should write a letter stating that the decision to publish was made on the basis of the manuscript's quality, without regard to the availability of a subvention, that it was subjected to normal refereeing procedures, and that the subvention is requested only because of the work's limited salability.

If you cannot raise the money and do not have it yourself, say so. The press may well go ahead anyway.

Author subventions present publishers with a difficult problem. On the one hand, they invite accusations of vanity publishing and the possibility of undue outside influence; on the other hand, they make possible the publication of much valuable but unprofitable scholarship and make it less necessary for presses to seek out semicommercial manuscripts. They also make it possible to keep the price of a book low enough to maximize sales and readership. I cannot see any ethical problems from the author's point of view – although raising the money is a practical problem. The book has been accepted on its merits, and the subvention in no way detracts from its quality. Of course, anyone would rather not pay a subvention, but it may be a wise investment. If, for example, being promoted to associate professor requires having a book published and brings a pay increase, the average subvention pays for itself pretty quickly.

Seeking Grants

Much academic research is supported by grants from government agencies or private foundations. Some of these same agencies and foundations also provide grants for publication costs, but most do not have special grant programs for this purpose. Others do have subvention programs but limit their grants to translations, critical editions, or other specific sorts of publications. In the appendix, I have provided names, addresses, and brief descriptions of some groups that do have special programs, but you and your publisher should not regard these as the only places to turn. The same agencies that supported your research may also provide a subvention for publication costs if they are approached properly. It is worth reminding grantors that the research they have supported is far more valuable if it is widely disseminated through publication, even if such dissemination is not likely to pay for itself.

The best time to approach a foundation or agency about funding publication is when you apply for the research grant. Depending on the regulations of the grantor, you may be able to apply in your original proposal for such publication costs as preparing illustrations; paying permissions fees; paying page charges; hiring an editor, indexer, proofreader, or word processor; or preparing camera-ready copy. You may also be able to request funds for a direct subvention to a publisher. But you must anticipate and estimate all of these costs at the time of the proposal.

If you do not ask for such funds along with your application for research support, it may be possible to go back to the foundation or agency with a later request. Even if they do not list such expenses among those they will support, they may do so if asked, particularly since the subvention is generally far smaller than the research grant. When making such a request after the research is completed, you would do well to have a publisher lined up who is willing to provide financial estimates justifying the subvention; most will do this happily. Of course, if you are fortunate enough to have some money left over from the original grant, you may be able to use that for the subvention. Do not do so, however, without asking permission.

It is also possible to find support for publication costs from fresh sources. If you are working with your home university press, you can jointly investigate local foundations, corporations, or institutions that might provide support. At some universities, as unlikely a source as the alumni foundation has funds for such projects. Otherwise, you can seek help from groups in your area, while the publisher looks for support in theirs. Your university's office of grants and contracts can provide assistance in this task. A publisher who is active in your field should be aware of any national foundations that support work in that field. The publisher should also know about the programs listed in the appendix, and you should familiarize yourself with these as well. In any case, it is important for you and the publisher to work together, or at least to keep one another informed of fund-raising activities. It is embarrassing to the author and publisher, and extremely annoying to foundations, when separate applications come from a publisher and an author seeking support for the same book.

Working with an Editor

When your manuscript is accepted, with final revisions completed, the acquiring editor will review it and decide whether it is ready to go into production. At this stage, the manuscript must contain all your revisions and responses to readers' and editors' comments. It must also be in acceptable physical condition so that the manuscript editor and designer can work with it.

Once your manuscript is judged ready for production, it will be assigned to a manuscript or copy editor and possibly to a production editor. The manuscript editor's job is to help you get the book into the most readable form possible. Depending on the state of your manuscript, this work will range from very minor corrections to extensive changes. You will have a chance to review these changes and, if necessary, discuss them with your editor. Throughout the editing process, keep four things in mind: (1) This is your book, and the ideas and general style should remain yours; (2) the editor is not an expert in your field, but he or she is an expert in scholarly publishing, and you should listen to advice of that sort offered; (3) editorial changes should not be taken as personal insults; (4) you and the editor are on the same side, and you both want the book to be as good as possible.

What sorts of changes will a manuscript editor suggest (or insist upon)? All editing, no matter how slight, attends to details of grammar, usage, punctuation, capitalization, and spelling. Chances are that the editor knows a good deal more about these subjects than you do, but if you see an error or do not understand a change, point it out and ask for an explanation. If your field has stylistic peculiarities (like the philosopher's eccentric spelling of *premiss*), let the editor know ahead of time.

Many words are spelled differently in the United States, Canada, and Great Britain, and there is some variation in usage and punctuation among these English-speaking countries. Publishers generally insist on the spelling and punctuation accepted in their own country, although they sometimes decide it is not worth the trouble to alter the author's work. No publisher, in any country, will allow a mixture of spelling systems. Books that are published in both the United States and Great Britain will almost always use one system or the other for both editions; rarely do publishers reset a book merely to alter spelling.

You should also know about "house style." This is a reference not to writing style but to such details as what nouns should be capitalized, whether terms should be in quotes or italicized, how to arrange notes, how to deal with foreign words, when to spell out numerals, and so forth. It is the kind of style referred to in the title of *The Chicago Manual of Style*, which is the bible of scholarly publishing. An editor will make your book conform to house style, to the style of your discipline, or to some consistent version of your own style. If, under the shelter of house style, the editor makes changes that conflict with the canons of your discipline, you should raise the issue. For example, political scientists like to refer to Representative Smith, whereas *Chicago* prefers Congressman. Another possible problem with house style arises through misunderstanding of special terms. In *Paradise Lost*, for example, Sin and Death are characters, so their names must be capitalized in a book analyzing the epic. An editor who does not know this may lowercase them. Fix them and explain why, lest they get changed back again. At some presses, the copy editor sends a style sheet to the author before beginning work, so that difficulties can be ironed out in advance. Some presses also send one or two edited chapters to the author for review before proceeding. British and U.S. styles differ, so if you work with a transatlantic publisher, you may find editorial changes of this sort more obtrusive.

Your own style is another matter. Wolcott Gibbs, an editor at *The New Yorker*, once instructed his editors to "try to preserve an author's style if he is an author and has a style."[2] You may or may not have a style in this grander sense of the word. If your style includes verbosity, pomposity, or pedantry, be grateful to the editor who refuses to preserve it. If you take justifiable pride in your writing (it's justifiable if people other than your parents have offered praise), then you probably will not be subjected to excessive tampering. If you feel your work is being overedited, say so.

Humor is a matter of style that deserves special comment. If your editor tells you that a joke or pun is in bad taste, not funny, or inappropriate, do not argue. Ninety-nine percent of the time, the editor is right.

Do not fight changes designed to make your manuscript more accessible. It may be true that everyone interested in corporatism in Brazil reads Portuguese, but if they are the only ones who buy your book, you are in trouble. Readers interested in corporatism outside Brazil may buy it if you make it possible for them to read it. So when your editor asks you to translate your Portuguese quotations, do so. Define terms when asked, and change jargon to English. Plain speaking never detracts from scholarly value.

You and your manuscript editor should deal diplomatically with each other. A good editor will ask polite questions and suggest changes without comment or with tactful comments. If you have written a book about twentieth-century France and misspelled de Gaulle, or called him Alfred, the editor will fix your gaffe silently, without pointing out what a dumb

[2] Quoted in James Thurber, *The Years with Ross* (Boston: Little, Brown, 1959; rept. ed., New York: Ballantine, 1972), p. 117.

mistake it is. You should also be polite in answering queries. Do not write, "No!!! You moron!!! Don't you know that cooking inactivates the avidin not the biotin?????" Just answer, "No, avidin is right."

Remember, too, that editors do not change things randomly. They have reasons. Perhaps your sentence was awkward, ambiguous, or just too long. When you do not like a change, or the change has altered your meaning, try to locate the original problem and offer an alternative solution. If you cannot figure it out, explain what is wrong with the editor's change and work it out together.

Occasionally authors feel they have been saddled with an incompetent editor. If you are having real problems, call or write to the copy editor and express your misgivings and explain your reasons. If this does not work, get in touch with the acquisitions editor who accepted your manuscript, who can then act as a mediator.

You will get the copy-edited manuscript back for review. The physical form of this manuscript will depend on the publisher's procedures and on whether your computer disks will be used for typesetting. You may receive ordinary hard copy, with the editor's changes written on it; this is the traditional process. Alternatively, you may received "red-lined" hard copy: a printout of the edited manuscript with alterations, deletions, and queries printed out like text, but distinguished typographically by certain symbols (for example, angle brackets). Each word-processing program uses different symbols, but they are not difficult to decipher. You may – though this is unlikely – receive a clean, edited copy that shows only queries, not editorial changes. Although some journals handle electronic manuscripts this way, most book publishers would not do so without consulting the author in advance. In any case, you will probably be asked to make changes and respond to queries on hard copy, rather than on disks, unless you are also entering typesetting codes or providing camera-ready pages. (Chapter 11 provides further details on handling electronic manuscripts.) After answering queries and reviewing the editing, give the manuscript one final, very careful reading. This is really your last chance to make changes. In proof, changes – if permitted at all – are costly, time-consuming, and risky. (The advent of desktop typesetting may reduce the cost and the risks.)

Some publishers employ production editors who oversee manuscript editing, design, and manufacture. The production editor is your liaison with the copy editor, the designer, and manufacturers. The production editor is particularly important to authors when the press uses freelance copy editors. Most presses use freelancers occasionally, and some use them for nearly all copy editing. This enables the publisher to maintain a smaller staff and to use editors who specialize in certain fields. For example, a press may not publish enough books in biology to employ full-time a first-rate life sciences editor; a freelancer fills this need. Freelancers are essential in textbook publishing, which is seasonal. If all copy editors and production people were employed full-time, they would spend several months a year twiddling their thumbs. Some authors are insulted when their books are assigned to freelancers, believing that they are not as good as in-house editors and that their own book must have been relegated to second-class citizenship. This is completely erroneous.

One of the production editor's main functions is to keep your book on schedule. To cooperate, you must be honest about deadlines. If you are asked to review the edited manuscript in two weeks, try to do so. But if you know this is impossible, warn the manuscript or production editor immediately, so that he or she can plan accordingly. Once the manuscript has been sent to the typesetter, meeting deadlines is crucial. The typesetter's schedule is fairly inflexible, and if you are late in returning proof, publication of your book may be considerably delayed. For example, returning galleys a week late may delay page proof a month or more, causing the typesetter to miss the printer's and binder's deadlines and thereby adding at least another month to the schedule. Take deadlines very seriously.

Manuscript to Bound Book

Once the edited manuscript goes off to the typesetter, you have two responsibilities: proofreading and indexing. Chapter 10 explains when and how to do both. In the meantime, your publisher's staff is tending to production and marketing.

Typesetting, the first stage of production, includes proofreading and corrections. With traditional typesetting, these processes take three to four months. If the type is set directly from the author's computer disks, several weeks may be saved, but proofreading will still be necessary. Strange things can happen between disk and proof. While final proofs are being prepared, the author must prepare the index. It is obviously important for the author to keep to the schedule in proofreading and indexing. Most authors, upon completing the index, expect their books to appear in a matter of days. Unfortunately, although the author's work is done, the publisher's is far from over. The printer has to make plates and print the books; the publisher must check final proofs and folded and gathered pages; the same printer or another must print the jackets; both pages and jackets must be delivered to the bindery. The binder must manufacture a die, stamp the binding, and bind the books. The quality of manufacturing is just as important as the quality of the writing, editing, and design, and all of these jobs must be done right.

The process involves a lot of suppliers and manufacturers, so there are many possible sources of delay. For example, paper may not be delivered on time, or shipping to the bindery may be slowed, or the publisher may discover an error that necessitates reprinting all or part of the book. The well-organized publisher will minimize the chance of delays and will allow for some slippage in the schedule. Nevertheless, if you do not receive a copy of your book within a couple of weeks of the date you have been given, call your editor to see what has happened. Publishers do not make a penny until the volume goes on sale, so they are as eager as you are to get finished books. You are suffering together.

The Ad in the *New York Times*

Published authors' most frequent complaint is that their books are not advertised enough. It is true that books do not sell if they are not promoted, but it is not true that advertising in the major media – or even in scholarly journals – automatically increases sales. When did you last buy a scholarly book just because you saw an ad? If you are like most academic readers, you buy books after reading reviews or hearing about them from colleagues. It is gratifying to see your book advertised, but it is not necessarily cost effective.

Every scholarly book has a finite sales potential, because the number of experts in the field is not large and because the number of research libraries is small. The publisher's goal is to make sure that every person who is likely to want your book is aware that it exists. Usually, the best way to inform the readers of scholarly books is to ensure that the book is widely reviewed and that the people and libraries most concerned with the subject of the book receive an announcement. Thus, university presses spend their marketing budgets on sending out review copies and doing mailings to appropriate lists. An ad in the *New York Times Book Review* will sell a collection of essays by Stephen Jay Gould; it will not sell a monograph on archeological analysis or quantum mechanics. (Textbooks and trade books are marketed differently; see Chapters 7 and 9.)

Authors can do a great deal to help publishers promote their books. You are most likely to know which journals will review your book, at which meetings it should be exhibited, and which organizations have mailing lists that might be appropriate. You can also suggest names of people who will offer enthusiastic praise that can be printed on the dust jacket and in mailing pieces. If your publisher (usually in the person of a marketing manager or director) does not ask your advice on these matters, give it anyway – preferably early, around the time you return the edited manuscript. The marketing manager or your acquiring editor may ask you to write a brief description of the book. Do this carefully and follow the instructions provided. Ask to see dust jacket, catalogue, and advertising copy before it is printed, and review it for accuracy. But try to be realistic in assessing the breadth of readership.

You can also send your editor a list of prizes for which your book is eligible. *Literary Market Place* lists the major prizes, and your publisher probably knows about those. But there are often less well known prizes specific to your field that offer small cash awards, prestige for you and your publisher, and some free publicity. Be sure to decline membership on prize committees for years in which your book may be nominated.

You will have to be realistic about how much the publisher can spend on marketing your book. A monograph that is expected to sell a thousand copies simply does not warrant a major campaign. In the case of trade books, for which demand is far more elastic, this prophecy may be self-fulfilling. A novelist may be right in claiming that more money spent on advertising or on a nationwide tour would have generated more sales. Scholarly publishers, though, cannot expect to sell to readers outside a small group that is usually easy to define – and to reach – without using expensive campaigns. Your efforts are best directed toward defining the audience and suggesting ways to reach it.

Keep your acquiring editor or the marketing department informed well in advance of any activities such as speaking engagements or participation in symposia that might generate interest in your book. If you are speaking on another campus, a lecture tour soon after publication may be worth arranging – the marketing department will try to get copies of your book into the campus bookstore. When you speak, mention your book by name and publisher, whenever relevant, and display it if possible. If you are unsure of the technique, watch a few best-selling authors on TV talk shows.

Use your campus news office to publicize your book. If the book has any link to your region, local newspapers may do an interview or feature story. Alumni magazines are another source of publicity.

In matters of promotion, you and the publisher have the

same goal: to sell as many books as possible. The more help you can offer, the better. But when the marketing manager tells you that the "Today" show is out, believe it.

After Publication

Even after your book is published and being sold, your relationship with the publisher continues. Journals will send copies of reviews to the publisher, who will forward them to you. You will get annual sales figures and royalty reports. You probably will have some new ideas about marketing to pass on.

Usually, some of the reviews your publisher forwards to you will be unfavorable, less favorable than you would have liked, or at least unperceptive. Some may even seem extremely unfair. What should you do when this happens? In 99 cases out of 100, the wisest course is to do nothing. Authors frequently overreact to criticism and feel the need to respond even to minor negative points in an otherwise positive review. It rarely does any good to object to a review. Even if the journal prints your objections (which it need not do unless they are substantial or the review was libelous), your response generally makes readers who may not have read the review assume that it was worse than it was. If you feel you must respond to a review, limit yourself to a straightforward correction of errors.

You may also discover errors in the book, either in your own reading or through the keen observation of friends and colleagues. Keep a record of these, on the chance that your book will be reprinted, and send them to your publisher from time to time. Many scholarly books are reprinted, and if yours is among them it may be possible to make minor corrections. For textbooks, which are more likely to be reprinted than are monographs, students are good detectors of error. Faculty members sometimes send students' comments and corrections to publishers. Some publishers even include tear-out postcards for students to use when they find mistakes or wish to make suggestions. If you write a revised edition of a textbook, such comments can help you correct errors and clarify misunderstandings.

Revised editions are less common than reprintings. A reprinting is simply a restocking, the printing of additional copies of the same book. A new edition incorporates major changes – an added chapter, a revised conclusion, overall updating, or the like. Only if your book is selling continuously in significant quantities, usually as a result of textbook adoptions, will a revised edition make sense.

The possibility of increased sales may also motivate your publisher to issue your book in paperback. Among publishers there is a great deal of debate and very little information about the advisability of issuing hardback and paper editions simultaneously, waiting six months to publish the paperback, or waiting longer. For most scholarly books, there is no justification for a paperback edition: Everyone who wants the book has bought the hardback edition. If your book comes out in paper, the price will be lower, and both the percentage and the actual dollars per book paid in royalties will be smaller (7.5 percent of list price is a common paperback royalty).

If you think there is justification for a paperback edition of your book, take the evidence to your acquiring editor. Market research can determine whether the edition is worthwhile.

Your publisher will notify you if your book is being remaindered. This means that sales have diminished to the point where it is not worth keeping the book in stock. The publisher will try to sell the unsold copies to a remainder house that in turn sells them at a large discount. Failing this, the publisher will sell your book for pulp. Authors are understandably horrified at such euthanasia. You can take some comfort in knowing that university presses postpone this moment of truth for quite a while (much longer than trade houses), and they will probably offer you the chance to buy the remaining copies at or near cost.

Sometimes authors feel that a publisher has not given their books a fair chance. If your book goes out of print and the publisher does not want to reprint it, you can have the rights revert to you (provided your contract contains such a clause, as explained earlier). At that point, you can try to convince another publisher to give it a second chance, either as a high-priced, small-edition reprint or as a paperback.

When you have completed the research and writing of a book, you are about two-thirds finished. You still must do a lot of planning and negotiating, and you must be prepared to work effectively with a publisher. Once your manuscript has been accepted, you and the publisher become partners. You both want the book to read well, look good, sell abundantly, and attract favorable reviews and publicity. In addition to cooperating with the manuscript editor, therefore, you should provide information and suggestions for promotion and advertising. You should contribute your own abilities and expertise, and your publisher's staff should contribute theirs. A book may be written and printed, but if it is not also distributed and read, your efforts become a pointless exercise. If you and your publisher do your jobs in a spirit of cooperation, the relationship will be rewarding for both of you.

Chapter 6

Multiauthor Books and Anthologies

I never could understand how two men can write a book together; to me that's like three people getting together to have a baby.

Evelyn Waugh

Multiauthor books are of two sorts: collections of original essays and anthologies of already published material. The first sort of collection is usually published by a university press or other scholarly publisher; it includes festschrifts, symposium proceedings, and commissioned volumes on current topics. The specialized encyclopedia is an especially complex variant. Although such books may occasionally include one or two articles that have been published elsewhere, the majority of the material must be original. The second sort of collection is most often prepared for use as a required or supplementary text for a course and is usually published by a textbook publisher. Some such anthologies, however – especially of literature and translations – are published by scholarly publishers. Because each sort of volume is prepared very differently, this chapter discusses them separately. In each case, the compiler must deal with legal or contractual problems, editorial problems, and mechanical problems. The chapter is written mainly for the volume editor or compiler, but contributors to such volumes will also find it useful.

Collections of Original Essays

Compiling and editing a collection of scholarly articles can be one of the most nerve-racking experiences of a lifetime. You are dealing with multiple egos, multiple addresses, multiple problems, multiple missed deadlines, and multiple tempers. You must negotiate between the publisher and the contributors, and that can be very difficult. In this chapter I discuss the various problems that can arise and offer alternative solutions. When possible, I suggest ways to prevent the problems from arising in the first place. Certain procedures can make publication quicker and relatively painless. No matter how careful you are, however, the book will take longer to compile and produce than you think. If you picture yourself as an amateur general contractor building a large house in an out-of-the-way place with the help of plumbers, carpenters, electricians, plasterers, painters, and others from around the country, you may be able to imagine the difficulties and delays that lie ahead.

If all the contributors to a volume have access to compatible computers, the process can be speeded up considerably: Contributors can send drafts to the editor on disk; the editor can easily make suggestions and revisions; and the completed manuscript can be sent on disk to the publisher. When you approach potential contributors, ask them whether they can prepare their work on a computer and, if so, what kind of hardware and software they use. If it is not possible for all contributors to produce electronic manuscripts, you may want to prepare the final manuscript on a computer yourself. This allows you more easily to make such features as footnote style consistent and gives you greater control over the project. As early as possible, consult with your acquiring editor about how such a manuscript should be handled; also see Chapter 11 for information on preparing electronic manuscripts.

Collections of articles generally do not sell as well as monographs, and to keep costs down, publishers frequently ask volume editors to supply camera-ready copy. Chapter 11 provides instructions for preparing such a manuscript. A special difficulty arises in the case of multiauthor volumes, however. Each contributor can prepare the copy of his or her chapter, but unless they all use matching typefaces and printers and follow directions carefully the result may be very unattractive. If the volume editor prepares the final pages, the result will be more consistent and pleasing to the eye, but this takes a lot of work.

Problems

Collections of scholarly articles are usually generated by inviting certain authors to contribute papers on designated topics. They are frequently invited to present the articles orally at a symposium or conference, with publication to follow, although sometimes no oral presentation is contemplated. Such collections may also be initiated by publishers who will contract with you to assemble the volume. At other times you, as an individual or as the representative of an association, will have to put together a proposal and find a publisher.

In the latter case, the first problem that arises is to interest a publisher. Because of the difficulties to be discussed shortly, publishers rarely commit themselves to an idea for a multiauthor book before seeing at least a complete table of contents and some of the articles. Even if the topic is current and the contributors are well known, the book remains a pig in a poke. Ask your prospective contributors for suggestions about publishers; they can sometimes provide useful contacts.

Whether you or the publisher initiates the project, the contract will be contingent on receipt of a manuscript satisfactory in form, content, and style. In addition, an author-initiated project will have to survive the normal refereeing process. A publisher may provide a list of topics to be covered and may even suggest specific authors. Make sure you understand what is expected in length, coverage, audience, and so forth. A misunderstanding at this point may catch up with you when it is too late to do anything about it.

You must also select contributors. You probably know who

is doing what in your field and what their general reputations are. That is a good starting point, but it is not enough. Read prospective contributors' *recent* publications and inquire discreetly among colleagues about their reputations for promptness and cooperativeness. When you write to the proposed contributors describing the project, make it clear that you are merely exploring possibilities. Ask whether they would be willing to submit an article of *n* words on specific topic *x* within *t* months. If they write back, "I have a marvelous article that's tangentially about *x* lying around; would you take that?" decline politely. If the letter says, "Your project sounds really fascinating, but I'm terribly overcommitted and couldn't get to it for at least a year. Can you wait that long?" say no. If the response is, "Well, I'm not really doing anything along these lines, but I probably could come up with something if you can't find anyone else," find someone else. The lack of enthusiasm will show up as a lack of quality.

If you are editing a specialized encyclopedia, you will also need to select an editorial board. The board serves two purposes: to add prestige and credibility to the enterprise and to give you help in defining topics and selecting contributors. Ideally, each member should provide both prestige and advice; if not, you need a larger board. Encyclopedias are longer (sometimes multivolume), contain more (usually shorter) articles, and include more contributors. Simply keeping track of such a project can be difficult, but the real problems are the intellectual ones of setting the limits of the subject and dividing it into manageable topics, with nothing superfluous included and nothing necessary left out.

An encyclopedia is such a large undertaking that it is vital to involve a publisher with reference book experience from the outset. Indeed, most such projects are initiated by publishers. If you have an idea for an encyclopedia or similar reference work, you should seek a publisher very early on. You might want to form a small editorial board and draw up a partial list of topics and possible contributors, but it is unwise to invest more time than that without a publisher's commitment.

For any multiauthor book, once you have contributors lined up, send each of them a letter of intent. Your publisher should provide these, or you can draw them up yourself. The letter should state the topic to be covered, the length of the article, and the date it is due. It should make clear that you can demand revisions or reject an unsuitable or unworthy submission. The letter should also point out that the publisher may also reject a submission or ask for revisions. In other words, publication is not guaranteed. The letter should include an agreement by the contributors not to publish their work elsewhere before the volume appears (and after it appears only with permission). The letter should also state whether the contributor is responsible for reviewing the editing of his or her manuscript and for proofreading galleys and pages. Finally, if a contributor is to be paid, the amount should be stated and it should be clear when payment will be made (on signature of the letter? after final acceptance? on publication?). The letter of intent should also grant book publication rights to the publisher or to you as volume editor.

Just because you have contributors and a publisher, don't think your worries are over. What happens when a contributor fails to write a chapter? If he or she backs out early enough, you can look for a substitute. Unfortunately, what usually happens is that the deadline arrives, the paper doesn't, and you are left holding the bag. After all, you cannot force anyone to write. The best thing to do is forget about that article. If the omission of the topic is glaring, then use your introduction to cover it as best you can. Let your publisher know that the essay will not be forthcoming. It is possible that you can find someone else to write on short notice, but it is not very likely.

To prevent this disaster, keep in regular contact with your contributors, remind them of deadlines, and ask how things are going. They may not tell you the truth, but they will at least have the task in mind. Periodic letters and calls may give you enough notice of impending failure to find a substitute. In any case, make sure deadlines are explicit, and make it clear that you intend to enforce them.

A more depressing problem is what to do with the article that is delivered on time but isn't any good. If the manuscript is not salvageable, you should admit this and return it diplomatically to the author. Never a pleasant task, it is better done early and mercifully than dragged out in the unrealistic expectation of a miracle. If the manuscript has some redeeming scholarly value but needs work, tell the author specifically and clearly what needs to be done and set a deadline for the work. Offer consultation and assistance. In this case, you should make a firm decision on the minimum quality you can accept and stick to it. Do not let time pressures force you into accepting garbage. The publisher's reviewers will catch the lapse anyway, and you will come in for a share of their criticism. The only way to prevent this problem is to choose your contributors carefully, as described earlier.

Unevenness in the volume often plagues multiauthor works – unequal quality in the articles, contributors writing for different audiences, overlapping coverage of topics, or gaps in coverage. These problems arise quite naturally, because each contributor is concerned exclusively with his or her own piece. It is your job, as volume editor, to see the big picture, to keep it in mind, and to convey it to the contributors. You must decide the central theme of the volume and how each article will contribute to it. You will probably write an introduction that sets this out for the readers. At the outset, you should write an overview that does the same for the contributors. Describe the prospective audience and define the level of sophistication and specificity it demands. Tell each contributor what the other articles do and who is writing them. Try to anticipate areas of overlap or conflict and settle border disputes in advance. Encourage authors to keep in touch with you and with one another. Send regular progress reports and suggestions. Periodically ask for outlines or preliminary drafts from each author, and ask permission to circulate these if appropriate. Try to make the venture a cooperative effort rather than a gathering of discrete projects.

If English is not a contributor's native language, you may need to polish the article a bit (or a lot) before submitting it to the publisher. Make sure the author understands and accepts your editing, and be prepared to do the work. If you yourself are not that good a writer, find someone else to do it. If the author's English borders on the nonexistent, you may want to have the article submitted in the native language and hire a professional translator. (Always give credit to the translator, whether professional or amateur.)

When the entire volume is complete, read it and edit it. It is very tempting at this point to rush it off to the publisher. Despite my admonitions and your efforts, the deadline has probably passed. You have seen outlines and drafts and made suggestions. Now read and edit again. This extra effort can make the difference between a jumbled set of essays and a coherent collection of well-written chapters.

Read each contribution separately and make editorial changes and suggestions. Then read through the volume as a whole. Does it hold together? Does the theme emerge logically and consistently? Does it seem reasonably even in tone and sophistication, or do certain essays leap out as extraordinarily difficult or insultingly superficial? Is there too much overlap? Make further revisions in each article to solve these problems.

Next, do what you can to pull the volume together. Make sure your introduction sets out the theme of the volume, explains how each article contributes to the whole, and covers any remaining gaps. If cross-references from one article to another would be helpful, add them. Consider writing brief introductions to each section of the book or to each essay.

If your review results in significant changes to any article, send it back to the author for approval. Only when this is done should you declare the book ready for publication.

Contributor impatience can be a headache. An author who submits a good manuscript on time wants a prompt publication decision and prompt publication. If the process is delayed through the fault of others, the model author grows impatient. The problem is that the impatience is justified. Your job is to minimize the delay. First, make it clear from the outset that the publisher's evaluation will take time. Second – repeating myself, as you will have to do – establish deadlines and enforce them. It is not fair that the cooperative author has to wait around for the dawdlers. The author left out in the cold because of missing the deadline may also be angry, but with much less justification.

You bear the responsibility for dealing with authors who object to the publisher's copy editing, who are out of the country when proof is to be read, and who did not know they had to supply camera-ready artwork. The initial letter should spell out these duties, but chances are your contributors will forget. Remind them in your regular communications. Whatever decisions you make about editing and proofreading, you must keep reminding contributors of their responsibilities and give them enough advance warning to save time for their chores.

Money is the last of your worries. A collection of essays probably will not make much money, and the royalty rate offered may be low. Since you will bear most of the responsibility and do most of the work, the royalties (if any) should go to you. Books that will generate more income may carry an advance large enough to make payment to contributors possible. If you do receive more than a token payment, you may want to offer contributors a small honorarium. In no case, however, should you pay some contributors and not others. Nor should you pay contributors unequally. Some publishers will offer a single payment, in lieu of royalties, either to the compiler or to the compiler and the contributors.

Encyclopedias are priced to make a profit, and the typical financial arrangements reflect this. The author is generally paid an advance to cover the costs of compiling the volume (postage, phone calls, secretarial help, etc.), as well as royalties. Members of the editorial board usually receive a small fee, and contributors are usually paid. The amounts depend on the length of the articles and range from a free copy of the book to perhaps two or three hundred dollars. The timing of any cash payment is important. Publishers prefer to pay contributors on publication. From the editor's point of view, it is better to pay contributors when their articles are accepted. This arrangement motivates contributors to meet their deadlines and makes them less likely to complain about publication delays. However, these payments add up to a substantial sum, and publishers may not be willing to change their policy. (It's also much easier to write all the checks at once, rather than piecemeal.)

To summarize, here is a suggested procedure for working with contributors to multiauthor volumes before the publishing process begins. The next section outlines a procedure to make things run smoothly during production. For an encyclopedia, steps 2 and 3 should be reversed.

1 Define the topic of the book and draw up a list of chapters needed.

2 Select potential contributors carefully and solicit their participation in a letter that describes the volume and their individual contributions in detail.

3 Seek a publisher for the volume.

4 Once contributors are chosen, send out letters of intent. Include a more detailed description of the book, the expected contributors and their topics, and what is expected of each author. Provide instructions on manuscript and artwork preparation, reference and note style, permissions, and other details. Tell contributors what sorts of computer disks (size and software) you can accept.

5 When signed letters of intent are returned to you, send all contributors the other contributors' names and addresses and remind them of deadlines. (This step is not necessary for an encyclopedia.)

6 Regularly circulate progress reports on publishers' interest, articles (or outlines) received, and deadlines approaching.

7 Telephone contributors periodically to check on progress and to remind them that you are there.

8 When you receive outlines, drafts, queries, or finished articles, read them carefully and respond promptly. Make your

suggestions as specific as possible and do not hesitate to reject the unsalvageable.

9 Be diplomatic in dealing with contributors, answer all correspondence promptly, and keep them informed of progress. The more closely involved they are in the book's creation, the more productive and cooperative they will be.

10 Do your own careful reading, review, and revision, including the composition of introductory and transitional material.

11 Once the manuscript is complete, notify all contributors that it is going to a publisher and keep them informed of the publisher's response. Final acceptance of the manuscript calls for a celebratory letter or phone call.

Production

Once a publisher accepts the final version of a multiauthor book for production, the press will send it through the usual sequence of editing, design, typesetting, proofreading, printing, and binding. You and the publisher should decide jointly who will perform the chores of obtaining permission to quote copyrighted material, reviewing copy editing, gathering illustrations, and reading proof – you or the contributors. *The Chicago Manual of Style* lists your responsibilities as volume editor (paragraphs 2.177–2.182), although publishers may prefer variations. Usually the publisher regards you as the author, so that any failure of the contributors to perform their jobs becomes your problem. The following division of labor makes sense in that the person who can do each job most efficiently is assigned the task. However, your book may be different, or special circumstances (a contributor on sabbatical in the wilds of Tibet) may dictate changes.

You should write for permission to reprint copyrighted material. The limit imposed on quotation under the "fair use" clause of the copyright act is cumulative for your entire book. Thus, if several contributors each quote a relatively small amount from the same book, you may need permission even though no single contributor would. You are the only person in a position to sort out permissions problems, and your contract with the publisher makes you responsible, so you should do it. (See Chapter 10 for details on permissions.)

You should ask contributors to sign letters of agreement or contracts with the publisher. These provide for the assignment of copyright (see Chapter 5) and set out other conditions. Usually the publisher will provide you with such a letter, with enough copies for each contributor. Alternatively, Figure 4.3 in the *Chicago Manual* is a sample letter that can be modified to make it suitable for your volume.

Contributors should generally review the copy editing of their own articles. However, since they have already reviewed your changes, this is not crucial, particularly if the copy editing is light. Especially when time is pressing (as it usually is), you might ask contributors to waive this right. If you do have contributors review the editing, those who cannot do so should designate a trusted colleague (preferably you) as a substitute, in writing. Notify contributors of changes in style that you have accepted, lest they change everything back. You should be prepared to mediate disputes between the copy editor and contributors if they arise and to enforce deadlines. A contributor overly sensitive to your suggestions is likely to take umbrage at a copy editor's changes, so warn the editor ahead of time. Similarly, the editor may want to work first on the contributions of the most dilatory, so that they will have more time for review without holding up the volume. It is a good idea for contributors to return their manuscripts to you. Then you can review them, handle queries from the authors, and make final changes before returning them to the manuscript editor. Leave time for this in the schedule.

Contributors must provide drafts of their own artwork, but you and the publisher must decide whether it is necessary for all drawing to be done by the same artist. If not, the publisher should provide specifications and directions and let the contributors fend for themselves. If the art is to be uniform, then hire an artist. Whether the contributors will take on the cost will depend on the usual practice in your field and on the letter of intent you signed with them. In the sciences, for example, where authors customarily pay journals page charges plus art fees, contributors will probably not balk at paying. You will have to negotiate such arrangements as early as possible.

You should generally take responsibility for proofreading. Although there is some value in having contributors proofread their own work, this is time-consuming and risky in that the contributors may want to start rewriting when it is too late. Let them know that the review of the copy editing (or of your editing) marks their last chance to make changes and that they will not see proof. If you are not a good proofreader, hire someone to do the work for you (the publisher can recommend a proofreader). You should still read the proof for sense, but you can rely on the proofreader for details. If your proofreading raises questions that only the contributor can answer, a phone call should resolve the problem. For highly technical manuscripts, however, the author may be the best proofreader. Send each contributor a copy of his or her proof and keep a copy yourself. Set a firm deadline, and if a contributor does not return proof on time, rely on your own reading. If contributors make excessive changes or argue about the style adopted throughout the volume, it is your job to tell them that the changes they want will not be made.

You are responsible for the index (see Chapter 10) as well as for providing a glossary or bibliography if the publisher requires it. In addition, you must gather biographical material on the contributors to be included in the volume. You must keep an up-to-date list of contributors' addresses and academic affiliations.

One final note: If you are sharing the volume editor's responsibilities with a colleague, divide up the chores sensibly and keep in touch. There is no point in wasting time and creating confusion by duplicating efforts.

Anthologies and Readers

The intellectual tasks to be performed in compiling an anthology are selection and presentation. The clerical tasks are permissions and physical preparation.

Before you can select materials for an anthology, you must have a clear idea of your purpose and audience. In what courses will the book be used? What time period should be covered? What topics must be included? Are you presenting one consistent view of an issue or illustrating conflicting opinions? Is your book meant to supplement a text or stand on its own? Is its purpose to provide information or to stimulate debate? What reading level and previous knowledge can you assume on the part of your readers? How is your anthology going to differ from existing ones?

You should think through all these questions and prepare a prospectus to send to potential publishers (see Chapter 7). First, formulate criteria for selections to be included. The criteria should reflect the goals that you have set out. As you review material for inclusion, check it against the criteria you have set. With any luck, you will have more material than you need. You can rank competing articles according to how well they meet your criteria and also on their secondary qualities. For example, perhaps two essays fill the same spot and are of roughly equal quality, but one is half as long as the other. Come up with a list of first choices and back it up with some alternatives. (Your list of alternatives can double as a list of supplementary reading.) For your benefit and that of an acquiring editor, you should write a brief description of each article (author, title, date, length, subject) and an explanation of its appropriateness for your collection. A prospectus that includes your understanding of the book's purpose and audience, your selection criteria, and this descriptive list should be all you need to sell the book.

You also need to decide how to present the selections. Will your written contribution be limited to a brief preface? Or will you provide a lengthy introduction to the volume plus headnotes for each selection? Will you write study or discussion questions? Will you annotate selections? Does the book need a bibliography? An index? Get all these issues worked out as soon as possible.

When you do find a publisher, your editor will want to review your selections and your decisions about such matters as annotation and may suggest a number of changes. Your list of alternative selections will be particularly useful at this point.

As soon as you have a publisher and have decided which selections to include, you must begin to write for permission to reprint. Your letters must state that you want to reprint the selection in its entirety in an anthology and should explain the book's nature and anticipated market. If the book is not intended for classroom use and will have a small circulation, make this clear so that the original publisher will charge less. You must expect to pay a fee, but your letter should not mention this; let them ask for it. In most cases, your contract will provide for your publisher's payment of this fee as an advance against royalties. (If you are being paid a lump sum in lieu of royalties, the publisher generally will pay permissions outright, up to a specified total. This arrangement is more common when the publisher initiates the project.) To determine who holds the rights to a selection, either look at the original publication or see where someone else got permission to reprint by checking the copyright page, acknowledgments, or credit line in another anthology. (Your text, of course, should come from the original.) If you are abridging the article, specify what you are omitting. You may need separate permission for art; check the credit lines in each selection. As explained in Chapter 10, prepare each letter in triplicate and send two copies to the publisher who holds rights. If permission is denied or the fee is too high, substitute another article and write promptly for permission. It is possible to bargain on permissions fees, and if you really want the original article you should try to get the fee reduced.

To prepare your anthology you will need reprints or high-quality photocopies of each page to be included. You may have to copy from a bound volume, and in these cases be careful to get the whole page copied without losing either edge. Each page of your manuscript should be an 8½- by 11-inch sheet, either a photocopy or a cutout page pasted or taped to the sheet. Use one side of the page only; if you have only one reprint you will have to photocopy the backs of pages. If the material was originally set in columns, cut the columns apart and paste one column to each 8½- by 11-inch sheet. Add your introductions, annotations, study questions, and credit lines where they belong, and prepare a title page and table of contents. Number the pages of your manuscript consecutively from beginning to end.

If the articles you are going to reprint contain figures or photographs, you will have to get original art or glossy prints. You can ask for these in your request for permission. If they are not available, you may have to have them redrawn; check with your editor about the possibility of duplicating the art from reprints before going to such expense.

You must read through your manuscript to see whether mechanical alterations are needed. For example, you should eliminate cross-references to material that appeared in the original but is not included in your anthology, and change cross-references to material that is in your anthology but on a different page. You may have to renumber tables and figures and alter the text references to them. Footnotes may need renumbering. You can correct obvious typographical errors, but you should not make any other changes without the owner's written permission. You should make only the deletions that you specified in your permissions letter, and you must mark these with ellipses. (See *The Chicago Manual of Style*, paragraphs 10.48–10.63, for the proper use of ellipses.)

Before sending the manuscript to your publisher, check the table of contents against the manuscript for the correct spelling of the authors' names and the correct and complete titles of the selections. Check credit lines against permissions letters to make sure you have all permissions and that you have placed and worded the credits as required. Make these two checks again in proof.

Self-publishing

If you are planning an anthology for an advanced course with a small enrollment, you may find it difficult to interest a publisher. Publishers may also turn up their noses at an anthology you are contemplating for use in your own introductory course if they think it is unlikely to be adopted elsewhere. In these cases, you may want to publish the book yourself. After selecting the articles you wish to include, obtaining permission, and writing introductory material, you must decide how elaborately to produce the book. If it is just for your own classes, you can paste up the original articles for inexpensive photocopying, shop around for the best price, and have them bound (looseleaf and comb, or plastic-spiral, bindings are not expensive). Some offset printers near college campuses offer this service regularly. A 200-page book can be produced for about $6.00 a copy, and you can sell it through your bookstore or the printer at cost or at a profit. (Your university may regulate such sales; check with your department chair.)

Even if the anthology is exclusively for the use of your own students, and even if you sell it at cost, you must get written permission from copyright holders. Failure to do so is a violation of the copyright law, and one that publishers are taking more and more seriously. Do not rely on the assurances of your campus copy shop. If they offer to obtain permisson for you, ask to see the permissions letters they have sent and received. Your permissions letter should explain the limited use you plan and the number of copies you will print. The fees that publishers charge should be included in your computation of costs and in the price you charge.

If you hope to sell your book beyond your own campus, you will have to write appropriate permissions letters to copyright holders and produce something more attractive. Read the sections in Chapters 10 and 11 on preparing camera-ready copy. Before beginning production, consult some local printers on the most practical page size and get estimates for printing and binding. You will probably not want to undertake a large-scale marketing effort, but sending a form letter and order blank to colleagues teaching in the same field is practical and effective. Be sure to do the mailing in time for them to adopt the book for the following semester.

Keep good records of your costs and sales both for your tax returns and to help you decide whether to continue your new venture.

In any self-publishing effort, there is an element of risk. Do not print more copies than you think you can sell in a year, and be sure to make this estimate on a day when you're feeling pessimistic. It is not difficult to reprint if you need to, and small printings require less storage space. They also allow for correcting mistakes and making worthwhile additions. Be realistic about the costs in time and money that you are expending.

If your book succeeds outside your own campus, you may then be able to interest a publisher in it. You can submit a copy of your book along with sales figures. Be sure to insist on a respectable royalty, because you will have done much of the publisher's work. You may, of course, decide to continue on your own. Before you invest large sums, however, be sure you want to spend time and money on a greater marketing effort, on maintaining a larger inventory, and on shipping and billing. The experience will give you a practical appreciation of what publishers do, but you may well be happier with a theoretical understanding.

Chapter 7

Finding a Publisher for the College Textbook

The book originated in the suggestion of a publisher, as many more good books have done than the arrogance of the man of letters is commonly inclined to admit.

G. K. Chesterton, on *The Pickwick Papers*

The College Textbook

A textbook is a book designed specifically to help an instructor teach a subject and students learn it. Although scholarly monographs and collections of articles are sometimes used as supplementary or even main texts in a college course, their primary purpose is to disseminate new thought or research findings. Textbooks, by contrast, rarely represent the culmination of research or what is traditionally considered "scholarly" activity. Instead, they summarize, organize, and analyze the accumulated wisdom of an area of knowledge, presenting it in a way that is comprehensible to students at a specific level of competence.

The writers of the most successful textbooks in a field are not necessarily – or even usually – at the cutting edge of research. They are more often, though not always, extremely good teachers. The skills required to write a good textbook are those of organization, synthesis, explication, and communication. However, the ability to communicate orally in a lecture class or seminar does not automatically translate into the ability to write effectively. As you write a textbook, you do not get instant student responses of understanding or befuddlement. You cannot carry on a conversation or discussion. You must decide, on the basis of logic and experience, what requires extensive explanation and what will be grasped quickly.

In writing a textbook, you must consider not only the student but also the teacher. After all, the teacher will decide whether to adopt your text or a competing volume. This means that your book must be easy for the teacher to use as the foundation of a course. To satisfy instructors, you must cover all the basic ground, the core material of the discipline. If using your text would force teachers to find supplementary materials for important subjects, they are not likely to adopt it.

At the same time, college faculty members are an independent lot, and they do not like to be dictated to. Your book should not, therefore, require a rigid course structure – particularly if it will mean that many teachers must radically revise lecture notes. In organizing your book, you should keep this in mind and, if possible, arrange the text in a way that permits it to be used flexibly. For example, it could be divided into units that can be taught in different order and that can be presented independently of one another. Your publisher will offer advice on such matters.

Teachers also adopt books for less rational reasons. They may like the way a book feels in their hands or lies on a lectern, or they may prefer a fat, impressive volume to a thinner book that uses less bulky paper and larger pages. They may hate green bindings. Publishers know about this sort of thing, and you should not be surprised when they raise such seemingly superficial issues.

Another general point about textbooks must be noted, too: The amounts of money involved in textbook publishing are far greater than those related to scholarly books. Textbook publishers must make a profit, and although they take risks, they do not publish books that are likely to lose money. Even textbooks for unusual or advanced courses are published in larger editions, with more elaborate design and larger marketing budgets, than are most monographs. Books for popular introductory courses are large-scale undertakings. Textbook publishers may invest as much as a half-million dollars in a basic text, and they expect to sell many hundreds of thousands of copies over the years. This naturally means that authors can expect to earn far larger royalties from basic textbooks than from monographs. It also means that publishers must consider very carefully where they are going to invest their resources.

Since textbooks with large anticipated sales demand large investments of money and effort, publishers usually conduct extensive market surveys and consultations with potential users. Textbook publishers know the market, and their decisions are based on economic considerations. A scholarly publisher may take a chance on an innovative bit of scholarship, a well-written biography of an obscure figure, or an intriguing but off-the-wall philosophical treatise. Textbook publishers cannot afford to take risks on excitement, experimentation, or artistry.

Finally, the timing of publication is crucial in textbook publishing. It may not matter whether your monograph hits the bookstores in July or November, but it certainly does matter that faculty members see a textbook early enough to make an adoption decision and that they can count on the books being on the shelf in time for classes. Deadlines are important in any kind of publishing, but they are doubly important for textbooks. The schedule for publishing a textbook may be very rushed, and there may not be time to dot all the scholarly *i*'s and cross all the academic *t*'s.

One result of the primacy of financial considerations is that textbook acquiring editors tend to be different sorts of people than university press editors. Usually they have arrived in the acquisitions department via sales and marketing rather than manuscript editing or academia. If all publishers are on a continuum between the worlds of scholarship and business, textbook editors are closer to the business end. A psychologist talking to the psychology editor of a university press will find the conversation running toward psychology; the same person talking to a textbook editor will end up discussing the market and rival texts. There are exceptions, of course, and some editors move between the two worlds. But on the whole, you will find that textbook publishing has an aura far removed from that of academe.

Textbooks for advanced or specialized courses, particularly those that represent one particular methodological or theoretical approach, may be more attractive to a university press or commercial scholarly publisher than to a textbook house. On such projects, you would do well to approach both sorts of publishers to see where the interest is greatest.

Choosing a Publisher

Many of the rules about finding a scholarly publisher also apply to selecting a textbook publisher, but there are some major differences. The most important is that textbook publishers rarely base their decisions on a completed manuscript. They prefer to begin working with an author at the earliest possible stage of the book's development. You are free to shop around and let publishers compete for your book; it is not like scholarly publishing, with its expectation of exclusive review. (Of course, once you have a contract, that's it.) Because you are not close to having a finished manuscript while you are seeking a publisher, the prospectus for the college textbook is far more important.

The Prospectus

The textbook prospectus is a more complicated document than the query letter for a monograph, but it has the same purpose. As you write it, remember that you are trying to sell an idea – and your ability to carry it out – to the publisher. You begin with broad descriptive material. First, you must explain the topic of your book and its theme or approach. Even an introductory survey text has a theme that differentiates it from other texts. A second important topic is coverage –

which topics will be discussed and which omitted. You should provide a rationale for any unusual inclusions or omissions. Third, what educational approach does your manuscript incorporate? For example, do you begin each section with an illustrative case study and then go on to discuss the theories and process it illustrates?

Next, you can cover market considerations such as the courses for which the book is suitable, how commonly such courses are offered, with what enrollments, and at what level; the kinds of students the book is written for (community college, freshman nonmajors, junior majors); and how the book differs from existing texts. This is the place to show your familiarity with what is available and to explain how you can do better. Some publishers expect a detailed comparison of your proposed book with all existing texts. I think that is their job – and one that they would be foolish to entrust to prospective authors – but gaining a variety of perspectives can be of value to you as you develop your own ideas. A general comparison with major texts should be adequate, along with a demonstration of differences in significant details.

You can also include any special features you plan, such as biographical sketches of notable figures in the field or brief first-person accounts of famous discoveries.

You must also convince the publisher that you are qualified to write the book. Do you have a record of publication? What courses have you taught, and for how long? Have you received teaching awards? Have you used any of the proposed material in class, and with what results? If you can provide duplicated class material and written student evaluations, these will be helpful.

Finally, estimate the length of your manuscript and the number of illustrations you expect to use, and explain the current status of your manuscript: How much is written, and when can you finish it?

All of this material can be presented as a prospectus or as a letter. If you write it as a prospectus, include a brief cover letter as well.

In addition to the prospectus or letter, enclose a curriculum vitae, a detailed table of contents, chapter outlines or summaries, and at least one sample chapter (the introduction plus two substantive chapters is ideal). You can send the prospectus to as many publishers as you like, but it saves time and money to select the ones most likely to be interested and to do a good job.

Shopping Around

You must find out which textbook publishers are active in your field. You can do this by looking at the texts you and your colleagues are using, by surveying the textbook ads you get in the mail, and by looking through the business cards of the college representatives who visit you each semester. Do not rule out publishers just because they already have a text in your field. Larger companies may publish several books in one area, especially for courses with large enrollments. Perhaps the current text is selling poorly or the publisher needs a text at a different ability level or with an innovative approach. Any company that publishes in your subject is a possibility.

College representatives (salespeople) for textbook publishers are valuable contacts. Part of their job is to sniff out new manuscripts. If you have a good idea for a textbook, they will be delighted to take it back to an acquisitions editor. But you do not need to wait for the college rep to appear at your door. Write a note or place a phone call. If you have been consistently unimpressed by a publisher's salespeople, you may want to cross the publisher off your list. After all, they are the ones who will be selling (or failing to sell) your book. However, there are other important considerations in choosing a textbook publisher as well.

Money may be a major factor for you. Larger publishers can offer larger advances, and that can certainly make a difference. Remember, though, that the advance is not in addition to royalties, just an early payment. Publishers will not advance you more than they think the book will earn, so the larger advance just means you get the money now instead of later. Royalties on textbooks are generally 10 to 12 percent of list or net. If you are not pressed for cash, you should evaluate the potential income from each publisher according to the royalty rate and how well and how long they will produce and promote the book. Read the textbooks the publishers have on their lists. Are they any good? Would you use them? Do other people use them? Publishers will tell you how well their texts are doing, but you should look at those numbers critically and compare statistics. How many copies were sold in the first year? In the second year? What share of the market does that represent? If the sales drop off dramatically in the second year and disappear in the third, that tells you something important about the quality of the book and the publisher's sales effort. There will always be some reduction in sales owing to the circulation of used books, but a good basic text that is well promoted and kept up to date with revised editions should continue to sell year after year.

Just as textbook publishing is expensive for the publisher, it can also be expensive for the author. If you must pay for permissions, illustrations, and indexing out of pocket, you will have to come up with a considerable amount of cash. See whether the publisher will pay permissions fees for quotations and illustrations. Will they pay an artist to draw special art for the book and a photo researcher to find existing photographs? Some may offer to pay part or all of these fees, and you should factor that into your calculations. If they will not pay or share any of these costs, ask them to advance the fees out of royalties so that you don't have to pay cash. (Further information on illustrations and permissions is provided in Chapter 10.)

Most textbook publishers employ developmental editors to help authors turn ideas into finished manuscripts. They fill in the gap between acquisitions and manuscript or production editors. Ask the acquiring editor how the developmental editors work. How much support will they provide? Will they read and comment on each chapter as it is finished? Will they send chapters out for specialists' suggestions? Can the

developmental editor help with illustrations? Will the publisher arrange classroom testing of material? Will they help
you to do so, or expect you to do it without help?

You also need to know whether the publisher's marketing
department can provide you with research reports on competing texts. If so, you and the developmental editor can
decide how to use the information to best advantage. Market
research can also help you determine the scope and level of
the text you write by telling you what prerequisites most
students will have had, what material they have generally
covered in earlier courses, and how advanced they are in
basic skills and in your academic field.

Determine, too, what each publisher will expect in the way
of supplementary materials, and whether you are required to
supply them. For example, will you have to write a lab manual, instructor's guide, sample exams, a study guide? Will
someone else write them, for your review? Will your textbook be sold with computer software, such as self-paced
exercises? Does the publisher want to offer a slide collection,
or a CD-ROM with art reproductions? How much help will
you get in preparing such exotic materials? Sometimes a collection of readings is considered supplementary to a text,
although it requires enough work to be considered a book on
its own. (See Chapter 6 on anthologies.) Introductory texts
are increasingly being viewed as packages, and you need to
know just how much work you are letting yourself in for.

You cannot always judge the quality of manuscript editing
by reading a finished book. A good editor's work is invisible,
and if a book is well written you cannot tell whether the credit
should go to the author or the editor. However, a poorly edited book is the publisher's fault. If you can spot grammatical
errors, stylistic inconsistencies, excessive repetition, and similar problems, then the book was badly edited. If the quality of
your writing is important to you, find a publisher whose
books are consistently well edited. Often a smaller publisher
will devote more effort to editing, but size is not an infallible
guide. Ask the acquisitions editor how copy editing is handled. Make sure the publisher takes it seriously, allows suffi-

cient time, expects you to review the editing, and provides advice on writing (and, if possible, written guidelines) to its authors. If the acquisitions editor promises not to touch a word of your golden prose, go elsewhere. No one's textbook prose is that golden. How high is the turnover in editorial staff? If editors keep quitting, there may be something wrong, and the production of your book is certain to be delayed. In addition, you may become frustrated as each new editor thinks of new revisions for you to make, or reinterprets previous understandings. Ask colleagues who have published with a firm about their experience.

Look at the design and special features of a publisher's books. Are the books easy to read and use? Are they attractive? Do they demonstrate innovative thinking in study aids and other special features? Are there enough illustrations? Are the illustrations well drawn or reproduced haphazardly from aging sources? Are elements like the glossary and index of good quality? See whether the book is well made. Is the paper of good quality? Is the printing clear, crisp, and even? Are photographs clearly printed? Is the binding likely to make it through the year?

Ask the publisher how your book will be promoted. Do they have an adequate sales staff? Are they good at their job? What about mailings and convention booths? If you have never seen a salesperson from a given company, probably other faculty haven't either.

Ask how soon the publisher would expect a first draft and when publishing the book is anticipated. They may be in too much of a hurry for you.

Finally, ask how long the publisher keeps books in print and how often revised editions will be issued. The need for frequent revision varies from field to field – astronomy changes faster than metaphysics – but you should be sure that the publisher is willing to revise as necessary. The loss of sales due to resale of used books is another motivation to revise. Remember, of course, that if the book does not succeed on the first try, the question will become moot. You will not get any guarantees on this point, but make sure the firm's general practice is not to let reasonably successful books die prematurely.

If you get more than one offer of publication, weigh all these elements – money (advance, royalty rates, and sharing of expenses), editorial support and capabilities, design talent, production quality, sales record and potential – and choose the publisher you would most like to work with. You will receive a contract, which you should read very carefully (see the section on contracts in Chapter 5). Given the amounts of money at stake, you may want a lawyer to review it for you. Your state bar association or a law school faculty member can refer you to an expert in communications law or in the law of intellectual property. As mentioned earlier, pay special attention to provisions about illustrations and permissions, which are an important part of textbooks. Whenever possible, have the contract permit prepublication costs such as permissions fees, artists' fees, and indexing to be paid for by the publisher or deducted from royalties rather than paid out of your pocket. Now all you have to do is write the book.

Chapter 8

Working with Your Textbook Publisher

> . . . As we were leaving he hinted
> That a student could hardly do less
> Than see how the volumes were printed
> At the time-honoured Clarendon Press.
> So I went there with scholarly yearning,
> And I gathered from kind Mr. Gell,
> Some books were to stimulate learning,
> And some were intended to sell.
> *Oxford Magazine,* 1892

Writing, reviewing, and revising a textbook manuscript are very different from the parallel processes in scholarly publishing. As noted in Chapter 7, the purpose and contents of a textbook are not those of the scholarly monograph. Textbooks also differ in the level of difficulty, in format, and in the degree of illustration. And as I also noted earlier, textbooks must please your colleagues or they will not use them. A monograph presents a unique viewpoint. If it is well documented and convincingly written, it will be read (and sometimes appreciated) even by those who disagree with its conclusions or approach. But a textbook must try to be all things to all teachers, and this necessitates a different review process and the consideration of a new range of writing issues.

Writing a Textbook

A textbook must be credible and authoritative. The key element in conveying credibility is, of course, your competence to write the book. You must know your subject thoroughly. The basic sources in your field, as well as the current literature, must be at your fingertips. Let us assume, though, that you would not attempt to write about a subject you do not know. Let us also assume that you can write clearly, at least with the help of an editor. What pitfalls must you avoid that can detract from the authority you should be able to convey?

The first is exaggeration. Do not say *all* when you mean *most*, or *most* when you mean *many*, or *many* when you mean *some*, or *some* when you mean *a few*.[1] If you must assign the status of "most exciting discovery of the decade," limit it to one discovery. In describing research, you will often have to simplify conclusions, but do not exaggerate the implications of a study or gloss over any significant limitations on its applicability.

A second threat to credibility is obvious bias, especially if it is unacknowledged. Students may not notice this, but instructors will. If your text is designed specifically to represent one school of thought, that should be explicit. It should probably even be part of the title: *Economics: A Supply-Side Analysis; Psychology: A Behaviorist Approach.* But in a general, all-purpose text, all schools should be represented evenhandedly. This does not mean one school, one paragraph. It does mean that your explications of various arguments should be objective and fair, and that respectable points of view are not neglected. Be careful not to overrepresent theories simply because their bizarre nature makes them more entertaining.

A third way to lose credibility is to make dogmatic and arbitrary statements. This is largely a matter of tone. You can say that there is only one right way to do something without ridiculing the alternatives or those who believe them, which

---

[1] Robert Graves and Alan Hodge offer a concise guide to such expressions on p. 140 of *The Reader Over Your Shoulder: A Handbook for Writers of English Prose* (New York: Macmillan, 1944).

might get you into libel trouble anyway. If you need to resort to "this is so because I say so," there is something wrong with your argument. Students respond better if they feel that they have discovered the truth themselves, and they resist having conclusions forced upon them.

In addition to credibility, you must strive for general acceptability. Your book will be considered for adoption and will be read by men, women, African Americans, whites, American Indians, Hispanics, Asian Americans, older people, teenagers, Republicans, Democrats, Libertarians, Socialists, fundamentalists, and atheists – among others. It cannot be all things to all people, and you do not want to be so fearful of offending that you become tongue-tied. You can, however, make an effort to be fair and to avoid such blatant offenses as stereotyping or ignoring minorities, ridiculing other people's religious or political opinions, or misrepresenting arguments.

Many of these issues are much easier to handle than people believe. A great deal of fuss has been raised about sexist language, more specifically the incorrect use of the generic *he*. Words such as *he, man, mankind,* and *salesman* do not include women. *Man* and *mankind* can be replaced by *human being, humanity,* or *civilization; salesmen* can be called *salespeople, sales agents,* or *sales representatives.* To avoid the he/she dilemma, sentences can be cast in the plural, or you can use the second-person *you.* A little imagination makes the problem go away. Many publishers and professional organizations offer guidelines on avoiding sexist language, and you can consult a useful book by Casey Miller and Kate Swift called *The Handbook of Nonsexist Writing for Writers, Editors and Speakers* or Rosalie Maggio's *Dictionary of Bias-Free Usage.* If you do not avoid sexist language, your copy editor will remove it for you.

Beyond the problem of language, you should avoid sexism in your examples, case histories, and illustrations. If you feel that making these elements sex-neutral renders them too vague or even inaccurate, you can divide them roughly equally by gender. When you do this, be sure that positive and negative examples are equally distributed between the sexes, unless of course the apparent inequities reflect genuine sex differences.

Avoiding racist language is not difficult, but there are more subtle issues to watch for. White authors tend to assume unconsciously that everyone is white. Remarks such as "Our ancestors came to America in search of freedom" become absurd when you remember that ancestors were of several colors besides white. You must, of course, avoid stereotyped images, examples, and illustrations.

It is no longer safe to assume that your readers are all between the ages of seventeen and twenty-two. Many older people are returning to college, and you cannot take for granted that they share the vocabulary and experiences of the current generation of adolescents. Of course, you may not share these either, and it is a mistake to try to write as if you do. A measure of dignity goes a long way toward avoiding this problem.

In some fields, religion is an issue. How the world was created and the factual status of evolution are again matters of dispute. These questions can be handled briefly, but they should not be ignored, dismissed, or ridiculed. On questions where religious belief is a major factor – abortion, for example – you must be extremely careful to present opposing points of view fairly. Choose the strongest arguments on each side.

Politics, the other issue we do not discuss in polite company, arises in many fields. You need not be bland, but you should present at least two sides to every issue and not hold any respectable argument up to ridicule.

In textbook writing, it may be difficult to draw the line between fairness and "political correctness." Some elementary and high school texts have been criticized for blandness and ridiculed for picturing not only the right ethnic mix in a classroom but the right vegetables in a salad. Although the pressure is less intense at the college level, authors need to be alert to editorial suggestions that are well meant but incorrect. For example, sex-neutral language may distort the account of a historical event or medical experiment, and attempts to include people of color when none were present will lead to justified criticism. Be fair, and be accurate.

On all of these issues, writing a textbook can be an opportunity for you to learn – to reexamine old prejudices, to read authors you have dismissed out of hand, and to rethink your position on a number of substantial intellectual issues. If you regard the problems of racial, sexual, religious, and political bias in writing as a genuine challenge rather than as a series of minor obstacles, you may find yourself enjoying the task and growing in its performance.

Reviews and Rewriting

Before you begin writing, you and your editor should work out a schedule and a plan for review. You should agree on a detailed outline and on a timetable for submitting chapters. Make sure you understand the reviewing process to be used and the kinds of revision you may have to undertake. Textbook publishers use a very different system of review from the one university presses employ, and the revisions they anticipate are far more extensive.

It is also at this stage that you and your publisher, usually in the person of a developmental editor, will set out the special features and organizational details that will make your book more useful and salable.

As I noted in Chapter 7, the instructors who will decide whether to adopt your book have a limited amount of flexibility. The published description of their courses determines what must be covered, and their own energy limits how much they are willing to revise a course from year to year. Usually, a textbook should be organized to follow the order in which most instructors teach the subject. It is often possible, however, to organize a text so that it can be used in various ways. This possibility can be explained to the instructor, with alternative tables of contents spelling out the details. The more flexible the text, the more it may be adopted.

Almost every textbook includes some sort of special material: glossaries, suggested readings, problems (both worked-out and unsolved), answers to problems, chapter summaries and reviews, inspirational essays by leading lights in the field, brief biographies, brief essays to highlight controversial or current issues – the possibilities are endless. You may already have discussed these matters with your acquiring editor, but now is the time to determine the nature, number, and length of these features. You and your developmental editor can use market research results and reviewers' comments to come up with an appropriate group of supplementary features. These details help attract students and instructors to the text, increase the students' interest, help them learn the material, and occasionally inspire a few students to further study. They are important selling points and also important learning aids. Consider their use carefully, and do them well.

It is also possible to use extra features to expand the market for the book. For example, by providing exercises at different levels of difficulty, you can make the book acceptable for classes of varying abilities. Supplementary materials can also provide ideas and challenges for more able or advanced students. Discuss all of these possibilities with your editor.

Although details may vary, the basic textbook editorial process includes three types of review: market, content, and editorial. The market evaluation is used first to determine whether a new textbook can be expected to sell. The publisher surveys existing texts and tries to learn how well they are doing, what faculty members think of them, which features make them appealing, and where they are vulnerable. The results of this research are then applied to your project, as the publisher determines the appropriate length, subject coverage, extent and type of illustration, level of difficulty, price range, and so forth. Many of these questions are interrelated. For example, a book for students who are not good readers may require heavier illustration, and a long book of complex design cannot sell for $7.95. Obviously, the market review must be done very early in the game, and the basic nature of the book must be decided before you have done much writing. Authors can contribute to this process, but the publisher is the real expert here. If you and your publisher disagree seriously at this stage, you should find another publisher.

Content reviews take place when the text is finished. (Sometimes various sections of a manuscript will be sent off earlier to experts in specific fields.) The reviewers are your academic colleagues, and they are asked whether your manuscript is accurate, balanced, up to date, authoritative, and complete. They will be asked to offer suggestions for additions and deletions, expansion and tightening, and other alterations. They may point out some recent research that would enhance your presentation or claim that you have spent too much time on one topic and too little on another. If you have your facts wrong, they will correct them (if you're lucky). They may detect errors in logic or confusion in arguments. The reviewers will be asked whether they would use the book in their courses and, if not, what is wrong.

Remember that the publisher will not take content reviews as gospel. The reviewers are experts, but they are not infallible. In fact, they will often disagree among themselves. If ten reviewers unanimously suggest the same change, your developmental editor (after recovering from the shock) will probably insist on it. More likely, however, suggestions will be weighed and evaluated, and some will be followed, while others are discarded.

You are an expert, too, and you must participate actively in this stage of the review. Your publisher has not solicited and paid for reviews to show you up or embarrass you. The purpose is to give you some advice, to anticipate criticism, and to improve your book. And it is still your book. If you think a reviewer is dead wrong, say so. You may agree with a reader's criticism but offer a different solution. The most important and difficult task at this stage is to consider the reviews objectively and use them wisely. You cannot do this if you are too easily insulted, too stubborn, not stubborn enough, or lazy. Ask yourself why you are resisting a suggestion. Is it because you know it is wrong or unworkable? Because you worked really hard on that section and – even though the change would be helpful – you cannot face it again? Because you do not like the tone of the criticism? Your developmental editor has tried to get you the best advice available, but your reaction will determine whether the advice will be put to good use. Remember, too, that the editor is on your side. You are in a hurry to get the book into production, but so are the acquisitions and developmental editors, production manager, and sales director. They are offering suggestions not to put obstacles in your path but to improve the final product. Even if a reviewer's comments are sarcastic or belittling (and they rarely are), your editor is not offering them in that spirit. Try to detach your vanity from the process, and it will go a lot easier.

Finally, the outside reviews are no substitute for your own careful reading. Reviewers will catch some factual and logical errors, but they will not catch them all. Your name is on the book, and it is, in the end, your responsibility to ensure its accuracy. If fatigue or haste led you to leave a quote or reference unchecked, an allusion vague, or a statement unverified, go back to the library and get it right. Someone will catch the mistake, and it is best if you do.

The editorial review is concerned with issues of style, tone, organization, and comprehensibility. The reviewer may be a member of the publisher's staff or an outside expert. Details and specific changes will be taken care of in copy editing, but alterations that require extensive reorganization or major writing problems that recur throughout the manuscript are best taken care of now.

Let me offer some examples of the kinds of problems that may be detected at this stage. In style, a reviewer may note that you are inconsistent in your point of view, sometimes referring to yourself as "the author," sometimes resorting to an editorial "we," occasionally lapsing into a chatty "I remember. . . ." You may refer to your readers as "you" in one chapter and "the student" in another, and include them in the "we" in still other places. This problem is easily corrected, but it is best handled as a conscious decision made jointly by author and editor.

A problem in tone might be a feeling on the part of the reviewer that you are being authoritarian rather than authoritative, that you are talking down to your readers by offering dogmatic statements rather than reasoned arguments. Or a reviewer might feel that your tone is too familiar and chatty, that you are inserting your personality in places where it does not belong. The reviewer will offer examples of these problems. Now, perhaps you have chosen the familiar tone deliberately and believe strongly that it makes your writing and teaching more effective. If so, you will want to discuss this with your editor. Chances are the editor will agree with your general tack but suggest that you may have gone overboard occasionally.

You are familiar with many kinds of general organizational problems in writing, but one or two are specific to textbooks. Here the reviewer may point out that students cannot understand Chapter 5 until they have read the first half of Chapter 12, or that a figure in Chapter 7 uses terms not introduced until Chapter 9. You will have to revise to correct such problems. Similarly, the reviewer may point out the difficulty of teaching a topic (say, photosynthesis) before you have introduced certain theoretical concepts (in this case, perhaps molecular and cellular structure). Again, you will have to rethink your organization.

Comprehensibility includes the question of how easy it is to understand various explanations in the text, but at this point the reviewer is more concerned with the general level of your writing and the adequacy of supplementary illustrative material. If you are writing a book aimed at first-year community college students, your vocabulary and sentence structure must be less sophisticated than those you would use in a book for junior or senior majors in the field. It is easy to lose sight of this as you write. On these questions, you should take the reviewer's advice very seriously. Of course you have no trouble understanding it. The class you tested it on did just fine, too, because they listened to your lectures and asked questions. But you are not a good judge of how easy it is to understand your own writing.

The reviewer may also point out places where you need an extended example, a graph, or a diagram, or suggest that certain material be treated as optional detail and placed in boxes or appendixes. You and your developmental editor should consider these suggestions and incorporate them when appropriate.

With all these suggestions flying around, it is important to decide exactly how you will go about revising your work. First, make sure that you and your developmental editor have the same understanding about what is to be done. Unless the revisions are to be extremely limited, it is a good idea to put in writing exactly what you are going to do – which suggestions you will incorporate, which you will ignore, what you will rewrite, what you will add, and so on. This ensures that you and your editor agree, and it also gives you a set of goals and a plan of attack.

Then do the revision. Tackle the major changes first – the additions, reorganization, and rewriting. Next make the minor, specific changes that are needed. When this is finished, if you have time, leave the manuscript alone for a week or two. Finally, sit down, reread the whole thing from beginning to end, and make sure you are satisfied with it. Then prepare a final manuscript, either according to the publisher's instructions or following the general instructions in Chapter 10.

Working with Your Editors

After all the reviews and revisions you have completed, you may be surprised to learn that yet another person is about to have a go at your manuscript, but here comes the copy editor. The earlier editorial review was designed to pick up general or recurring problems. The copy editor, however, goes over your work word by word, sentence by sentence. Grammatical and spelling errors, awkward phrasing, and poor diction must be corrected, and stylistic consistency will be imposed. Logical inconsistencies will be eliminated and ambiguities clarified. If an example does not make sense, or a process is poorly explained, or chronology is unclear, the copy editor will catch your lapse.

Copy editors sometimes ask what seem to be stupid questions. The copy editor working on a scholarly book tries to view the work through a scholar's eyes, but a textbook editor views your work through the eyes of a student. If your textbook is for freshman chemistry, an effective copy editor will try to read your explanations as a freshman would. If the editor cannot understand something, students will not be able to either.

Review the edited manuscript carefully, checking changes and answering all queries. Return the manuscript promptly, so that production can begin.

In textbook publishing, the roles of author and editor overlap in many places, and the relationship lasts for months or even years. There are a number of ways to make communication between you and your editors more effective and pleasant, beyond observing the normal, everyday rules of civility and decency.

As I have stressed before, remember that you and your publisher are on the same side. Conflicts may arise over copy editing, money, schedules, and other matters, but they will be easier to resolve if you view them as arguments within a sound marriage rather than as flare-ups in a cold war. Be firm on important issues, but do not dig in your heels at every opportunity. Recognize your editor's expertise in publishing matters just as you expect your own professional knowledge to be respected.

Now that I have released the dove of goodwill, let me tell you how to keep it from treating you like a statue in the park. *Get it in writing.* Editors work on many books, and they change jobs a lot. They may also promise more than their bosses will want to deliver. Do not rely on phone conversations or casual assurances. Your basic guarantees are written into your contract. Beyond that, summarize in writing your understanding of subsequent promises and send it on. "It is my understanding that you will pursue permissions for the Lovejoy graphs," or "In our phone conversation yesterday, you agreed to deduct the indexer's fee from my royalties rather than having me pay it immediately," or "We agreed that the editorial changes in Chapter 4 to which I objected in my previous letter will not be made." If the editor disagrees with your interpretation, you will hear about it and you will be able to straighten out the matter quickly.

Be prompt about permissions and illustrations (see Chapter 10), and meet your deadlines. Do not agree to a deadline you know you cannot meet. Textbooks must be published on time, and the publisher must work out a realistic schedule. Honesty and realism on your side are vital. By the same token, if you are expecting proof or other material and it fails to arrive, call and check on it. Your editor should notify you of delays, but things do get lost in the mail or sent to the wrong address.

Finally, I urge you to express appreciation for work well done. If the copy editing was brilliant, say so. Tell the designer if you love the cover. When the graphs come out looking ten times better than you hoped for, send thanks. Praise the editor who saves you from mortification by spotting a factual error, and the typesetter who spots a misspelling. If you are like most people, you are quick to complain or criticize. It's nice to be nearly as quick to praise.

Teacher's Manuals and Study Guides

In some fields a teacher's manual for your textbook is nearly obligatory; in others, such supplementary material is rare. You and your publisher should share the decision on whether to prepare an instructor's manual and, if so, what kind.

A minimal teacher's manual provides answers to the problems given in the textbook if these are not printed in the book itself. Other possibilities include exam questions (essay, multiple choice, or true/false) with answers, discussion topics, take-home exercises, paper topics, and lecture outlines.

Teacher's manuals are not elaborately produced. They are usually printed from typed or laser-printed copy, with only the simplest design and binding. The production does not take long and is usually begun at about the same time as the index. Nevertheless, you should have the material written well ahead of time. A teacher's manual will have to be copyedited, and it may take longer to write than you think. The rules for manuscript preparation still hold: typed, double-spaced, on 8½- by 11-inch bond; follow any specific instructions your publisher provides. The use of a computer and laser printer can improve on the usual appearance of these materials (see Chapter 11).

The main consideration in an answer key is, naturally, accuracy. Check and double-check your answers, and proofread carefully, reading aloud with another person if possible. One reason for preparing the instructor's manual early is that you may find that the problems you wrote for the text itself contain ambiguities – or even that they are unanswerable. That is a good thing to discover before the problems are in print. In proof, check and recheck all cross-references to chapters, pages, and problems in the textbook. It is embarrassing to provide answers to thirty-two problems when the text contains only thirty-one.

You and your publisher may also decide that you should prepare a study guide for students using the textbook. This may offer general study hints, summaries, study questions, review outlines, and suggestions for supplementary reading. Study guides are produced in the same way as teacher's guides, and on a similar schedule.

It is very tempting to regard supplementary materials like study guides and instructor's manuals as unimportant or even as minor nuisances. They certainly lack glamour. But if you have decided to do one, do it right. Write carefully, be accurate, double-check all answers, and proofread scrupulously. Many instructors will ignore the manual, but those who rely on it expect it to be accurate and useful. If it is not, they may never use your text again.

Revised Editions

Textbooks are more likely to be revised and published in new editions than are trade and scholarly books. One reason for frequent revision is economic: There is a flourishing trade in used textbooks on which neither author nor publisher makes any money. This is not the only reason, however.

In many fields, particularly the sciences, new information must constantly be assimilated into textbooks or they become obsolete. In other fields, such as history, methodological and sociopolitical changes require that texts be modified. For example, no survey of U.S. history is now marketable unless it includes material about the roles of women and minority groups; books on modern Russian and East European history must be updated. Sometimes books must be revised because of trends in teaching (such as increased use of discussions in place of lectures) or because the students have changed. The most notable example of this last problem is the move toward simplified vocabulary and sentence structure in response to reduced literacy.

You should begin working on a revised edition as soon as you have finished reading the proof of the current edition. You do not begin writing, of course, but you do begin a file of articles to be added to the bibliography, ideas for new topics, new illustrations, and so forth. You should not wait to do all your catching up at once.

When you and your publisher decide to prepare a revised edition, you should make sure you know the purpose of the revision. Your publisher's representatives will have been discussing your book with faculty members who use it and should have some ideas about which features are consistently praised and which are repeatedly criticized. Important omissions will have been noted. Your editor will also know what other publishers have been up to and how a revised edition might increase your competitive advantage. At the same time, you will have gotten criticism from colleagues and students, and you will have developed some ideas about what you wish you had done differently. You will also be aware of new research that should be reflected in your book.

You and your editor need to sit down and agree on what sorts of revisions should be made and how extensive they will be. You should discuss the need for new illustrations. If the book is to be redesigned and typeset from scratch, the production process is just as time-consuming as if you were writing a completely new book. However, if the revisions are minor or are limited to a few parts of the book, only the affected parts may be reset, and the whole procedure will be a good deal less complicated (see Chapter 10 for instructions on preparing copy for a revised edition). If the revisions are extensive, your editor may want to have the new version reviewed all over again. And, of course, you must set a schedule for revision that you can follow and that will allow the publisher to get the book out on time.

Preparing a new edition is not just a physical task of cutting and pasting. Nor is it simply a matter of correcting errors. Even when you have made the revisions and additions that you and your editor decided on, you must again read through the manuscript to make sure it is coherent. Details to watch out for include cross-references to pages, chapters, tables, and figures in the book that will change; time-related references ("this decade," "a few years ago," "in 1990 we will probably . . ."); presidents who have become former presidents; the use of the present tense with people who have died or governments that have fallen; and language or allusions that were current but have since become dated. Tables and figures should be included in this check. The bibliography should be reviewed for outdated material. If you used a notation system with parenthetic author-date references in the text and a reference list at the end, you must make sure that new text references have corresponding entries in the list and that references completely omitted from the text have also been omitted from the list. Check, too, for books or articles that were "in press" or "forthcoming," and put in the dates of publication.

Finally, sit down and read the whole book afresh (to the

extent that's possible). Make sure you are happy with it. If you do not have the time, energy, or imagination to do this now, be sure you do it after the manuscript has been copyedited.

Textbook writing can be an intellectually and financially rewarding activity, but it is not as easy as it looks. It is very difficult to organize massive amounts of material, to simplify complex ideas, and to provide explanations, examples, and illustrations that help students learn. The review process can also be trying, both physically and emotionally, since accepting criticism and reworking what you thought was a finished product are rarely pleasant. Your investment in time and effort will be high. You may also have to make a significant financial investment in artwork if your book is heavily illustrated.

Because of the length of time and intensity of the involvement, you should make every effort to find a publisher with whom you can work comfortably. If you are writing with a coauthor or as part of a team, make sure you like and respect your colleagues. Be careful to see that everyone involved has compatible ideas about the project and that responsibilities are clearly assigned.

There are few publishing endeavors in which the gratification is delayed as long as it is in textbook writing. (The *Oxford English Dictionary* comes to mind, but not too much else.) Be prepared to work hard and to wait a while for both the praise and the royalties.

Chapter 9

Books for General Readers

> In the idea of *literature* one essential element is some relation
> to a general and common interest of man – so that what ap-
> plies only to a local, or professional, or merely personal inter-
> est, even though presenting itself in the shape of a book, will
> not belong to literature.
>
> Thomas de Quincey

Serious nonfiction – whether written by journalists, professional writers, or academics – has become very popular in
recent years. Allan Bloom's *Closing of the American Mind* and
Stephen Hawking's *Brief History of Time* both appeared on the
New York Times best-seller list for weeks on end (Hawking's
for nearly two years), and books by scholars such as Stephen
Jay Gould, Deborah Tannen, and John Kenneth Galbraith
have made frequent, if briefer, appearances. Still more books
by academic writers, though not best-sellers, have sold in
respectable numbers, sometimes for several years.

Academics have many reasons to write for general readers. Trade books bring their authors more money than
monographs do, though usually not as much as textbooks.
They also allow scholars to communicate with people other
than their colleagues and students. Writing for a nonspec-
ialized audience conveys a researcher's own discoveries, the
state of a discipline, enthusiasm for work, or the urgency of
an issue or cause to significant numbers of people. It is
another way to make a difference: to influence public policy,
interest people in an important subject, reduce ignorance

about a discipline, or bring readers up to date on important research.

Because books for a general audience are usually published by trade houses, it is important to understand their acquisitions, editorial, and marketing practices. When trade books are published by university presses, they should be edited and marketed differently than monographs. And, most important, books for general readers must be written with a different audience in mind.

Economic Realism

By dangling the *New York Times* best-seller list in front of you, I may have created fantasies of wealth that – alas – I must now dispel. The nonfiction best-seller lists are dominated by books about diet, self-improvement, life after death, or the deeds and misdeeds of celebrities. Serious nonfiction rarely appears. No one can be sure which books will become best-sellers, but there are some fairly good predictors of success for academic authors. A nonfiction book is most likely to become a best-seller if the author has had a best-selling book before, has won a Nobel Prize, has a television show airing when the book is published, or receives extensive media coverage, usually because the book is timely and controversial. Few authors meet these requirements, and even if they do, their books may sell only moderately well. The author's previous best-seller may have been a fluke: *The Closing of the American Mind* was Bloom's only best-seller. A Nobel laureate in physics or chemistry may have little idea of what would interest a general reader. And even a much-discussed, highly controversial book may not sell as well as you might expect: controversial books are often discussed apparently knowledgeably by people who have read the reviews and news coverage, but not the book.

Of course, a publisher who believes a book has a good chance to become a best-seller will risk a great deal of money to acquire it. Some science books have brought their authors advances of more than $250,000, and in many cases the publisher has not regretted the decision. Advances of $50,000 to $100,000 are offered to significant numbers of authors in the sciences. For most first-time trade authors, especially those who are not scientists, an advance of $10,000 to $25,000 is more realistic, with university presses usually offering even less. Of course, if a book with a small advance really takes off, the author will get additional royalties.[1]

I would encourage every writer who wants to reach a large audience to be optimistic, but it is a serious miscalculation to think that you can retire on the proceeds of one moderately successful trade book. Buying a new car, remodeling a kitchen, or paying a year's Ivy League tuition for one child is a more realistic financial goal. And you are unlikely to get a large advance unless you have a literary agent negotiating for you.

Finding a Literary Agent

Finding a literary agent is much like finding a publisher, and unless your manuscript shows strong promise of profitability you are unlikely to succeed. As explained in Chapter 4, literary agents charge fees that are a percentage of the author's royalties. They cannot afford to spend time trying to sell manuscripts that will bring them only a few hundred dollars. Nor are they likely to take on a project that will require a lot of editorial work before it can be submitted. Agents who handle nonfiction are looking for well-written, salable manuscripts on topics with a wide potential readership. As a result, most agents accept fewer than 10 percent of the manuscripts submitted to them. However, they almost always place the manuscripts they accept and are able to convince publishers to offer better terms and larger advances than an unrepresented author can negotiate.

---

[1] Information on advances and print runs is drawn from Laura Wood, "Targeting the Educated Lay Audience: Publishers' Perceptions and Strategies" (M.A. thesis, New York University, 1994).

To earn their 10 to 15 percent fees, literary agents submit manuscripts to publishers, negotiate contracts, persuade publishers to increase their marketing efforts, review royalty statements, either sell subsidiary rights or encourage publishers to pursue such sales more aggressively, and generally act as the author's advocate. Agents may offer editorial advice, but they do not do extensive revision. Some will refer an author to an editor, a coauthor, or even a ghostwriter, all of whom charge separate fees. In addition to their commissions, agents usually charge clients for expenses such as photocopying and long-distance phone calls.

A minority of agents charge fees to read manuscripts. Although such fees may be substantial, they are not meant to cover the cost of a thorough editorial review. Rather, the fee pays for a reading that determines whether the agent will take on the project and may include some general suggestions for revision. The more selective and better-known agents generally do not charge reading fees.

If you think you need an agent, the first place to turn is either *Literary Market Place* or *Literary Agents of North America* (both are in the bibliography and should be in your university or public library). These directories provide names, addresses, phone numbers, and types of manuscripts handled; tell whether an agent accepts unsolicited manuscripts (more about this in a moment); and note whether an agent charges a reading fee. *Literary Agents of North America* is more detailed and generally lists commissions charged as well as typical or recent clients and books. It is indexed by subject, location, policies, and size.

Once you have identified a few agents who handle manuscripts in your field, you must note carefully what each expects as a first submission. Few agents accept unsolicited complete manuscripts. Rather, they want to see a query letter and a prospectus, an outline, or perhaps a sample chapter. They will want to know whether you have had other books published. Your letter or prospectus should not only describe the book but explain why it will appeal to a trade publisher and a lay audience. As in seeking a publisher, you may send queries to more than one agent at a time, but if you are asked to send a manuscript, you must send it to only one agent.

Reputable agents explain to prospective clients exactly what they will and will not do for them and spell out all commissions and fees. When they accept a client, they offer a contract that sets out all of these matters. You should read such a contract even more carefully than you read a publisher's contract. You should clarify just how much advice an agent is prepared to offer on your writing. Most will offer general suggestions, and almost none make line-by-line corrections, but there are many possibilities in between. Some agents are very comfortable with the literary side of their work; others prefer to devote almost all their attention to the business side. You must understand the agent's obligations and your own, and you must be able to trust your agent with your money and your reputation. I strongly recommend a personal meeting with an agent before signing a contract.

Once you sign a contract with an agent, you must submit all manuscripts through the agency unless you and the agent have agreed otherwise. For example, the agent is unlikely to want to handle your submissions to nonpaying scholarly journals but will probably want to take care of submissions to popular magazines. Any requests that come to you for foreign rights, translations, or reprinting in anthologies must be referred to your agent. Other issues to be clarified include which communications with publishers may go directly to you and which should go to your agent. All financial matters are in the agent's province; copy editor's queries are in yours. But many things fall in the middle, including review of catalogue and advertising copy and jacket design. Most agents will want to participate in decisions that relate to marketing.

The fact that most authors remain with the same agent throughout their careers testifies to the care that both parties must use in establishing the relationship and to the trust and respect that it generates. If you plan to write more than one trade book in the course of your career, your agent will become a very important part of your professional life.

Agents may accept clients on the basis of book outlines or summaries, and they may secure a publication contract on that basis as well. If a book is on a salable topic and there is reason to think the author can live up to the promise of the outline, publishers are willing to make a commitment early on to secure the manuscript. Of course, established authors have an advantage here, but an agent may be able to get a contract and an advance for an inexperienced author with a good idea. If, however, your agent does not wish to seek a publisher until the project is further along, you should be guided by that advice.

Writing for General Readers

When you write a monograph, your audience is your peers and perhaps some graduate students. When you write a textbook, your readers are undergraduates. But when you write a trade book, the audience is harder to define. People who buy and read serious nonfiction are mostly college educated but not professional academics. They may have developed certain interests in college that they have retained but do not pursue in their careers. A lawyer, for example, may remember an astronomy course fondly, while an industrial chemist becomes an amateur archaeologist because of a particularly interesting freshman course. Other readers are seeking to fill in gaps in their education. Those who took physics as their laboratory science may wish to understand heredity and evolution better, or former English majors may want to catch up with their teenagers' more advanced knowledge of mathematics. Some serious nonfiction buyers are attracted to books simply because they are being talked about, despite a lack of personal interest in the discipline of the author. Television series create spillover interest in their topics:

viewers of *The Civil War* bought not only the book derived from the series but other books by Civil War historians and biographers.

It is vital to keep the audience in mind as you write, but how can you keep a steady vision of so disparate an audience? One way is to think of them as alumni – your students of ten or twenty years ago, for instance, back for a reunion with your book instead of with you. As students, they varied in ability and interest, so you must now write to appeal to as many as possible. When they were students, of course, you had more power over them than you have now, and you cannot require them to buy your book. You must instead arouse their interest, pique their curiosity, answer their questions, and keep them reading.

Another way to think of your audience is to imagine a dozen or so real individuals who might read your book: a colleague in another field, your tennis partner, your child's teacher, a cousin, a neighbor, a colleague's spouse, your doctor, and so forth. When you have to make a decision about how much background to provide or how to explain a phenomenon, you can imagine speaking to one or two of these people and then write to meet their needs. You can even use them as guinea pigs occasionally.

How do you define a subject for a trade book? A monograph is usually the report of a research project, and a textbook's subject is defined by the courses in which it will be used, but the limits of a trade book are not set down anywhere. You cannot say that a book for "general" readers should be more "general" than a monograph: many successful trade books are extremely focused and specific. In history, for example, Natalie Davis's *Return of Martin Guerre* is simply a very effective recounting of a single legal case, and Laurel Ulrich's *Midwife's Tale: The Life of Martha Ballard* is an imaginatively edited diary from the turn of the nineteenth century. To determine what to write about, you must look at your reasons for writing and your audience's reasons for reading and then find a solution that satisfies both.

What are the possible intellectual motivations for writing a trade book? You may want to demonstrate the relevance of your field, explain recent developments and changes, set out competing theories (or argue in favor of one), alert readers to a serious problem that your work has uncovered, influence public opinion and policy, or simply share an insight or discovery. Each of these motivations would lead to a different kind of book.

Why might readers want to read what you have to say? Perhaps they want to educate themselves concerning a field about which they know nothing: they will be looking for a book that sets out the relevance, history, current approaches, and underlying knowledge of the field. Other readers may want to know what has happened recently in a field in which they have some background. They will be looking for books that set out new developments in evolutionary theory, the impact of computers on epistemology, or what literary critics mean by "the new historicism." Readers may want to know what researchers think about controversial public policy issues like race and intelligence, global warming, or international human rights. Some readers are looking for an inside view of research: how do geneticists, forensic anthropologists, or archaeologists go about their business, and what are they like? Books designed to meet these needs are likely to succeed in a trade market.

Providing Context

Writing a trade book raises other questions that writing a monograph or textbook does not. The first is where to start. How much context must you provide? How much knowledge can you assume? The answer, of course, lies in that imaginary audience. One way to think about context and background is that it roughly substitutes for the literature review plus what you assume your peers know. Whether it is called an introduction or something else, the relevant chapter or chapters must provide all the information the reader needs in order to understand the heart of the book, including competing theories, underlying consensus, and basic terminology. It must also explain why your subject matters, perhaps because it is new, important for public policy, or just interesting.

A common and effective approach to attracting readers is to begin with a short, dramatic statement of the importance of the topic, perhaps opening with an account of a recent event or discovery and the controversy surrounding it or with the possibilities it creates. This becomes the introductory chapter, followed by a longer chapter or section of necessary background and explanations. Sometimes the first chapter wins over readers by showing the disastrous effects (upon individuals or society) of failing to understand the subject of the book. However the problem is handled, the author of a trade book has only a few pages to attract readers and then perhaps a chapter to ensure that they do not drop out before they get to the important part.

Structure

Organization is important. Most serious nonfiction that succeeds in attracting readers and keeping them reading tells a story. It may be a single sustained narrative or a series of shorter ones, but it should have continuity and connections. Like a novel, the nonfiction story can use flashbacks to provide background, side plots to provide suspense and enhance interest, and hints about interesting things to come. Whenever possible, it should have well-developed characters and thoroughly described settings. In a scientific journal article, you might summarize an earlier study in one sentence, but in a trade book it might be worth several pages, including an analysis of the researchers' personalities and relationships, a description of the laboratory or its setting, and a sense of the excitement the results created among the researchers and, later, their colleagues. Indeed, you might begin with the excitement generated by the public announcement of the findings and then flash back to the work that went into the discovery. A historical or sociological monograph might summarize economic or demographic changes in a community with tables and explanatory text. In a trade book, the author would do well to choose a few individuals who experienced or typified these changes and tell their stories.

Not every book can be organized as a sustained narrative (although nearly every book can include "short stories" now and then). Other organizational schemes may be geometric. For example, you may think of your book as a pyramid, with a broad explanatory base underlying increasingly specific understanding. Or perhaps your book is a series of concentric circles of diminishing diameter, beginning with a broad sweep and gradually focusing on particulars. Or perhaps you should begin at the center of the circles and work outward. Your book may be a group of circles that overlap one another, or perhaps a Venn diagram.

Your book may, in fact, not have very much unity. It may be the nonficiton equivalent of a collection of short stories sharing a very general theme. In that case, you can organize it by writing an introduction that sets out the theme, making that theme apparent in each chapter, and ensuring that each chapter is itself a coherent, interesting narrative. Mario Salvadori's *Why Buildings Stand Up* and *Why Buildings Fall Down* (written with Matthys Levy) are good examples of this approach.

If you have written only journal articles or monographs, the idea of "envisioning" a book in this way is probably new. With monographs, we generally think in terms of outlines and do not worry too much about the overall shape and motion of the book. Monographs are frequently rather static; geometrically, they look like rectangles. They are meant to convey information to people who need it and expect to find it in a predictable package, and both publishers and readers will be satisfied if they do this efficiently. Trade publishers and general readers expect something more attractive and original, and that presents exciting opportunities for the writer.

Tone

The next important consideration is the tone of the book. How formal do you want to be? Trade books are supposed to be accessible, and to many writers that means informal, casual, or chatty. If you are comfortable with informality, and if it suits your subject, then this approach will work well. You can address the reader as *you*, for example, and throw in casual asides and humorous anecdotes. This will not work if it is forced or if it is inappropriate for your subject. Books about morally sensitive issues generally require a degree of formality to be credible. A casual approach to a book about genocide, for example, is unthinkable.

When the subject matter can be treated at any level of formality, the purpose of the book should help determine the author's approach. For example, John Allen Paulos's *Innumeracy*, a book that seeks to allay math phobia and show people that mathematics is useful and even necessary, works because it is casual, friendly, and funny. John D. Barrow's *Pi in the Sky*, which is mathematically no more difficult than Paulos's book, is also entertaining, but it is far more formal. Barrow assumes that his readers are already interested in (though not necessarily knowledgeable about) math and provides a history of counting and of approaches to mathematics. The two books cover many of the same topics, but reading them creates two completely different reading experiences and impressions of the authors.

You must also consider your own personality. If you are generally formal in your dealings with colleagues and students, it is unlikely that you can write convincingly in a casual, intimate style. The result would be forced and unnatural. If your usual approach to writing and speaking is relatively informal, an attempt to be more distant from your readers may end up reading like a parody. You must write in a style that is natural to you, or at least not uncomfortable.

Think about your subject, your audience, your purpose, and the kind of relationship you want to establish with your readers, and then decide how formal you wish your book to be. This decision, in turn, will determine the voice and tone you use.

How Much Is Too Much?

Trade book authors need to make certain mechanical decisions as well. In trade publishing, short is better than long. Although some historians and biographers find publishers for five-hundred-page books, it is safer to aim for no more than three hundred book pages (roughly five hundred manuscript pages). If you write a long book, you need a very strong unifying principle, tight organization, and a continually magnetic presence (yours or your subject's) – a performance hard to sustain over several hundred pages. It is sometimes difficult to distill what you have to say, but many pages can be saved through discipline: finding a single, perfect example rather than offering two or three weaker ones; seeking out one crucial event to summarize or symbolize many; and keeping a tight rein on digression and verbosity.

Editors and writers generally agree that equations, tables, and diagrams deter readers. In the acknowledgments of *A Brief History of Time*, Stephen Hawking pokes fun at this idea, while at the same time following the advice it suggests: "Someone told me that each equation I included in the book would halve the sales. I therefore resolved not to have any equations at all. In the end, however, I *did* put in one equation, Einstein's famous equation, $E = mc^2$. I hope that this will not scare off half of my potential readers." There is no magic formula for determining how many equations or tables are too many. (If there were, I would have included the equation.) Although they probably should be minimized, do not lose sight of the fact that we use equations and other mathematical expressions because they are the most economical way of conveying information and relationships. As long as these elements are used for that purpose and are thoroughly explained, most readers can cope with a few numbers. The test is whether they are *necessary* for the reader's understanding, *clearly explained,* and *better* than a nonnumerical alternative.

Footnotes and endnotes are also assumed to discourage readers, but a strict rule against them would be silly. The fact that you are writing for general readers does not reduce your obligation to give credit to others. However, credit can be given in the text, as I did with Stephen Hawking a moment ago, reducing the need for source notes. Other uses of notes should be avoided. Notes that amplify or qualify should either be brought into the text (if needed) or omitted (if merely nitpicking or overly finicky). Notes that are in fact brief bibliographical essays should also be eliminated. Some publishers suggest or accept note systems that eliminate superscripts but provide the sources in a commentary at the end of the book referring back to the relevant pages and lines (see *The Chicago Manual,* section 15.52 and figures 15.7-15.9). This allows readers to proceed through the text without being distracted but nevertheless provides the information they might want.

Drawings and photographs are generally considered to be assets in a trade book. They should be carefully chosen and executed to illustrate precisely the point you are trying to make. A picture can be worth a thousand or more words, if it is exactly the right picture. A trade publisher's editor will want to work with you, a photo researcher, or a graphic artist to develop the most useful art. Think carefully about where in your text illustrations can replace or enhance examples and explanations.

A bibliography is useful in a trade book, but it should generally be brief and suggest further reading for those who want to learn more about your subject. Supplementary materials like a glossary, chronology, or genealogical table should also be considered if they will help the reader. An index is almost always required. Indexes in trade books are usually shorter than those in monographs, but the main consideration should still be the needs of the reader.

Language

In thinking about the needs of their readers, authors new to trade publishing tend to focus on avoiding technical language and jargon. That is a worthy goal, but it should not be overdone. Nor should it be regarded as a panacea. Some words that general readers will not understand must be used. You will not get very far in writing a physics book without using the word *mass*, but many intelligent, well-educated people do not remember exactly what it means. Use it, by all means, but explain it the first time you use it and put it in the glossary if you provide one. Use ordinary words when possible, but not at the price of clarity or specificity.

Trade editors say they are looking for writing that is *accessible, lively,* and *engaging.* You can help make your work accessible by avoiding or defining technical terms, but that alone will not do the trick. It is easy to write inaccessible prose in everyday words. Accessibility depends on clarity of thought and language. The words composing each sentence must relate clearly to one another; each sentence must have a logical connection to the sentences that precede and follow it; each paragraph must be a coherent whole and relate logically to the paragraphs surrounding it. All of this must be accomplished without obvious signals, yet the reader must have a sense of motion – of getting from A to B to C – and of accomplishment. If people read serious nonfiction to learn something, then they should be able to stop at the end of each chapter (should they wish to do so) and explain briefly what they have learned. Imagine your reader as a passenger seated next to you in an airplane who puts your book down at the end of a chapter and says casually, "Did you know that. . . ." If a reader can do that, your book is *accessible:* well organized, logical, and transparent.

Liveliness depends on a number of qualities. One is brevity: short books are *usually* livelier than long ones. Brevity depends on not repeating oneself more than necessary, avoiding unnecessary words, and sticking to what is relevant (even digressions should be purposeful). A second quality that promotes liveliness is precision of language. The most specific nouns should be chosen over more general ones, and adjectives and adverbs should be used to make nouns and verbs more precise. Specific words are usually livelier and more colorful than general words: *leap* is livelier than *move; anemone* is more colorful than *flower; Saturn* evokes a clearer image than *a planet.*

You can find all of these rules and suggestions in any good writing handbook. The point here is that these rules apply more strictly when you write for general readers than when you write for your peers. Academic readers are tolerant of (or resigned to) a certain degree of uniformity, or even drabness, in their professional reading. As long as a book conveys the information they need or explains the author's thinking clearly, they are satisfied. General readers are more demanding. Your book will have to compete not only with similar books but with other media. It has to be informative, but also entertaining enough to convince readers to spend a weekend reading it instead of watching television or going to a movie. You want them to buy your book, begin reading it, finish reading it, and recommend it to others. So you must choose words and put them together thoughtfully and carefully.

Writing a trade book is very different from writing a monograph. Most people find the actual writing, though not the research, far more difficult. Selecting and defining a subject, organizing and controlling the material, and expressing information and ideas clearly to nonexperts draw on skills that many academic authors have not developed. For most, however, the oportunity to reach thousands of readers makes the effort worthwhile.

Finding a Publisher for the Trade Book

Authors who have literary agents send their proposals or manuscripts to their agents and let them handle submissions and negotiations. Agents generally know which editors at which houses are likely to be interested in a project and can get quicker decisions from those editors than an unrepresented author can expect. Agents keep their authors informed about progress, though they do not report every detail. (Some authors, in fact, like having an agent because they do not want to hear about rejections.) Once an offer is made, the agent will discuss it with the author and give advice on whether to accept it. Even when represented by an agent, the author must make the final decision about whether to sign a contract.

Authors who are not represented by agents can also approach trade houses. In order to find the right editors to approach, you can ask colleagues who have had trade books published or you can look at the acknowledgments in trade books in your field. You should then send a carefully written query letter and prospectus to these editors. An editor may well ask to see the manuscript, and a contract may follow. The advice on contracts offered in Chapter 5 still applies, with some special cautions. A trade contract should always offer a royalty of at least 10 percent of retail or net on the casebound edition. Carefully read the provisions for paperback rights to see what royalty you will receive if the publisher exercises these rights (5–7.5 percent or a sliding scale is usual) and what percentage of the proceeds you will receive if paperback rights are sold to another house (at least 50 percent). Also look especially carefully at provisions pertaining to sales of subsidiary rights (serial rights, foreign rights, and so forth). If a television production is even remotely possible, look carefully at those provisions. If the book is to be illustrated, try to get the publisher to pay those costs.

Trade publishers are more likely than university presses to pay advances, and you should try to negotiate such a provision. If you are not an established author, and are not represented by an agent, you may have some difficulty getting a significant cash advance on the basis of an outline or a partial manuscript. It does no harm to ask, however, especially if a relatively small advance would allow you to work on the book during the summer and complete it more quickly. If you are writing on a subject of great public interest or if you are well known and respected in your field, publishers are more likely to make a financial commitment. Sometimes publishers will agree to pay a small portion of the advance when the contract is signed, with the balance to be paid when the manuscript is accepted. Occasionally, the advance will be divided into several parts, payable when specified deadlines are met.

Trade publishers frequently seek authors to write on subjects for which they feel books are needed. The advance then becomes, in essence, a commission to write the book. (Additional royalties will still be paid, of course, if they exceed the advance.) Trade editors will look for authors among the clients of the literary agents they work with, but they will look beyond that group by reading journal articles and news articles about research in the field. A publisher who commissions a book will provide a respectable advance and a great deal of advice and guidance on writing. As we shall see shortly, writing a trade book is almost always more collaborative than writing a monograph, but this is especially true for books initiated by publishers.

Even if your search for a trade publisher fails, your book may find a home with a university press that publishes books in your field for general readers. University presses publish many successful trade books, including those of Edward O. Wilson, John Rawls, and Peter Gay. In order to identify prospects, you should see who publishes books in your discipline that are reviewed in magazines like the *New York Times Book Review*, the *New York Review of Books*, *Harpers*, *Scientific American*, and the popular magazines in your field. Also examine the shelves of your local off-campus bookstores. Then follow the procedure described in Chapter 4, making it clear in your correspondence that you view your work as a trade book. At most presses, the acquisitions and review procedures are identical for trade and scholarly works. It is important, however, that you and your potential publisher have similar views on marketability and sales potential.

If a university press agrees that your book should reach a large general audience, you will be offered more generous royalty terms than would be offered on a monograph, and you may be able to get a modest advance. Your most important concern, however, should be with the press's commitment to selling subsidiary rights and to marketing the book. A royalty is simply a percentage of revenue, and a high percentage is worthless if the book does not sell. Before signing a contract, you should be convinced that the press will spend enough on marketing and that they have a track record of selling trade books. Publishers will not give you sales figures for a specific title (that is no one's business but the author's), but you can ask them how many copies they generally sell of their trade titles in your field, and you can ask for details of the marketing campaigns they have conducted for their trade titles. As we shall see, trade books are edited and designed differently than monographs, but the most important differences in their publication are in marketing.

Editing and Design

Editors take two approaches to trade books. Some look only for extremely well written books that require very little editorial work. Especially in large trade houses, few editors have time for painstaking reviews of manuscripts, and schedules are rushed. Other editors, especially those at smaller trade houses and at university presses trying to build their trade lists, seek out manuscripts that have sales potential because of their subject but may require editorial work to make them attractive to general readers. These editors may work directly with the authors or hire freelance editors who are skilled at this kind of effort. Each acquiring editor takes a different approach, and even editors who prefer to avoid extensive editing may make an occasional exception for an especially promising or interesting manuscript.

Trade book editors who prefer to be actively involved frequently ask to see early drafts so that they can provide suggestions for extensive revisions before authors have invested a lot of time on material that may not be included. These suggestions are like those made by developmental editors in textbook houses. New chapters may be suggested, and others may be deleted. Editors may want more (or less) background and context, more (or fewer) examples, more (or less) formality, and more (or fewer) personal asides. They may note that some features of the manuscript do not work. They may suggest reorganizing the whole manuscript or individual chapters. To the author used to dealing with university press editors about monographs, this level of editorial intervention will be unexpected and possibly insulting. Trade publishing is very much a collaboration, a melding of the talents and knowledge of the author and those of the editor. You know astronomy, history, or economics; your editor knows readers' expectations and how to meet them. The editor could not write your book, but without editorial help you cannot make it as salable as it must be. Expect a lot of advice, and take it seriously.

You should consult your editor as you revise, whenever major questions arise. Do not be surprised if even a second or third version comes back with a lot of suggestions.

When your editor thinks the book is ready, it will go to a copy editor who will do a sentence-by-sentence review. This editing is unlikely to require much revision on your part, but it may take a lot of time to answer the editor's queries and review the changes. The copy editor may have been given a specific charge beyond the normal instructions. For example, if you have been unable to get the manuscript down to a desired length, that job may fall to the copy editor. You will have an opportunity to review the copy editor's work, and you will also have to review proof, as you would with a monograph or textbook.

While your book is being copyedited, it is also being designed. Trade books always have dust jackets, and these are generally more elaborate than those for monographs. For trade books, the jacket is a major marketing tool. It usually appears in advertising, and it must appeal to booksellers and to prospective readers. Your suggestions may be sought early in the design process, and you may get to see sketches of possible jackets. You will probably be asked to send a photograph of yourself for the back or flap of the jacket and for other publicity material.

The paperback edition of your book may use the same design or start over. If it is to have a new design (most likely if the paperback is issued by another publisher), you may again be consulted.

The inside of the book may be more elaborately designed than that of a monograph, too, with illustrated or ornamented chapter openings or part-title pages. Trade books are generally typeset professionally, so authors' disks are rarely used. A paperback edition will not be reedited, but it may be redesigned (less elaborately) for the smaller, less expensive format.

The editorial, marketing, and design departments – and the author – will all be involved in creating a title. Titles are very important in trade publishing. A memorable title helps sales in many ways: the person who reads a review goes into the store and asks for the book by name instead of asking for "that new book on the Civil War" and ending up with the wrong one. It is also easier to recommend a book to a friend if you can remember the title. Trade book titles must be memorable, but they must also be accurate and not promise more than they can deliver. This seems to be a special problem for university presses, which frequently use a title to grab the reader's attention and only in the subtitle disclose the book's limitations (an imaginary example: *The Meaning of Life: Deconstructing the Magazine's First Five Issues*).[2] You should contribute as many ideas as you can, offer your opinion on the short list, and object if the final choice does not really reflect what your book is about.

Marketing

A trade book is sold to readers in bookstores, where it competes with thousands of other new titles. The publisher's job

---

[2] Wendy Doniger discusses university press trade publishing, including titles, in "The Academic Snob Goes to Market," *Scholarly Publishing* 24, no. 1 (October 1992): 3–12.

is to get the book into the store, encourage the bookseller to promote it, and make sure that as many customers as possible walk into the store and ask for it. Marketing departments work at these tasks from the moment your book is accepted.

The marketing department will solicit information from you about your book, who you think will want to read it, whether you have any contacts in the review media or among booksellers, whether any famous authors might be willing to say something complimentary about the book for the jacket, catalogue, and advertising, and so forth. Your literary agent's help will also be sought. You will probably be asked to write book summaries of different lengths which the marketers will use as the basis for jacket, catalogue, and advertising copy.

If the publisher has grand expectations for your book, you may be asked to participate more directly in its marketing. Authors are occasionally asked to address the publisher's salespeople, attend booksellers' conventions, or even make bookselling tours (autographing books in bookstores, for example). The marketing effort may include trying to book you onto radio or even television interview shows. You can help by telling the publisher about media opportunities in your own city. But if you are not willing to do any of these things, say so early. Shy people can be successful authors, too.

Most of the marketing effort is less visible and demands far less of the author. Marketers focus on writing good catalogue and advertising copy, selecting the best places to buy advertising space, soliciting useful comments from well-known experts or public figures, getting review attention, and encouraging bookseller enthusiasm. Trade publishers may join booksellers in paying for local advertising, for example, or offering a cardboard display that can be placed near the cash register or in some other prominent place. When early reviews are favorable, marketers may mail or fax them to major bookstores. (For serious nonfiction, "major booksellers" often means the successful independent stores as well as the superstore chains.)

A minimum marketing budget for a trade book is about

$25,000. That may sound like a lot, but advertising in the major review media is very expensive. What really sells books, though, is the kind of publicity that you cannot buy: lots of favorable reviews, word-of-mouth recommendations, and bookseller enthusiasm. Advertising can help all of this along, but it cannot guarantee results.

The best thing an author can do to help sell a book is to offer suggestions, cooperate with the marketing staff, and become sensitive to promotional opportunities. Use your campus news bureau to help generate local media interest. An interview in a local newspaper or on a local television program may attract national attention, and booksellers in your city talk to booksellers in other cities. Anything that gets the word out will be helpful.

Are You Ready for This?

Most academic authors wait until they are well along in their careers before writing for general readers. In part, this may be because they do not feel ready before then, but it is also because trade books do not usually help much in gaining tenure or promotion. Some people claim that they actually detract from one's chances for academic advancement. The disdain academics express for "popularization" may come from misunderstanding, snobbishness, or just plain jealousy, but it does discourage many younger writers.

Of course, actually writing a trade book is daunting. Yet most authors who write one successful trade book write at least one more. A few authors write many. Apparently the rewards are worth the difficulty.

Chapter 10

The Mechanics of Authorship

Describing the rhythm method of birth control in her latest book, . . . sex therapist Ruth Westheimer, Ph.D., incorrectly tells her readers that "the safe times [for sexual intercourse] are the week before and the week of ovulation." While proofreading, "I read the word 'unsafe' in my mind," says the tiny tycoon. "These things do happen."

Newsweek, January 13, 1986

Many of the tasks involved in publishing are mechanical, uninteresting, and frustrating. They are also crucial. This chapter does not make proofreading, indexing, and the like painless, but it will help the diligent author perform these jobs efficiently and well. If you yourself do not want to fulfill any of these functions, your publisher can help you find people to do them for you, but the cost of delegating all this work would probably be prohibitive. In many cases, too, the author is the best-qualified proofreader and indexer.

This chapter is directed at authors preparing either a traditional or an electronic manuscript. If you are preparing an electronic manuscript on disks that may be used for typesetting, or if you are preparing camera-ready copy, you should also read Chapter 11.

Preparing the Typescript

The instructions for preparing a typescript are the same regardless of the sort of book you are writing. However, many textbook publishers provide their authors with specific instructions on the preparation of the manuscript. If your publisher gives you such instructions, follow them. If you have not received instructions, request them.

Keyboarding

Whether prepared on a typewriter, word processor, or computer, *all* material in a book manuscript – including notes, bibliography, tables, and appendixes – should be double-spaced. Double-spacing leaves room for interlinear editing and makes for easier reading by referees, the copy editor, and the typesetter. Notes and bibliographies must often be heavily edited for form and style, and this is impossible on single-spaced copy. Also, typesetters frequently impose a surcharge for single-spaced copy. Change to a fresh ribbon and make sure that your printer produces copy that is legible and dark enough to photocopy well. A laser printer, "letter-quality" daisywheel printer, or 24-pin dot matrix printer will work; a 9-pin dot matrix printer usually will not. Use a good-quality, 8½- by 11-inch, white 20-lb paper; lightweight paper tears, and because manuscripts are handled a great deal, they can quickly become illegible. It is all right to submit a good-quality dry-process photocopy. Leave ample margins, so that there is room for editorial comments, queries, and changes, and for typesetters' marks. Number the pages consecutively straight through the manuscript, not chapter by chapter, to make length estimates easier and to avoid confusion. Do not number table or illustration pages.

If you use a computer, do not justify the right margin or divide words at the ends of lines. Because the lines will end in different places in the typeset version, the copy editor will have to mark each end-of-line hyphen for the typesetter. End-of-line hyphens are all right only if they are permanent hyphens that occur in compound words. Chapter 11 provides more detailed instructions for preparing a manuscript that may be typeset from the author's disks.

What to Include

Make sure the manuscript includes the following elements:

1 A title page
2 A dedication if desired
3 A table of contents
4 A preface and acknowledgments if needed
5 Lists of maps, illustrations, and tables if needed
6 The complete text
7 Maps, tables, and illustrations if needed
8 Glossary or list of abbreviations if needed
9 Notes
10 Bibliography

Note that the manuscript should not contain an index. Book indexes cannot be prepared in final form until you have at least preliminary page proofs, because entries must provide page numbers. Even if you use an indexing program to make it easier to check spelling and style, the product cannot be put into final form until your manuscript has been edited and set in pages. The sole exception is a book that is indexed by numbered items or paragraphs, rather than by pages, such as a bibliography.

The title page should contain the title and subtitle (if any) and your name. It is advisable, though not vital, to include the standard copyright notice: Copyright © 1990 by Leslie J. Author.

Dedications are optional. If you want to dedicate your book to someone, by all means do so. But avoid flowery, overly personal, or cute tributes. A lot of people are going to read your book, and few of them need to be told in detail of your spouse's adoration, your parents' sacrifices, or your children's brilliance. Keep it short and simple. The dedicatees will be grateful for the recognition, no matter how few the words.

The table of contents can be brief (just chapter titles plus notes and bibliography) or more detailed. If your chapters are long and have major subdivisions with descriptive headings, include these headings if they will help the reader locate material more easily or determine whether the book is of interest. Only highly technical works need greater detail. When a manuscript is divided into parts as well as chapters, the parts should be included in the table of contents. Figures 1.9–1.11 in *The Chicago Manual of Style* illustrate the varieties of tables of contents.

A preface is useful in explaining the inspiration for the book, origins and evolution of the project, and so forth. It should be regarded as optional reading, however, and should not include anything such as methodology or theoretical background that the reader needs to understand the book. Acknowledgments, when included, should be brief and relatively formal. Personal thanks, particularly if effusive, should be handwritten in an inscription.

Be sure that your lists of maps, illustrations, and tables are accurate – that is, that they conform to the actual numbers, titles, and placement of the figures and tables.

The text should be complete. If you have left out a date, first name, or piece of data, fill it in. You do not want to give an impression of sloppiness or haste, and you are going to have to complete it eventually anyway.

Each table should be typed neatly, not handwritten, on a separate piece of paper, with correct alignment of columns. Tables should be numbered and titled. You can place the pages in the text where they belong or group them separately. For the latter alternative, be sure to indicate the number of the manuscript page where the table belongs. Short, simple tables can be typed within the text.

Instructions for preparing and mailing illustrations are provided in the next section. When submitting a manuscript for consideration, however, you may simply send photocopies.

Type the glossary and list of abbreviations, if needed, in proper alphabetical order, double-spaced. Make sure such elements are complete and accurate, and that they contain all the foreign words, technical words, or abbreviations as they are actually used in the book.

Notes should not be inserted at the foot of the text page. This is true no matter where the notes will appear in the finished book. Even if they are to be set at the foot of the page, the copy editor and typesetter can deal with them more easily if you prepare them as a separate entity. Type them like the text, double-spaced, each beginning as an indented paragraph with a number typed at line level followed by a period (i.e., 32., not [32]). Make sure you have the same number of notes as you have note numbers in the text. Number notes consecutively by chapter.

The bibliography or reference list should also be typed double-spaced. Each entry begins at the left margin, with further lines indented three to five spaces. Such lists are alphabetical, author's last name first, and entries are not numbered. When more than one work by the same author is listed, use three hyphens instead of the name for all listings after the first. Figures 15.10–15.16 and 16.1–16.3 in *The Chicago Manual of Style* illustrate form and style of bibliographies and reference lists.

Changes and Corrections

The manuscript you submit to a publisher has almost always been revised and reworked from an original draft. It should be neat and carefully proofread, but it need not be perfect. Of course, if you have prepared the manuscript on a computer, there is little excuse for a sloppy manuscript. Even with a computer, however, it is all right to correct misspellings and other minor errors by hand – unless, of course, the typesetter will be using your disks. If you have used a typewriter rather than a computer, and revision has led you to eliminate sections or paragraphs, it is all right to cross them out firmly (or white them out and photocopy the page); you need not retype to fill out the page. Minor corrections that fit between the lines and are legible are acceptable. Figure 3.(a) shows acceptable corrections. (In proofreading, corrections are made in the margins, but in the manuscript they should be interlinear.) Inserts may be added by cutting and pasting, but keep the page size at 8½ by 11 inches. It is best to send photocopies of such pages. Never write in the margins, on the backs of pages, on little slips of paper, or vertically up or down the margins. Figure 3.(b) shows some unacceptable practices. Such changes may be missed by the copy editor or typesetter, and they may result in penalty charges for typesetting. It is best to use a single typewriter or printer throughout, but using the same size of type will do. Do not use 10-point type for some chapters and 12-point for others. It is difficult for designers and compositors to estimate length and costs if the manuscript is not uniform.

The Chicago Manual of Style, Chapter 2, provides further details on manuscript preparation. However, the discussion is concerned with a manuscript accepted for publication, and not all the instructions described are required by all publishers. If your manuscript has not yet been accepted, you will probably need to make further changes, so it is a waste of time to produce a *Chicago*-perfect manuscript at this point.

Send the manuscript in a corrugated cardboard box (a padded bag is all right if you are not enclosing artwork or computer disks). Disks should be mailed in rigid cardboard mailers or plastic cases. Use first-class mail or a commercial delivery service. Overnight delivery is rarely necessary.

Revised Editions

The method used to prepare a revised edition will depend on the method used to prepare the previous edition. If the earlier edition was typeset traditionally (that is, not from your disks), then you can work from the existing book. If the publisher has unbound copies, ask for two. If not, you will have to cut apart two copies of the book (one for left-hand pages, one for right). Then, using paste, rubber cement, or tape – not paper clips or staples – put the new edition together on 8½- by 11-inch paper, conserving as much of the original type as possible. For example, if you just need to

tion, having met the standards of impartial reviewers. The disadvantage is the amount of time it takes. Even assuming that no one involved has anything else to do, which is never the case, a manuscript of average length will take from one to ~~two~~ eight weeks for inhouse review (depending on how through this is and whether cost estimates are required), a month per outside reader (usually at least two readers, sometimes as many as five), a week or two for recommendations to the faculty committee, and a week to a month before the faculty committee meets. Add in mailing time, and you are up to a minimum of four months. If a summer intervenes, you're up to six or seven. ~~And that allows no time for reviewers' tardiness.~~ Sometimes review takes more than a year.

University presses are also distinguished by greater emphasis on substantive and copy editing, and (often) by higher standards of design and production (better paper and sturdier bindings, for example). They also keep books in print longer than trade publishers, who may dispose of them after a year or two.

Trade Publishers

Trade houses publish scholarly works that are also of interest to the general public. Professional publishers and some trade publishers issue more specialized books in series (for example, Praeger Special Studies), or technical books in certain fields (Academic Press, Jossey-Bass, and Addison-Wesley are good examples). Their reviewing processes vary, but their decisions are usually more prompt than those of university presses. However, an unsolicited manuscript will often get short shift from a commercial publisher. It may go into a slush pile, to be read when and if someone has the time. Unless you can get some sort of introduction to an editor, or make sure through correspondence that your manuscript is expected and desired, you may not save any time at all.

~~The prestigious trade houses generally carry the same clout with administrators as does a university press. They may be less impressed by run-of-the-mill publishers. If you are worried bout promotion or tenure, check out the attitudes of the powers that be.~~

Figure 3(a). Acceptable and unacceptable manuscript corrections. The page above, although extensively marked up, is legible.

tion, having met the standards of impartial reviewers. The disadvantage is the
amount of time it takes. Even assuming that no one involved has anything else
to do, which is never the case, a manuscript of average length will take from
one to eight weeks for inhouse review (depending on how thorough this is and
whether cost estimates are required), a month or two per outside reader (usually
at least two readers, sometimes as many as five), a week or two for recommendations
to the faculty committee, and a week to a month before the faculty committee meets.
Add in mailing time, and you're up to a minimum of four months. If a summer
intervenes you're up to six or seven. And that's allowing no time for reviewers'
tardiness. Sometimes review takes more than a year. ①University presses are also distinguished
by greater emphasis in substantive and copy editing, and Copteri by higher standards of

Trade and Professional Publishers design and production (better paper and sturdier bindings, for example). They also keep books in

Trade houses publish scholarly works that are also of interest to the

general public. Professional publishers and some trade publishers issue more
(for example, Praeger Special Studies) (Academic Press, Jossey
specialized books in series, or technical books in certain fields, their Wesley are
reviewing processes vary, but their decisions are usually more prompt than those
of university presses. However, an unsolicited manuscript will often get short
shrift from a commercial publisher. It may go into a slush pile, to be read when
and if someone has the time. Unless you can get some sort of introduction to an
editor, or make sure through correspondence that your manuscript is expected,
submission to a trade publisher may not save any time at all.

Insert paragraph from back of page
You should consider a trade publisher only if you honestly believe that your
work to be of interest to those outside academia. Otherwise you are wasting
your time and the publisher's. Professional publishers should be considered if
they are active in your field. They aare generally interested in books for
practitioners in the behavioral, medical, physical, and life sciences, in business,
or in engineering.

Figure 3(b). This page shows such unacceptable corrections as writing in the margin, cramped writing, and instructions to look at the back of the page.

change a word or two, paste up the old type and make the corrections by crossing out and writing in ink in the margin; indicate clearly where the correction belongs and use standard proofreaders' marks. If you are inserting material, cut the old page where the new information belongs and paste it and the newly typed addition onto a sheet of paper. To delete a paragraph or two, paste it up with the rest of the page and then cross it out. To delete whole pages, just leave them out. When changes are so extensive that cutting and pasting is cumbersome, retype the whole page, double-spaced. (If your book was set in two or three columns, cut the columns apart and paste them up in sequence, each column on a separate sheet.)

Tables and figures to be retained should be pasted in place. Note the placement of new tables and figures in the margin, and prepare new artwork just as for the original edition.

You must prepare new front matter (title page, preface, acknowledgments, table of contents, list of illustrations, and so forth). Renumber the pages of the manuscript. You will also have to redo the index when page proof is ready. If you were granted permissions that applied only to one edition, you will have to reapply. Check your files and ask your editor's advice.

If the previous edition of your book was set from your disks, you can revise on the disks. Ask your editor to send you copies of the disks from which the book was set in a form that is compatible with your software. Agree with your editor on a method to highlight the revisions on screen and in hard copy. For example, in doing the revisions for the second edition of this book, I surrounded all changes, deletions, and additions with tildes, a symbol not used for any other purpose in the manuscript: ~this is new material~. The tildes printed out in the hard copy, and I circled them in red to make them easier to find. Depending on how you work best, you may want to print out a copy of the unrevised manuscript, edit on that, and then enter the changes on the disk; or you may prefer simply to do your revisions only on the disk. In either case, your editor will probably want hard copy as well as disks, so you will have to print out the revised version of any chapter in which you made changes. Your manuscript editor can enter further changes directly on the disks as well. It is certainly easier, quicker, and cleaner to revise a book on disks than with scissors and paste.

Illustrations

Whether your book is a biography with a frontispiece as the only illustration, an economics treatise with a dozen graphs, or a textbook with hundreds of illustrations, you need some basic understanding of the acquisition and preparation of the kinds of artwork you are using. If you are writing a heavily illustrated textbook, you must also figure out a way to keep track of all those graphs, cartoons, charts, and photographs.

You and your editor should discuss the number and kinds of illustrations to be included from the very beginning of your association, and before production of the artwork begins, you must agree on this. Compile a very specific list, chapter by chapter. Often the number and type of illustrations will be stipulated in the contract; certainly the use of color illustrations must be agreed upon in writing, well in advance.

To work intelligently with your editor, you should learn the technical differences among illustrations, discover where artwork comes from, and understand exactly your responsibilities for providing illustrative material that is appropriate and of good technical quality. (Two excellent guides to developing and preparing illustrations are *Graphics Simplified,* by A. J. MacGregor, and the Council of Biology Editors' *Illustrating Science: Standards for Publication*, both listed in the bibliography.)

Types of Artwork

From the point of view of printing technology, there are three types of artwork: line drawings, halftones, and color plates. In all likelihood, the artwork in your book will be either line drawings or halftones. Line drawings are black and white, with no shading (cross-hatching or dots may be used to simulate shading, however). Examples are maps, graphs, and cartoons. Line drawings are the cheapest and easiest illustrations to reproduce. Halftones are illustrations with gray tones; examples include photographs and drawings with pencil shading. Some artwork can be reproduced as either a line drawing or a halftone, and the production editor will make this decision. Few books require color illustrations, and since they are extremely expensive, they are used only when absolutely necessary, most commonly in art books. (You will often see color printing in textbooks – headings in red or line drawings printed in brown or blue. This is not the same process as printing full-color photographs; it simply requires the use of two inks. It is more expensive than using just one color, but it is not nearly so costly as reproducing color photographs.)

Producing Artwork

Whether a given illustration is a halftone or a line drawing, it does not come from thin air. You must produce it yourself, have it produced, or acquire it from someone who already has it. Producing your own artwork is not a good idea unless you are an accomplished cartographer, graphic artist, or photographer. Sketches and snapshots will not do. Of course, you will have to provide the content of the artwork: the data for graphs, sketches for diagrams, subjects for photographs, and so forth. These must be complete, accurate, drawn to scale, and as detailed as necessary. You cannot just tell a cartographer that the Ohio River goes over here someplace. All keys, labels, numbers, names, and any other text that is part of the artwork must be legible and correctly spelled. It is a good idea to provide a separate, typed list of these as well. You should write out any additional instructions or explanations that the artist might find helpful, and, when possible, provide photocopies of similar art that shows what you have in mind. (Such photocopies should be marked clearly "Not copy.") Remember, the artist cannot be expected to do your research, check your facts, or clarify your data. If you submit inaccurate or vague sketches, incorrect or rough numbers, or maps with cities on the wrong bank of the river, you will not get good illustrations.

Computer technology facilitates the production of maps and graphs. Cartography programs are expensive, complex, and difficult to learn, so it is still best to have a professional produce maps. However, most graphs can easily be produced with software in common use. You can do these yourself, or hire someone familiar with a graphics program, and print them using a laser printer.

Textbook publishers usually prefer to have their own artists, or free-lance artists under their supervision, produce the final illustrations. If this is the case, working from the list you and your editor developed, you must submit sketches of each illustration that is to be drawn from scratch. The art editor and copy editor will review and revise these, sometimes returning them to you with requests for further information or clarification. The artist will then draw the final art, and you will get photocopies for checking. Depending on the way your contract is written, you will be billed for all or part of the artwork or the fee will be deducted from your royalties. If you are paying for the artwork, you would be wise to ask for an estimate before work begins and for an itemized bill when it is finished. As I suggested in Chapter 5, it is a good idea to try to get the publisher to share the costs of illustrations. This should be done at the contract stage. When the bill comes, it is a bit late to reopen negotiations.

If you decide to hire an artist on your own, she or he will have to follow the specifications set by the publisher. These vary, so you should get detailed instructions on size and type of paper, ink, style of lettering (typeset or hand-lettered? in what face or hand? supplied by whom?), and the size the artwork will be in the finished book. To avoid confusion, ask the editor to send specifications directly to your artist and to provide advice to the artist when questions arise. Do not have the artist begin work before your sketches have been edited. It is a good idea to have the artist submit to your editor for technical approval a sample of each category of illustration before proceeding. You should check the final artwork very carefully for accuracy.

Perhaps some of the line drawings you need have been drawn and published in other books or in journal articles. A very clear original from the journal may be adequate for reproduction, but only if it is highly contrasted, unsmudged, without ink from the other side showing through, and so forth. It is much better to borrow the original artwork from the author or the journal. In some cases, though, you will have to have it redrawn or scanned. No matter which of these courses you choose, you must get written permission from the owner of the illustration, a procedure explained in the section on permissions.

Photographs

Unless you have a large budget and a contemporary subject, the photographs you use will come from existing collections. Your publisher may have photo files, and you may have seen usable photographs in other books or articles. Photographs should not be reproduced from publications if you can avoid it; you should obtain a black-and-white print (preferably glossy) or negative. When photographs are printed in books they go through a process called "screening." This is obvious in newspaper photos, where visible dots appear, but you can see it in finer printing if you use a magnifying glass. If you take a screened photo and rescreen it, you get a moiré pattern which can obscure detail. Therefore, if you are using halftones, you must get prints from the original publisher, the photographer, the photo service, or the depository that owns them.

Finding appropriate, high-quality photographs can be very difficult. It would be impossible to list the sources in every academic field, but I will provide some general ideas, and I have listed further sources in the bibliography. First, if you have seen the perfect photograph already in print, consult the credit line or acknowledgments section of the book for the source. If none is listed, write to the publisher. Second, look through other books in your field and see where they got their photographs. You may not want to use the same pictures, but you will get some leads. Third, try free or inexpensive sources. These include federal agencies like the Library of Congress, the National Archives, the Smithsonian Institution, and NASA; public libraries, historical societies, and museums; and trade associations, businesses, and foreign countries' information offices. Fourth, commercial photo agencies will supply photos for a fee. United Press International, Black Star, and Magnum are examples of such companies. *Literary Market Place* provides a longer list.

To use any of these sources effectively, you must begin early. The Library of Congress, for example, always has a backlog of requests, and it may take several months to get your photographs. It is a good idea to call or write and ask what each collection's procedures are: Must you send a deposit for reproduction and mailing costs? Do they have a catalogue? What information must you supply? What will they send initially – descriptions, photocopies, or glossies? (You will need glossy black-and-white photos for actual production, but photocopies may be adequate for making your selection.) Can they recommend a free-lance photo researcher who knows their collection? Procedures vary, and advance preparation saves time.

The second key to success is to make your request as specific as possible, including all relevant details. Do not just ask for a picture of Franklin Roosevelt. Do you want an informal pose or a portrait? At what age? Alone, with family, or with the Cabinet? In the White House or elsewhere? Instead of asking for a photo of a mine, tell what sort of mine (coal? diamond? salt?), in what region (the American West? Appalachia? South Africa? Siberia?), with or without people, when (now? mid-nineteenth century?), and for what purpose (to show working conditions? technology? environmental impact?). The more specific you are, the more suitable the photos you receive will be.

You need to evaluate photographs not only for appropriateness of content but also for aesthetic qualities such as composition and for technical qualities such as contrast and clarity. Your editor, with help from the production staff, can provide guidance on these issues, and the books by MacGregor and the Council of Biology Editors offer good advice.

Before paying agency or permissions fees, have your editor approve the photographs for inclusion in the book. Photo agencies may charge a great deal of money, and even the small reproduction fees collected by nonprofit agencies can mount up, so make sure photos are acceptable to the publisher before you invest. Also find out when permissions fees are due. Most agencies are willing to wait until publication.

A word of warning on photo fees is in order. Your publisher may volunteer to provide photographs, but you will still have to pay the fees (read your contract). When you are paying, the publisher may not be as motivated to seek out free or inexpensive photos. If you decide to let the publisher do your photo research, ask for a list of photos, sources, and fees well in advance. You can then take the time to find cheaper substitutes for expensive agency selections if necessary. If you do not do this, you may be in for a shock when the bill comes. It may also be less expensive for you to hire a free-lance photo researcher who can find what you need and who will keep within a budget you set. *Literary Market Place* has a list of picture researchers, or try the New York or Washington, D.C., phone book. Some researchers use computer searches and can compile a list of free or inexpensive photos with amazing speed.

Keeping Track of Illustrations

Once you have identified the line drawing or photograph you need, you must make sure it is properly identified, placed, and credited. Your publisher may provide a form or checklist for this purpose. If not, and if you have many illustrations to keep track of, make up one. Figure 4 shows a form you may find helpful. Use pencil rather than ink to fill in whatever form you use. If you like, you can use a database program to perform this chore. Ideally, such a program should be able to renumber, reorder, and print out captions and credits separately.

First, number each illustration. Do not put the number on the front of a photograph. Use the back or a tissue overlay. If you mark the back of a photograph, use a fine, soft felt-tipped pen or write the number on a sticky label and then apply it to the back. Pressure on the back of a photo from a pencil or ballpoint pen will mar the front. Do not use paper clips; they, too, will mar the photo. It is all right to number a line drawing in the margin. If possible, though, be consistent about placement of numbers (e.g., back, upper right-hand corner) so that they are easy to find. If your publisher has a system for numbering, use it. If not, I recommend that you adopt a chapter-by-chapter double-digit system (1.1, 1.2, etc.) rather than try to number straight through the book. It is easier to make additions and deletions that way. Your working number system need not correspond to the published numbers, although it saves work if it does.

Now, go through the manuscript and note in the margin where each illustration belongs. On your form, fill in the manuscript page number. When you have finished this, the illustrations have been placed.

The next task is to write a caption for each illustration. A caption should be a brief identification of the subject of the illustration. In addition, it may have to explain the process being illustrated or identify detail. Perhaps it will state the conclusion drawn from the illustrated data. If the illustration is not vital but simply emphasizes a point in the text, then the caption may simply restate the point being made. The caption should include the final figure number (just leave space for this if you do not know it yet), and the working

Working no.	Final no.	MS page	Description	Source	Final copy	Editor's OK	Perm. asked	Perm. rec'd	Caption written	Credit written

Notes:

Figure 4. Art inventory form.

number should be written in the margin. When you have completed the caption, indicate that on your checklist.

Now write the credit lines. Check the permission letters. If a letter requires a certain form, use it. If not, adopt a simple formula: "Courtesy of the Library of Congress," "Used with the permission of National Sticky Wicket." Federal agencies or museums may provide photographs free, but you should nevertheless acknowledge their contribution.

Finally, type up the captions and credit lines, chapter by chapter, double-spaced, on regular typing paper. Type or write your working number in the margin and leave space in the caption itself for the final number: Figure . George Washington, in a portrait by Charles Willson Peale. Courtesy of the Pennsylvania Academy of Fine Arts.

Preparing the art manuscript or art package for a textbook can be a nightmare if you are disorganized. Here is a summary of the procedure that may help you keep things straight:

1 Work with your editor to develop a list of illustrations, specifying whether a photograph or drawing is preferred.
2 Compile the artwork:
   (a) Prepare sketches of all new line drawings; submit them for editing; have them drawn to the publisher's specifications; proofread all final artwork.
   (b) Locate existing line drawings; write for originals and permissions; make changes, redraw, or scan if necessary.
   (c) Locate desired photographs; get editor's approval; make sure you can afford fees; write for permission and glossy prints.
3 Organize artwork, using a checklist:
   (a) Number each illustration.
   (b) Indicate placement of each illustration in the manuscript.
   (c) Prepare captions and credit lines.
4 Pay permissions fees when due.

Permissions

Whenever you quote or otherwise draw on someone else's work, you must acknowledge the source. That is a simple matter of honesty and good scholarship. When your quotation exceeds what is vaguely defined as "fair use" (explained shortly), you must obtain the written permission of the copyright holder. Obtaining permission is vital for the writer of any book or article, and your contract will make clear that it is your responsibility. It is especially complicated for the textbook writer because textbooks are written for profit (one of the considerations mentioned in the copyright law) and because they tend to draw on a greater number of sources than do monographs.

When to Request Permission

Permission is not needed when your quotation is "fair use," but there is a good deal of debate about what this means. The copyright law is purposefully vague; since the provision is brief, I will quote it:

> Notwithstanding the provisions of section 106, the fair use of a copyrighted work, including such use by reproduction in copies or phonorecords or by any other means specified by that section, for purposes such as criticism, comment, news reporting, teaching (including multiple copies for classroom use), scholarship, or research, is not an infringement of copyright. In determining whether the use made of a work in any particular case is a fair use the factors to be considered shall include
> (1) the purpose and character of the use, including whether such use is of a commercial nature or is for nonprofit educational purposes;
> (2) the nature of the copyrighted work;
> (3) the amount and substantiality of the portion used in relation to the copyrighted work as a whole; and
> (4) the effect of the use upon the potential market for or value of the copyrighted work.

These four factors are generally interpreted in terms of the nature of your use (a free class handout versus a profitable textbook); the nature of the quoted work (a speech versus an unpublished letter, a news release versus a limited-circulation investors' letter); the proportion – whether by length or significance – of the original work being reproduced (a single paragraph from a lengthy novel versus an entire sonnet; an example of an author's style versus the author's summary of an original theory or technique); and the potential economic effect of the use on the owner of the original work (will people decide not to buy the poet's own slim volume if the most famous poem is reproduced in your paperback anthology?).

The important point to note is that the law gives no maximum number of words or other hard-and-fast rules that you can rely on. Any such guidelines – including those that follow – are simply collections drawn from practical experience. Few, if any, have been tested in the courts.

Your publisher will give you rules of thumb at least about when you need to request permission, and the bibliography lists handbooks on copyright law. I will give a brief summary here, which combines the variety of rules I have heard over the years. It is not a lawyer's advice, which you and your publisher should seek in difficult cases. The best general advice I can give is to remember that permissions are your responsibility, and when in doubt, err on the side of caution – especially if you are writing a textbook. Transgressions by authors of textbooks are considered much more serious than those committed by authors of unprofitable monographs.

1 When do you need permission for quotations?
- In the case of a monograph, for quotations of a total of 500 or more words of prose from any published book or book-length document
- In the case of a textbook, for quotations of a total of 150 or more words of prose from any published book or book-length document
- For shorter quotations of prose from shorter works (e.g., 50 words from an article of 1,000 words)

- For quotations of 3 or more lines of poetry or 8 measures of a song
- For any exact reproduction of a table, graph, or other illustration, including photographs of paintings or sculpture (data may be used without permission, though the source must be credited)
- For any unpublished material (letters, diaries, manuscripts; recent court decisions have construed this very strictly)
- For material obtained in interviews (ideally, a release should be obtained from the subject at the time of the interview)
- For examples, problems, or the like written by your students, friends, or relatives
- For your own work published by another company

2 When do you definitely not need permission?
- For quotations from material first published in the United States 75 or more years ago
- For quotations from material first published in a U.S. government publication (but watch for reports by individuals; these are sometimes protected)

3 When have you done enough?
- When you have received written permission and paid any required fees

Remember: Be cautious, begin early, and keep good records.

How to Request Permission

Your publisher may provide a form letter for you to use in seeking permission. If not, *The Chicago Manual of Style* provides a sample letter (Figure 4.4). At a minimum, you must give the author, title, and publication date of the work from which you are quoting; the pages on which the material appears; any changes or deletions you propose to make in the quoted material; the author, title, and approximate length of your own book or article; and the publication date, price, and size and type of edition (paper and/or cloth) of your book. If a future paperback edition is likely, ask permission to quote in that, too. Ask your publisher whether the book is to be sold outside the United States. If so, you will have to obtain "nonexclusive world rights in the English language." If your book is likely to be translated into a foreign language, you can also ask for these rights so that you can sell foreign rights without complications. This can be postponed, however, until someone is actually interested in doing a translation. Figures 5 and 6 are permissions requests for a monograph and a textbook, with possible publishers' responses. Figure 7 is a permissions request for an anthology, also with a response.

Some publishers go through the manuscript and provide you with a list of material requiring permission. If your publisher does not do this, or does not do it early, you yourself should compile such a list. To make the job easier in the case of books requiring large numbers of permissions, use index cards or a database program instead of a single list. That way, you can compile the list as you go through the manuscript and then order the requests by publisher or journal to facilitate letter writing. After that, you can more easily check the status of each request. Make at least three copies of each letter: one for your files, one for the files of the publisher granting permission, and one for the publisher's signature, to be returned to you.

As in compiling illustrations, the keys to obtaining permissions are starting early and staying organized. Begin the permissions process as soon as you have a book contract in hand and send follow-up letters if you do not get responses. The author or publisher may deny permission (this is rare but possible) or ask an excessive fee, or you may have difficulty locating the person or company that holds the rights. You may have to send a copy of the pages in which the material appears, or the publisher may send you a form to complete. All of this takes time. As soon as you run into trouble, ask your editor's advice; do not wait until the last minute.

52 Sequoia Drive
Redwood, California 94444

May 10, 1995

Permissions Department
Ambleside Publishers, Inc.
2122 East Concorda Drive
Tempe, Arizona 85282

Dear Permissions Editor,

I have written a scholarly monograph, *Math Anxiety and Career Choice*, to be published by the University of Antarctica Press in September 1996. The book will be published in an edition of 1,500 copies and priced at $34.95.

I would like to quote approximately 750 words from pages 115-120 of *Psychology: Strategies for Success*, by David Cantrell, which you published in 1988. Although no paperback edition is planned at this time, I would like permission for a future paperback edition, as well as world rights in case the book is translated and published abroad. If you agree to this use, please sign and return one copy of this letter. I would be happy to include any credit line you specify.

Sincerely,

Leslie J. Author

We grant permission for the uses specified in this letter.

_____

for Ambleside Publishers, Inc.

_____

Date

Figure 5. Permissions letter for a monograph. The publisher granted permission by signing the bottom of the letter and adding one condition.

52 Sequoia Drive
Redwood, California 94444

May 10, 1995

Permissions Department
Ambleside Publishers, Inc.
2122 East Concorda Drive
Tempe, Arizona 85282

Dear Permissions Editor,

I have written a scholarly monograph, *Math Anxiety and Career Choice,*
to be published by the University of Antarctica Press in September 1996.
The book will be published in an edition of 1,500 copies and priced at $34.95.

I would like to quote approximately 750 words from pages 115-120 of
Psychology: Strategies for Success, by David Cantrell, which you published
in 1988. Although no paperback edition is planned at this time, I would like
permission for a future paperback edition, as well as world rights in case the
book is translated and published abroad. If you agree to this use, please sign
and return one copy of this letter. I would be happy to include any credit line
you specify.

Sincerely,

Leslie J. Author

We grant permission for the uses specified in this letter.

Susan Publisher
for Ambleside Publishers, Inc.

10 June 1995
Date

No special credit line needed -
just usual note citation.

Figure 5 (*cont.*)

52 Sequoia Drive
Redwood, California 94444

May 5, 1995

Permissions Department
Ambleside Publishers, Inc.
2122 East Concorda Drive
Tempe, Arizona 85282

Dear Permissions Editor,

I am the author of a text in introductory psychology to be published by
Mammoth House. The first edition will be 50,000 copies, with a retail price
of $29.95. It will be published in cloth only, sometime in 1997.

I am writing to request world rights, in the English language, to quote the
section on reading statistics in David Cantrell's *Psychology: Strategies for
Success,* which you published in 1988. The section I wish to quote begins
with the first full paragraph on p. 116 and ends with the third full paragraph
on p. 118. This material will appear in a box.

If you agree to this use, please sign the form below and return this letter to me.
I have enclosed a second copy for your files.

Sincerely,

Leslie J. Author

We hereby grant permission for the use described above.

_____

for Ambleside Publishers, Inc.

_____

Date

Figure 6. Permissions letter for a textbook. The publisher in the
reply (facing page) attaches conditions to the permission. The fee is
undoubtedly negotiable.

Ambleside Publishers, Inc.
2122 East Concorda Drive
Tempe, AZ 85282

June 2, 1995

Leslie J. Author
52 Sequoia Drive
Redwood, California 94444

Dear Professor Author:

Thank you for asking to use the section on reading statistics from David Cantrell's *Psychology*. We will grant the rights you requested with the following conditions:

    1. Within the box containing this section, you must print the following credit line: From *Psychology: Strategies for Success* by David P. Cantrell, ©️ 1988, Ambleside Publishers, Inc.

    2. On publication of your book, you will send us a fee of $500 plus two copies of the book.

    3. You will request renewal of this permission should you wish to use this section in subsequent editions.

Sincerely,

Susan Publisher

Susan Publisher
Permissions Editor

Figure 6 (*cont.*)

52 Sequoia Drive
Redwood, California 94444

April 4, 1995

Permissions Department
Ambleside Publishers, Inc.
2122 East Concorda Drive
Tempe, Arizona 85282

Dear Permissions Editor,

I am writing to request permission to include chapter 8, "Reading and Writing Papers in Psychology," of David Cantrell's book, *Psychology: Strategies for Success,* in an anthology I am compiling. The book, a reader for introductory psychology, will be titled *Winning Techniques for Understanding Psychology.* It will be published in paperback by Collegiate Publications in an edition of 10,000 copies. It is tentatively priced at $12.95.

If you agree to this use, please sign and return one copy of this letter to me.

Sincerely,

Leslie J. Author

We hereby grant permission for the use described in this letter.

_____

for Ambleside Publishers, Inc.

_____

Date

Figure 7. Permissions letter for an anthology. The publisher's response (facing page), which is perfectly reasonable, illustrates the need to develop alternative selections early in your planning.

 Ambleside Publishers, Inc.
2122 East Concorda Drive
Tempe, AZ 85282

April 24, 1995

Leslie J. Author
52 Sequoia Drive
Redwood, California 94444

Dear Professor Author:

On March 22, you requested permission to reprint chapter 8 of David
Cantrell's *Psychology* in your anthology, *Winning Techniques for
Understanding Psychology.* I have consulted Dr. Cantrell, and I am afraid we
must deny your request. Your anthology appears to be in direct competition
with our book, which is still in print, and the chapter you want constitutes 16
percent of our volume.

Sincerely,

Susan Publisher

Susan Publisher
Permissions Editor

Figure 7 *(cont.)*

Proofreading

If you want your book to appear with all the words spelled right and in the right order, with no words missing, and with the pages in the right order, you must proofread carefully. The typesetter proofreads, but that isn't enough. Your publisher may or may not provide proofreading (university presses are more and more frequently leaving this entirely up to the author). In other words, if you don't do it, it is quite possible that no one else will. In theory, books that are set from the author's computer disks need not be proofread, although page makeup, running heads (the lines at the tops of pages, usually shortened chapter or section titles), and folios (page numbers) must be checked. In fact, it's a good idea to do a thorough reading anyway. Your disks, after all, may have contained mistakes, and errors can be caused by damage to the disk, static electricity, and gremlins.

Proofreading is not intellectually challenging. It merely requires good eyesight and patience. *The Chicago Manual* provides detailed instructions, and I will explain when you have to proofread and what to expect, as well as offer some pointers.

You must read at least one set of proofs. If your book is first set in galleys (generally long sheets not divided into pages and without properly placed tables and illustrations), you will have to read both these and the subsequent page proofs. If the book is set directly into pages, you will receive only page proofs. Whichever form it takes, the first proof usually appears between one and three months after the edited manuscript goes to the compositor (another word for typesetter). Your publisher will give you as much advance notice as possible.

Proof will arrive either alone or with the edited manuscript, depending on the practice of your publisher. (If you know in advance that your publisher will not send the edited manuscript, you may want to make a photocopy when you review it.) You will also receive instructions, which you should follow to the letter. If you do not get the edited manuscript, then all you need to do is read the galleys very carefully and mark them for corrections. If you do receive the manuscript, then you must compare the manuscript and the galleys, to make sure the typesetter has reproduced the manuscript exactly. The best way to do this is to recruit a friend to read with you. The person holding the manuscript should read aloud, and the person holding the galleys should mark the corrections, using the standard proofreader's marks found in *The Chicago Manual* or any good dictionary. No marks of any kind should be made on the manuscript. Nor should you attempt to re-write your book. If you see an error that you should have caught earlier, fix it; but do not make optional changes. Such changes will cost you money (remember the contract clause about alterations to proof), delay the book, and increase the chances that new errors will be introduced when the corrections are made. In theory, vital changes can be made up to the last minute before the book is printed. In fact, they have to be awfully important to be done after page proof.

If your first proof is page proof, you can now fill in page numbers in the table of contents and the lists of maps, tables, and illustrations and possibly in the running heads for the notes section. Any cross-references to other pages of your book must also be filled in (these will usually be set as "see pp. ooo–oo" and can now be completed).

Some authors believe that the best way to proofread is to read backward – from the last line to the first – with the line above covered by a card or ruler. The theory is that you are less likely subconsciously to read in correct spellings or punctuation instead of accurately seeing errors. This practice (if, indeed, anyone has ever practiced it) is either masochism or sadism, depending on whether you read alone or with a companion. I do not recommend it. Reading frontward through the proof, checking carefully against the manuscript, is far more effective.

Here are a few commonsense hints that will improve your proofreading. Work at it for no more than two hours without a break, and when you take time off do something that does not tax your eyes or your concentration. Pay special attention to the following error-prone areas: chapter titles and headings, tables, numbers, proper names, foreign words, block quotations, footnotes, and bibliographies. If parts of your manuscript were particularly messy, read the proof set from them one extra time. Make sure all your corrections are legible and complete; for example, if you have deleted a word that has a comma after it, make sure that the comma is saved and put in the right place. Use a dictionary to check words that have been divided at the ends of lines.

The typesetter and your production editor will check type size and technical details, but if you see anything of that sort that looks peculiar – a heading that should be italic or larger or centered, for example – point it out in a query to the editor. Do not mark splotches or lines that are clearly the product of a dirty photocopying machine.

Finally – again – return the proof on time.

If you proofread galleys, you may also be expected to read page proofs. Your editor will let you know whether and when to expect them. If you are really pressed for time, you need proofread only those sections where corrections were made. Read from the galleys to the pages, and wherever a correction was to be made, check the new type. For safety's sake, read the whole paragraph, since several lines may have been reset and not all typesetters let you know where resetting begins and ends. You must also fill in cross-references to other pages of the book. Proofread running heads and folios. It is better, though, to read all of the page proof, because the more often proof is read, the fewer errors you end up with. If you can, when you have checked the corrections against the galleys and filled in the cross-references, read the whole thing through one last time.

Generally, the editor takes care of subsequent stages of proof – revised pages, bluelines (or the equivalent photographic proof), and folded and gathered pages. For a very few kinds of books, it may make sense for the author to check these as well. Books in this category might include documentary or critical editions, where apparent errors are in fact correct. They might also include highly technical works with many symbols if galleys and page proofs contained many errors, or heavily illustrated books if the illustrations and captions did not appear in page proof. If you wish to read later proof, you should include such a provision in your contract. And because adding authorial readings for later proof extends the schedule by a week or two, make sure that you have reminded your editor about this well ahead of time.

At any stage in proofreading, if you have a major question, or if something appears to have been done consistently wrong, call your editor and discuss the problem. Sometimes the apparent error is just a technical shortcut (especially in galleys), and you can save yourself a lot of worry and time by checking. You can also avoid needless marking of the proof that will confuse and delay the typesetter.

Indexing

When page proof arrives, it is time to compile the index for your book. Almost every scholarly book and textbook has an index, although anthologies and collections of essays are sometimes exempt. You should decide whether you want to index the book yourself or hire an indexer. This decision should be based partly on whether you have the time to do it yourself and partly on whether you can afford to hire someone else. In part, however, the decision must be based on the nature of your book. If it is difficult and highly technical or theoretical, you may be the best indexer. If you want to hire someone, your publisher can recommend an indexer and let you know what the cost will be. You and your editor should let the indexer know the type of index you want, its approximate length, and its depth of coverage. You can provide a list of important topics, sample entries, and suggestions on how to handle difficult material. You may also want to review the completed index.

You must decide what kind of index is appropriate for your book: The main possibilities are a name index plus a subject index or an index in which names and subjects are combined. Sometimes a name index alone is adequate. The combined index is the most common, although the separate indexes may be helpful in a long, complex work. Separate indexes might also be added for titles of works (musical, literary, or artistic); first lines of works (as in poetry anthologies); or authors cited (separate from people as subjects). The nature of your book should determine which sort of index you compile, and your acquiring, manuscript, or production editor can provide guidance.

Preparing an index is not difficult, but it must be done carefully, sensibly, and quickly. It is usually due two weeks after you receive page proof. Your publisher can supply some guidelines, and *The Chicago Manual* and Judith Butcher's *Copy-Editing* have sections on indexes. The best brief, practical guide on how actually to go about the process is Sina Spiker's *Indexing Your Book*. I recommend that you read it before beginning your index. You might also want to look at indexes of books similar to yours to see their general approach, strengths, and weaknesses.

I will not attempt to duplicate *Chicago* or Spiker, but I can add some practical advice. Most authors overindex their own books. They include everything – even things that no one will look for – and they provide too much detail in modifications (e.g., "Communism, Reagan speaks frequently against" instead of "Communism, Reagan on"). If you compile your own index, here are some things to omit:

1 Items that people will not look for in that book. For example, a biology text tells the story of John Dillinger painting a gun carved out of a potato with iodine, so that the potato turned steel gray; iodine is a test for starch. You do not index *Dillinger, John*. (There is an argument for including it, however: Dillinger's name may be the only thing a student remembers.)
2 Items that will not give the reader any relevant information when looked up. For example, a book on Watergate has an index entry for the Taft-Hartley Act. When you look on the page given, it reads "Cox . . . had become close to John [Kennedy] when they worked together on revisions to the Taft-Hartley Act."

3 Mere mentions without content. For example, the only entry for Good Neighbor Policy turns out to be "Historians instinctively employ many insidious analogies without a second thought – or maybe even a first one. All of the following examples have caused trouble: [32 names], Good Neighbor Policy, [58 more names]."
4 People and institutions mentioned only in the acknowledgments.
5 Mere source citations, such as authors of articles cited in notes (in some disciplines these are included).
6 Tables and illustrations. These will be included in the entries for the text where they are mentioned. The exceptions are art books and any book where the illustrations will be sought independently, as in a botanical manual or field guide.
7 Part and chapter titles.

Let me also offer some hints that make the process of generating the index a bit easier. First, use index cards or a good indexing program as your working tool. For example, if you have not decided which of two headings is better, put the alternative at the end of the entry. Or write possibilities for cross-references at the end of the entry as you think of them. Another possibility is to add your own symbols for such things as "this is marginal; use only if other entries turn up."

Second, if you are using cards, write very clearly, especially page numbers. You do not want to have to go back to the page proof to see whether you meant 91 or 97. Third, as you write each card, toss it upside down into a pile so that your cards are in page order. Then do your checking of page numbers, spelling of names, and so forth as you go along, every ten pages or so. Finally, in writing the entries, whether on cards or on a computer, err on the side of inclusiveness. It is much easier to discard entries than to go back through the proof to find what you left out. By the same token, write a "modification" (the descriptive part of the entry, as in "Democracy, *rise of*") for every entry even if you end up not using it. Otherwise you will find you have to go back to modify entries that you thought would not need modifications.

A computer can be an enormous help with the more tedious aspects of indexing. If the only index you need for your book is a simple, unmodified name index, there are programs available that can generate one automatically. For a more complex index, you need a program that will at least alphabetize, order and combine page numbers, and combine entries. Many such programs are available. The "search" function is helpful for indexing names of people and places if the manuscript itself is on the computer. Unfortunately, you will always have to do the hardest part yourself – generating the entries and modifications.

An index is worthless if it is not accurate, so proofread your typed copy against your cards very carefully; shanghai a friend or student to read aloud with you. Once you have sent in your index, your production responsibilities are probably over. Some publishers send authors index proof, but usually the editor will read it when it comes back from the typesetter, and the book will then go on to the printer. You can relax now.

Chapter 11

Electronic Manuscripts and Electronic Publishing

It is important that the workman should not have to watch his instrument, that his whole attention should be given to work.
Eric Gill, *An Essay on Typography*

When an author submits computer disks or tapes to a publisher, to be used for setting type with a typesetting machine or a laser printer, the manuscript is called an *electronic manuscript*. At the time I began the first edition of this book, it was virtually unheard of for a publisher to typeset a book from an author's computer disks or tapes. Some authors were using computers for word processing, but even they were simply generating cleaner, more easily revised manuscripts to send to their publishers. Now, as I complete revisions for the third edition, most scholarly publishers are sending authors' disks to typesetters and some are "typesetting" books in-house, using the author's disks and their own laser printers. (That is the way the first two editions of this book were produced.) It is still difficult to set complex tables and technical material from an author's disks, but it is also very expensive to prepare such material using traditional methods. With better software for technical text available, the use of authors' disks for technical works is becoming increasingly common.

Textbook publishers are less likely to want electronic manuscripts because of the complex layout and design of their books, and because typesetting is a small percentage of their production costs. They may well want electronic manuscripts for supplementary materials, such as study guides, however. Trade publishers usually rely on traditional production methods because, as in text publishing, typesetting is not one of their larger costs. (See Chapter 12 for a more detailed explanation of costs.)

Improved, less expensive laser printers and new editing and page-layout software are being introduced almost daily, but the choices for book publishers are more limited than those for newsletter publishers, and two or three sophisticated page-makeup programs have been nearly universally accepted. Book publishers and manufacturers have been working together to agree on a uniform standard for coding computer-generated manuscripts. In addition, conversion software is available that makes manuscripts produced using one kind of hardware compatible with other systems. At least for scholarly books, the new technology is making a significant impact. It is becoming increasingly likely that the manuscript you write on your computer will be treated as an electronic manuscript.

Authors should keep in mind, however, that even the most carefully prepared electronic manuscript may not be used for typesetting. A publisher may decide to use traditional typesetting for a number of reasons. It is generally impractical to use an author's disks for a book that is heavily illustrated or has an elaborate layout, because most of the cost and effort comes in laying out pages rather than in keyboarding. Even for a simple manuscript with nothing but straightforward text, using an author's disks may not be economical. The disks cannot simply be "plugged in" to a typesetting machine; they must be checked, coded, and corrected. The savings will be small if much coding or correction is needed because a typesetter's keyboarding staff is paid at lower rates than the staff that handles the typesetting of disks provided by the author and publisher. Even desktop typesetting provides only marginal savings if higher-paid members of the publisher's production staff (or the author!) do the work. And, as we will see in Chapter 12, the cost of typesetting is a fairly small percentage of the cost of publishing a book, particularly if the print run is large. The monetary savings may be inconsequential.

Nor is a great deal of time always saved. The actual typesetting time may be reduced from roughly four weeks to two, but over the nine months that it usually takes to produce a book, two weeks is not very much.

The decision to use the author's disks for typesetting is largely an economic gamble, and the publisher may simply decide that the savings on a given book will not be high enough. Nevertheless, you can improve the odds that your disks will be used by preparing them carefully. Whether the publisher uses them or not, you can save yourself and your editor some time in preparing the manuscript for publication, and you can reduce the chance that error will be introduced. Assume that your electronic manuscript will be used for typesetting, but do not be too disappointed if it is not.

Electronic publishing may begin with an electronic manuscript, but the final product is not a traditional book or journal. Instead, it is a publication that is not printed on paper: The medium in which the reader receives it, like the medium in which the author created it, is electronic. Electronic publishing, which includes electronic journals, databases, and optical disks, is creating opportunities for scholarly communication that are described at the end of the chapter.

Planning the Electronic Manuscript

Because efficient use of computer technology requires compatibility of hardware and software, it is best to talk to your prospective publisher as early as possible about the practicality of typesetting from your disks. If you sign an advance contract before you have done much writing, you are in an ideal position to work successfully with your publisher on an electronic manuscript. You can agree on the word-processing program to be used and establish keyboarding rules and codes for headings, block quotations, and so forth. You can decide how to handle the mechanics of editing, who will enter the typesetting codes, and how to handle other details.

If you do not find a publisher until your manuscript is completed, all of this will be more difficult, but it is far from impossible. However, if you are going to do a significant amount of writing before finding a publisher, it will be especially important to follow the keyboarding rules given in the next section.

Publishers who are experienced in using authors' computer disks or tapes generally send authors questionnaires about the preparation of their manuscripts or instructions about their preparation; they may also ask you to send a sample disk. Figure 8 is the Cambridge University Press instructions. Such questionnaires, along with sample disks, provide the publisher with enough information to decide whether your disks can be used.

Producing an electronic manuscript may require more work on your part (or your typist's) than the traditional process. You will have to make all your changes on the disk – no more pencil corrections of typos or last-minute insertions. The disk must be letter-perfect. You may be asked to put in codes (abbreviations signaling the beginning and end of chapter titles, headings, block quotations, and other manuscript elements) and perform other tasks that authors in the good old days never knew were necessary. If you are not prepared to do any of this extra work, make sure your publisher understands that.

In fact, discussions about your responsibilities for creating an electronic manuscript should be part of your contract negotiations. Some authors do not want to spend their time entering editorial changes or codes, and they must be sure that their contract does not require them to do so. At the other extreme, some authors prefer the kind of control that this gives them and consider it to be worth the extra work. Similarly, the publisher may decide a book is publishable only if the author does a great deal of the work, while on another project no production work from the author beyond a typescript is desirable. After reading this chapter, you should have a clear idea of how much effort is required for various alternatives. If you do not want to do much of it, you will need to find a publisher who does not expect it.

If this proves impossible (for example, if your book is expected to sell few copies and would be uneconomical to produce traditionally), you may want to hire someone to do the keyboarding for you. An experienced word processor or freelance editor is a likely candidate. Some freelance editors will also produce camera-ready copy. These services may be expensive if your book is long or complex, but it may be worth paying someone rather than learning the skills and spending long hours that you would prefer to spend on research or writing. Your publisher should be able to help you find assistance, or there may be qualified people on your own campus.

The suggestions in the following sections assume that, as you are preparing your manuscript, you do not know who your publisher will be, whether your computer-generated manuscript will be used for typesetting, whether (if it will be used) it will be sent to a typesetter or fed into the publisher's own laser printer, or if you yourself may end up preparing camera-ready copy from it. Under this assumption of maximum uncertainty, you need to produce a readable, attractive typescript for referees and other readers (one that meets all the standards described in Chapter 10), yet you do not want to make it difficult for your future publisher to use your electronic manuscript. This assumption complicates matters. For example, no referee or editor wants to work with a manuscript whose pages are unnumbered, but no typesetter wants disks with page numbers already set up. Unfortunate though these complications may be, most scholarly authors must face them.

The suggestions that follow also assume that you are able to use a computer for word processing but do not require that you have any technical understanding of how computers, software, and printers work. This level of knowledge is adequate for any task you need to undertake as an author.

CAMBRIDGE
UNIVERSITY PRESS

NEW YORK OFFICE
40 West 20th Street
New York, NY 10011-4211
U.S.A.

Some Notes for Authors
on Electronic Manuscripts

If the manuscript that you are preparing for the Press is being keyboarded on a computer, it is possible that we may be able to use your disks for conversion and phototypesetting, without total rekeyboarding. Or, if the output from your printer is of sufficiently high quality, in some cases we may be able to reproduce that output directly, photographing it page for page as camera-ready copy.

We would like to examine these possibilities as early as we can during the preparation of the manuscript, so that we can decide if either of these methods would offer more efficient and economical production of your book.

If you are using a computer, may we ask that you answer as many of the questions on this questionnaire as you are able. Send the completed form to your editor as soon as you can. Even if you do not yet have any of the materials typed into the system you plan to use, we would like to learn about that system.

Please enclose a sample page or two from your printer when you return the questionnaire, so that we can assess whether the output from your printer is sharp enough to be used for reproduction directly in your book, as well as examine the structure of technical or math displays, and quality of tables and charts.

When we receive the answers to these questions and if the system you are using might be compatible with that of our typesetter, we may ask you to send us a sample diskette. This will be tested by our typesetter to see if they can be used.

Please note that whether or not we use your electronic output for typesetting, your final manuscript should be sent to your editor in the form of two hard copies. Set your printer to print double-spaced with an unjustified right margin and there should be no wordbreaks at the end of lines. All the notes should be printed double-spaced in a separate listing by chapter at the end of the manuscript, and not be printed at the foot of the manuscript pages. Please refer to our 'Notes for Authors' for more information on manuscript preparation.

For some word processing systems it is possible that the Press can provide macros or stylesheets that automatically produce our house and series styles (eg. for TeX and LaTeX). Please indicate on the questionnaire if you believe that you could use one of these packages and the preferred format (disk size and format, electronic mail etc.).

Figure 8. The Cambridge University Press electronic manuscript instructions.

CAMBRIDGE
UNIVERSITYPRESS

Electronic Manuscript Questionnaire

Author_____

Title_____

Date_____ CUP Editor _____

Your Computer

Make and model (e.g. Mac IIci, NEC 386)_____

Word processing software (include version number)_____

Graphics software (include version number)_____

Peripheral packages (e.g. BibTeX, Formulator, MacEquation)

Your Disks

Size: 5.25"   3.5"

Density: single   double   high

Format (e.g. DOS, Mac) _____

Files: Formatted using the   ASCII   Both
             above listed software

Your Text

Does your text contain:
_____technical notation   _____foreign accents   _____other special characters

Has your text been:
_____spell-checked   _____grammar-checked   _____other special checking

Would you be willing to input CUP editorial revisions directly onto the disks yourself after the copyediting is complete? ___Yes   ___No   ___Uncertain at this stage

Other Information

Figure 8 (*cont.*)

Manuscript Preparation

Even in the absence of specific advice from a publisher, you can avert future problems by following some basic rules as you write at your keyboard.[1] Actually, these rules are worth following even if your disks will not be used for typesetting: They are just good procedure to avoid disaster and disorder. These instructions will produce a manuscript that referees will be able to read without distraction but that can easily be edited and coded for electronic typesetting.

1. Select a commonly used word-processing program and, if possible, use the most recent version. Avoid systems specific to your campus or your department, as well as any free experimental programs floating around. The most popular programs are the ones that page-makeup and typesetting programs can adapt to most easily. Having chosen a program, do not switch software in midstream. If you begin a book using one program, stick with it, no matter how exciting a newer one may be. Even if material prepared with the old program can easily be exported into the new program, don't do it. This process can create a variety of minor, often unpredictable, problems later on.

2. Use disks sensibly. Label all disks to show your name and the contents of the disk. Keep your electronic manuscript in order, with only contiguous chapters sharing a disk. In other words, do not put chapters 2, 5, and 8 on one disk, with 1, 3, and 7 on a second, and 4, 6, and notes on a third. Never divide a chapter between disks. Use as few files per chapter as possible; one file per chapter is best if length permits. Keep notes in a separate file (unless you're compiling a multiauthor book, in which case each chapter should have a separate note file). The bibliography, too, should be in a separate file, as should tables, captions, glossary, and any other

[1] Association of American Publishers, *An Author's Primer to Word Processing* (New York, 1983), provided some of the advice offered here.

special elements. Do not overload a disk. What constitutes overloading depends on your software and your disks, but make sure to leave plenty of space to edit what is there. Save your copy frequently and keep *current* back-up copies of all your disks. It does not do much good to have copies of only the unrevised disks if the ones with your revisions and the copy editor's work are lost or destroyed.

3. Type carefully. Do not type zero for the letter oh, one for the letter ell, brackets for parentheses, zeros for bullets, or any other substitutions. If you use any special character (e.g., asterisks before items in a list), use it for one purpose only. Use the word wrap feature, reserving carriage returns for places where lines must also end in the finished book – that is, at the ends of paragraphs, headings, lines of poetry, items in a list, formulas or equations set off on separate lines, chapter titles, epigraphs, and so forth. The publisher will expect all hard copy to be double-spaced, including notes, bibliography, and block quotations; you can accomplish this by double-spacing everything as you type, by reformatting before printing, or by having your printer switch from single-spacing to double-spacing. (The last alternative is best, because the material on the disks to be used for typesetting should be single-spaced.) The publisher will also expect your manuscript to have adequate margins: An inch on the sides and at top and bottom is fine.

4. Avoid your program's bells and whistles. Under no circumstances should you use justification or hyphenation features. Do not break any words at the ends of lines except genuine compounds with permanent hyphens (e.g., English-speaking). Do not put notes at the foot of the page, even though your program can do it magnificently. Type notes in a separate file, paragraph style, with the numbers at line level rather than as superscripts. (You can use superscripts in the text itself, however.) The bibliography, too, can be typed paragraph style, again in a separate file. Because page and line breaks will be different in the final book pages, any extra

formatting commands will simply have to be removed anyway. You will save time and prevent error by not using them in the first place.

5. Type consistently. Use the tab key to generate the same number of spaces for all paragraph indents (or use your program's special paragraph indent command); use two spaces at the ends of sentences. If you put extra spacing above or below headings (which is not necessary), always use the same number of spaces. Never add spacing to avoid an awkward page break.

6. Keep the manuscript simple. Do not put headings in italics, boldface, or all capital letters; capitalize only the initial letters of nouns, pronouns, verbs, adjectives, and adverbs. You can differentiate levels of headings by centering the major ones, placing the next level flush left, and running the third level into the text. Do not use a different font or size for block quotations, notes, or any other special element. For the sake of readability, it is all right (though not necessary) to center headings and to indent block quotations, but do not do anything more elaborate. Use italics or underlining only as necessary, for book titles, special terms, foreign words, and the like. (Remember that underlining will turn into italics when your manuscript becomes a book, because – in the absence of good reasons to do otherwise – the commands for underlining and italics will both be read as italics. To make the hard copy more attractive and consistent, use one or the other.) Do not add elements like running heads that are meant to make the manuscript look more like a book. A manuscript should look like a manuscript.

An editor may return the electronic manuscript to you if your disks have been prepared in a way that makes typesetting difficult. Failure to follow instructions (either the publisher's or those given above) might increase the amount of work for the publisher or typesetter to the point where the savings would evaporate. In such cases, the responsibility for revision is clearly yours, just as it would be if you submitted a single-spaced or messy typescript. You might even be asked to make these changes before editing begins. At whatever stage this occurs, follow directions carefully.

What Software Can and Cannot Do

Although some word-processing features, such as automatic hyphenation at the ends of lines, should be avoided in preparing an electronic manuscript, many of them are helpful. If you can search the manuscript automatically, then you can fix spelling errors, replace one term with a more precise one, check for overuse of a word or expression, and check for consistency. A novelist, for example, can easily make sure that the hero's eyes do not change from steely gray to melting brown between chapters 2 and 5.

Remember, however, that the computer is not as smart as you are. Monitor your use of such functions as search-and-replace very carefully. At first glance, for example, it seems reasonable to tell the computer to replace, say, *man* with *human* – a quick and easy solution to one problem of sexist language. If you do not phrase your search precisely (in this case by searching for *man* surrounded by spaces), you will end up with such linguistic marvels as *comhumand*, *humandatory*, *ehumancipation*, and *rohumance*. Even if you tell the computer to make the change only when *man* stands as an independent word, you are likely to get strange sentences, such as those about the discovery of Peking Human and Shaw's play *Human and Superman*. It is safest to avoid such global commands in favor of searching out each use and making the decision to replace yourself. (One instance in which the global replace command is useful is in coding, as I will explain later.)

Spelling checkers are also a boon to authors and copy editors. If you are not a good speller or a good typist, the spelling checker will find your most embarrassing errors. It will not, however, correct the sort of spelling error most common among even good writers – choosing the wrong homonym.

Even a good spelling checker will let you use *discreet* when you meant *discrete* and allow you to "martial your resources," although the better ones will alert you to the possibility of error. Nor will a spelling checker find typos that happen to be correctly spelled words – though not the ones you intended. For example, if you type *casual* instead of *causal*, the checker will not take notice. Nor will accidental plurals be spotted.

One drawback to spelling checkers is that their vocabularies may be inadequate for specialized writing. Fortunately, most of them allow you to add technical terms, proper nouns, and so forth to their dictionaries. (Be sure to spell them correctly when you add them.) Nevertheless, spelling checkers remain too cumbersome to be of much use in manuscripts that contain material in foreign languages or that quote extensively from documents replete with inconsistencies or misspellings, such as seventeenth-century theological treatises.

Software versions of thesauruses are available, but – like their printed equivalents – they may not be very discriminating. Use them with caution.

The grammar checkers now available vary greatly in usefulness and sophistication. Most were designed for business correspondence and reports and are inadequate for scholarly writing. Before purchasing a grammar checker, read the reviews in computer magazines and test the alternatives carefully. The best test is to subject a brief manuscript on disk to the checker. See how long it takes (some are extraordinarily slow) and how much of what it does is useful. For example, some programs claim to spot "unusual" words or words that are not readily understood by students at, say, the level of college freshmen. Unfortunately, such a program may merely list every proper noun (e.g., Europe) along with everything else that is not in its vocabulary. Test, too, what it does when it finds a problem. Does it highlight it in some way, tell you specifically what is wrong (double negative, passive construction, or whatever), offer suggestions, or provide all of these kinds of assistance? More of these programs are being developed all the time, and they are getting more sophisticated. You may find one that is helpful to you.

Editing

Electronic copy editing is possible but is viewed more cautiously in book publishing than in newspaper or magazine publishing. One problem that you have probably come across in writing and editing your own work is that the screen does not hold enough type for you to visualize problems of organization. Unless you can see a larger context than most computer screens offer, you cannot tell what will happen when you move a paragraph from one page to another. However, the main problem with on-screen editing has been making the editor's changes and queries easily visible to the author, and the author's responses easily visible to the editor. Programs are now available that resolve this difficulty by using "red-lining systems," a split screen, or other devices. If both author and editor are comfortable with these innovations, and equipped for them, on-screen editing works well.

In a red-lining system, the editor will make changes on the disk, which will be typographically highlighted when the manuscript is printed out (details vary from program to program). The author can then approve changes, answer queries, make alterations, and so forth on the hard copy. The editor cleans up the disk for coding and typesetting. Editors do not usually send edited disks to the author, but if you receive edited disks you will need instructions specific to the software in order to review them.

If the editor does not use a system that allows you to see changes, an alternative procedure works as follows. You will have submitted both electronic and hard copy to your publisher. (Mail disks in heavy, rigid cardboard or in plastic cases.) The copy editor will probably edit on paper, sending you a manuscript marked up with changes and queries as though no computer had been involved. Your review will be easier, especially if the editing has been light, if your editor uses colored pencil or ink. You must then check the changes and respond to the queries. At this point, you and your editor have a choice: Either you can enter the changes from paper to disk, or your editor can do so. My own preference is for the editor to create the final copy because that adds another layer of checking for consistency and correctness. (Will you have absorbed the fine points of house style well enough to make sure you have adhered to it in the paragraphs you added?) Alternatively, you can return the hard copy for the editor's review and then get both electronic and hard copy back to enter final changes.

If the editor enters editorial and authorial changes, you have nothing to worry about. If you do it, however, you must be careful to enter all changes fully and accurately. Do not regard this as an opportunity silently to reverse editorial changes that you found objectionable. Nor is it a time to make additional changes that your editor has not approved. At this point, no alteration to the disks should be made that you and your editor have not agreed on. You must also be sure to create safety copies of the revised disks. Again, be sure to mail disks in protective packaging.

Sometimes authors express interest in transmitting their manuscripts electronically over phone lines. Although this may be manageable for short journal articles, the time required to transmit a book manuscript and the risk of introducing error in the transmission are both excessive. It is also very difficult to retain tabular material in a usable format. There is rarely that much of a hurry in any case.

Coding

Once the electronic manuscript is edited, with all the editor's changes and yours entered, it must be "coded" to provide instructions to the typesetting machine or laser printer. The elaborateness of the codes depends in part on the design of the book: The more complicated the design, the more codes are needed. It also depends on the typesetting process chosen: Page-makeup programs use simpler codes than typesetting machines. The procedure that is easiest for the author is for the publisher or typesetter to enter the codes. In some cases, however, authors are asked to do this chore. (Sometimes the task is divided: The author enters simple codes for routine matters like new paragraphs and italics, and the publisher or typesetter codes the more sophisticated elements.)

If you understand a little bit about the design and typesetting processes, the need for coding becomes clearer. Each element of a manuscript needs to be designed. For the text itself, a designer must select the depth and width of the type page, the size of the type, the typeface, and the amount of space (or "leading") between lines. For each level of subheading, the size and face of the type must be chosen. In addition, decisions must be made about whether the heading will be italic, boldface, roman, or small caps; whether it should be centered, flush left, flush right, or in some other position; whether it will be set in initial caps and lowercase (as in book titles) or sentence style; and how much extra space will be inserted above and below it. Similar decisions must be made for running heads, page numbers, block quotations, equations, epigraphs, notes, chapter numbers and titles – for every design element the manuscript contains. The purpose of the initial coding, which has been done for decades, independent of computer technology, is simply to identify each of these elements, regardless of the designer's decisions. That is, a first-level subheading is a first-level subheading, no matter what typeface the designer selects or whether it is to be centered or flush left. This part of the coding is frequently done by an editor before the designer looks at the manuscript, so that the designer can quickly see what elements must be designed. The editor writes simple codes of one to three letters on hard copy that is sent to the designer. Figure 9 is an example of one page of a manuscript coded by an editor for the designer.

The designer's choices are conveyed to the typesetter or the person setting up the page-makeup program in a list of specifications, which spells out the various elements the book includes and describes their design, and in the coding of the manuscript. Obviously, no one would like to have to write out in full the instructions for each element each time. (The description for a subheading, for example, might read: 10 pt. Baskerville, italic, caps and lowercase, centered, 12 points space above, 6 points below.) The codes convey this information in shorthand. Thus, upon reading the code for level 1 heading, the typesetting machine or page-makeup program sets the words that follow in 10-point Baskerville, italic, caps and lowercase, and centers them, leaving 12 points of space above and 6 points below.

In the traditional typesetting process, when the typesetter receives the manuscript and the design specifications, more complex codes are substituted for the simple mnemonic codes and further codes are added for italics, accent marks, and other special characters within the text (see Figure 10).

When the author's disks are used, a similar system can easily be adopted. You have probably already recognized how a search-and-replace command could be used to change short mnemonic codes entered by an author or editor to the more complex typesetting codes. Once you know which elements need to be coded, it is relatively easy to code an electronic manuscript. However, unless you are trained in book design, you will need some help from your publisher. And you will need to be very careful about formulating and entering codes. If you undertake to code your manuscript, you can use three types of code: one you make up yourself, one specified by your publisher (or, if you are self-publishing or preparing camera-ready copy, by your page-makeup program), or the Standard Generalized Markup Language (SGML), an international standard code. Each has its requirements and its advantages, and each must be used exactly.

Do-it-yourself Codes

Making up your own code has the obvious advantage of allowing you to use a code that is easy to remember: If you make it up, you ought to be able to use it. It has the disadvantages of any idiosyncratic system: Perhaps no one else will understand it. Certainly, nonhumans such as page-makeup programs and typesetting machines will not know what you are up to. However, you can use your own comfortable codes and then substitute more universal ones with your software's search-and-replace function.

Your own codes must follow certain rules. First, each must be unique. You cannot use the same code for a paragraph indent and a list indent. Duplication can be avoided by creating a complete list of elements to be coded and following it carefully, as I will explain shortly.

Second, each code must be distinguished from text by symbols called "delimiters." These must be used uniformly and must be characters that are not used in the text itself. The most commonly used delimiters are angle brackets, which are rarely needed in ordinary text and which meet the criterion of providing an opening delimiter that is different from the closing delimiter. For mathematical text, where angle brackets are used to symbolize "less than" and "more than," other delimiters may be chosen.

Finally, you must remember to insert codes everywhere they are needed. If you have ever had the experience of forgetting the command for "end italics" when you typed a bibliography on your computer, you have experienced the havoc that such carelessness can wreak.

To avoid duplication, and to help create a code that has some internal consistency, you should begin by making a list of all elements that must be coded. The considerate and experienced publisher will provide a checklist, but if you do not get one, you can use the following list as a starting point. (Note that it covers only the text, not front matter like the title page and table of contents, which are especially complicated and for which the publisher should provide special instructions.)

(CO)

(CN) 15

(CT) Coding a Manuscript

(TX) When an electronic manuscript is coded for typesetting--whether by the author, the publisher's production staff, or the typesetter--two types of elements must be coded. The first are design elements that designate parts of the text, such as chapter titles, subheadings, and lists. The second are typographical elements that occur within the text, such as italics, boldface, accents, and other special characters.

(A-HD) Design Elements

Every element that is to be designed must be coded. Beginning at the beginning (though after the frontmatter), most books will contain chapter numbers, chapter titles, first paragraphs of chapters, paragraph indents, subheadings at various levels, lists, extracts (sometimes called "block quotes"), tables, figures, figure captions, glossary, notes, bibliography, and index.

(A-HD) Typographical Elements

Some typographical elements that must be coded are special forms of type: italics, boldface, and small caps are the most common. Others are special characters, such as superscripts and accents. Others are characters that do not appear on the computer keyboard but are available in type, for example, dashes (--) and "opening and closing quotation marks." These, too, must be coded.

Some of the coding may take place without intervention. If the page-makeup or typesetting equipment can "read" your word-processing program's commands for italics, for example, then no coding is needed for italics.

(Drop FOL)

1

Figure 9. Manuscript page coded for the designer. Note that only design elements are coded. If the manuscript had included unusual typographic elements, such as a foreign alphabet, that would also have been noted.

15

Coding a Manuscript

When an electronic manuscript is coded for typesetting--whether by the author, the publisher's production staff, or the typesetter--two types of elements must be coded. The first are design elements that designate parts of the text, such as chapter titles, subheadings, and lists. The second are typographical elements that occur within the text, such as italics, boldface, accents, and other special characters. Each code must have forms for entering and exiting.

Design Elements

Every element that is to be designed must be coded. Beginning at the beginning (though after the frontmatter), most books will contain chapter numbers, chapter titles, first paragraphs of chapters, paragraph indents, subheadings at various levels, lists, extracts (sometimes called "block quotes"), tables, figures, figure captions, figure credits, glossary, notes, bibliography, and index.

Typographical Elements

Some typographical elements that must be coded are special forms of type: italics, boldface, and small caps are the most common. Others are special characters, such as superscripts and accents. Others are characters that do not appear on the computer keyboard but are available in type, for example, dashes (--) and "opening and closing quotation marks." These, too, must be coded.

Some of the coding may take place without intervention. If the page-makeup or typesetting equipment can "read" your word-processing program's commands for italics, for example, then no coding is needed for italics.

1

Figure 10. Manuscript page coded by a typesetter. Both design and typographic elements are coded.

1 Chapter number
2 Chapter title
3 Title without number (e.g., "Foreword")
4 Epigraph
5 Source of epigraph
6 First paragraph of chapter
7 Level 1 heading
8 Level 2 heading
9 Level 3 heading
10 Extra space (e.g., to substitute for a heading)
11 Prose block quotation
12 Poetry block quotation
13 Numbered list
14 List with bullets
15 Equations
16 Chemical formulas
17 Table numbers
18 Table titles
19 Table column headings
20 Table stub elements
21 Table text
22 Table notes
23 Figure numbers
24 Figure titles
25 Figure captions
26 Figure credits
27 Notes
28 Subheadings for notes section
29 Block quotations within notes
30 Bibliography
31 Subheadings for bibliography
32 Glossary text
33 Appendix number
34 Appendix title
35 Appendix text

Not all of these will be necessary in every book. For one thing, your book may not contain all of these elements. Equally likely, the book's design will be such that some of these elements will be identical. For example, subheadings may be the same in text, bibliography, and notes, so that a single set of subheading codes will be adequate. If your publisher provides a list of elements that need codes, your job will be made easier.

In addition to the codes for design elements, you will need codes for some characters within the text. The following list includes the most common such elements:

1 Italics
2 Boldface
3 Small capitals
4 Paragraph indent
5 Em dashes (those usually typed as two dashes)
6 En dashes (used for inclusive numbers and for other specific purposes that your copy editor will mark)
7 3-em dashes (used in bibliographies and occasionally in quotations)
8 Opening quotation marks
9 Closing quotation marks
10 Opening single quotation marks
11 Closing single quotation marks
12 Superscripts
13 Monetary symbols (dollars, cents, pounds sterling, etc.)
14 Accent marks (acute, grave, tilde, cedilla, etc.)
15 Greek letters
16 Cyrillic letters
17 Mathematical symbols

Again, not all of these codes will be needed in all books. In all likelihood, you are not using the cyrillic alphabet. More important, by testing a sample disk, your publisher can determine whether their typesetting program can understand your word-processing program's commands for such elements as italics, superscripts, accents, and paragraph indents. If it can, no special coding will be needed for those elements.

Once you have created a list of elements that you will need to code, you can make up opening and closing codes that are easy for you to remember. Enter them wherever needed, being sure to have a closing or exit code to end each coded command. Figure 11 shows a page coded in an author's code. It is an example, not a model: Your memory may work very differently than mine. Print out your manuscript and proofread the coding very carefully. (I would advise using a colored pen or pencil and marking each code with a checkmark as you go.) Correct any mistyped codes, delete any extra ones, and add any that are missing. Then, if it is your job to enter the publisher's or typesetter's codes, you can do so by using the search-and-replace command.

Using the Publisher's Codes

Using the publisher's codes will ensure that your disks can be used easily in whatever typesetting process the publisher has chosen. It may or may not be significantly harder to assimilate than a code that you might invent. The publisher's code may in fact be the code set up for a page-makeup program. In this case, the codes will not be too complex, and you may find it easier simply to use them than to invent your own codes. If they are true typesetting codes, however, they will be more complicated, so that it may be worth the time it will take to make up your own codes and replace them electronically.

Publishers who expect authors to enter their own codes will provide directions. One example of such directions is the *Chicago Guide to Preparing Electronic Manuscripts*, although it is far more elaborate than most such instructions, and it is specifically geared to authors publishing with the University of Chicago Press. Generally, all you need is a list of elements and the corresponding codes. Read through the instructions, make sure you know what each element is, and call your editor with questions before you begin. Make sure there are codes provided for every element in your manuscript. Then study the codes more closely. Even the most complex codes are not arbitrary, and by spending some time with the code and instructions you can learn enough about how the code was designed to make memorizing easier. For example, exit

```
(CN)15

(CT)Coding a Manuscript

(NOP)When an electronic manuscript is coded for
typesetting(DSH)whether by the author, the publisher's production
staff, or the typesetter(DSH)two types of elements must be coded. The
first are design elements that designate parts of the text, such as
chapter titles, subheadings, and lists. The second are typographical
elements that occur within the text, such as italics, boldface,
accents, and other special characters.

(SH1)Design Elements

(NOP)Every element that is to be designed must be coded. Beginning at
the beginning (though after the frontmatter), most books will contain
chapter numbers, chapter titles, first paragraphs of chapters,
paragraph indents, subheadings at various levels, lists, extracts
(sometimes called (OQ)block quotes(CQ)), tables, figures, figure
captions, glossary, notes, bibliography, and index.

(SH1)Typographical Elements

(NOP)Some typographical elements that must be coded are special forms
of type: (OI)italics,(CI) (OB)boldface,(CB) and (OSC)small caps(CSC)
are the most common. Others are special characters, such as
superscripts(OUP)1(CUP) and (AA)accents. Others are characters that do
not appear on the computer keyboard but are available in type, for
example, dashes ((DSH)) and (OQ)opening and closing quotation
marks.(CQ) These, too, must be coded.

(PI)Some of the coding may take place without intervention. If the
page-makeup or typesetting equipment can (OQ)read(CQ) your word-
processing program's commands for italics, for example, then no coding
is needed for italics.

                                  1
```

Figure 11. Manuscript page coded by an author using an idiosyncratic mnemonic code.

codes are often identical to opening codes except for the addition of a single keystroke. Your word-processing program may also allow you to program the function or other keys so that you can use them for the codes that appear most frequently. Your editor can make your job easier by marking various elements to be coded on the hard copy of the manuscript, at least for the first chapter. Some publishers mark all the codes on hard copy for the author to enter. As noted in the instructions for using your own code, enter codes carefully and proofread thoroughly. Figure 12 is a page coded for Ventura, the page-makeup program used to produce the first two editions of this book.

The Standard Generalized Markup Language

By now you are probably thinking that all of this would be much easier if authors, publishers, and typesetters could agree on a single, simple method of coding. Publishers and typesetters have been cooperating in an effort to create such a method, and the result is the Standard Generalized Markup Language, or SGML, whose use is illustrated in Figure 13. It has been accepted as an international standard by the relevant agencies, but it has not yet been universally adopted by publishers and typesetters. (The agencies that create standards do so by convening international teams of experts, publishing their recommendations, and promoting them, but they have no enforcement powers. Their recommendations become truly "standard" only when they are voluntarily adopted by the relevant industries. The ISBN, or International Standard Book Number, which appears on the copyright page and back cover of this and virtually every book, is an example of a fully implemented standard.) SGML is undoubtedly more complex than a mnemonic code that an individual author might create, but it is not difficult to understand. If your publisher wants to use SGML, your editor will send you a list of the relevant codes, along with instructions. (If you are publishing your manuscript yourself and are having it typeset, your typesetter may use the SGML codes and can provide a list.)

If SGML is more widely adopted, it may become possible to eliminate altogether the need for coding manuscripts manually. Software is being developed that automates the insertion of SGML codes, and some major software manufacturers are testing programs that embed the SGML codes in word-processing software, so that the codes are entered automatically or optionally. That is, you can enter the usual command for a paragraph indent or italics, and the program records the SGML command. This renders the task completely painless for authors, and makes the use of author-coded disks much easier for publishers and typesetters.

SGML is commonly used by producers of electronic publications such as CD-ROMs. For such products the codes are used, not for typesetting, but for hypertext and other searching and organizing functions. This kind of SGML mark-up can become extremely complex and is best left to publishers. Again, however, software is being developed to make it easier to code electronic documents using SGML.

Proofreading

Even if proof has been set from your disks, and regardless of who entered the codes, it must be read carefully. Many possibilities for error remain. After all, your manuscript may not have been error-free, even after your careful preparation and your editor's careful reading. When you see the type set in its final form, the errors may be easier to catch. Also, this is the first time that you can actually see the results of coding errors. You must read carefully to see that headings, italics, chapter titles, block quotes, and other elements have been set properly – and that they end where they are supposed to. Your editor will check all of these technical matters carefully, but you should look out for them as well. Remember,

```
@CN = 15
@TITLE = Coding a Manuscript
@FIRST PARA = When an electronic manuscript is coded for typesetting
<196> whether by the author, the publisher's production staff, or the
typesetter <196> two types of elements must be coded. The first are
design elements that designate parts of the text, such as chapter
titles, subheadings, and lists. The second are typographical elements
that occur within the text, such as italics, boldface, accents, and
other special characters.
@HEAD LEVEL 1 =   Design Elements
@FIRST PARA = Every element that is to be designed must be coded.
Beginning at the beginning (though after the frontmatter), most books
will contain chapter numbers, chapter titles, first paragraphs of
chapters, paragraph indents, subheadings at various levels, lists,
extracts (sometimes called <169>block quotes<170>), tables, figures,
figure captions, glossary, notes, bibliography, and index.
@HEAD LEVEL 1 = Typographical Elements
@FIRST PARA = Some typographical elements that must be coded are
special forms of type: <MI>italics,<D> <MB>boldface,<D> and <>small
caps<> are the most common. Others are special characters, such as
superscripts1 and accents. Others are characters that do not appear on
the computer keyboard but are available in type, for example, dashes
(<196>) and <169>opening and closing quotation marks.<170> These, too,
must be coded.
     Some of the coding may take place without intervention. If
the page-makeup or typesetting equipment can <169>read<170> your word-
processing program's commands for italics, for example, then no coding
is needed for italics.
```

                                          1

Figure 12. Manuscript page coded for the Ventura page-makeup
program.

```
<chp><no>15

<ct>Coding a Manuscript

When an electronic manuscript is coded for typesetting&mdash;whether

by the author, the publisher's production staff, or the

typesetter&mdash;two types of elements must be coded. The first are

design elements that designate parts of the text, such as chapter

titles, subheadings, and lists. The second are typographical elements

that occur within the text, such as italics, boldface, accents, and

other special characters.

<h1>Design Elements

Every element that is to be designed must be coded. Beginning at the

beginning (though after the frontmatter), most books will contain

chapter numbers, chapter titles, first paragraphs of chapters,

paragraph indents, subheadings at various levels, lists, extracts

(sometimes called &ldquo;block quotes&rdquo;), tables, figures,

figure captions, glossary, notes, bibliography, and index.

<h1>Typographical Elements

Some typographical elements that must be coded are special forms of

type: <it>italics,</> <b>boldface,</> and <scp>small caps</> are

the most common. Others are special characters, such as

superscripts<fnr>1</> and &aacute;ccents. Others are characters that

do not appear on the computer keyboard but are available in type, for

example, dashes (&mdash;) and &ldquo;opening and closing quotation

marks.&rdquo; These, too, must be coded.

<p>Some of the coding may take place without intervention. If

the page-makeup or typesetting equipment can &ldquo;read&rdquo;

your word-processing program's commands for italics, for example,

then no coding is needed for italics.
```

1

Figure 13. Manuscript page coded in SGML, the Standard Generalized Markup Language.

too, that electronic typesetting is prone to nonhuman errors, resulting from static electricity, faulty disks, gremlins, and other mysterious causes. Proofreading remains important. Usually, when an author's disks are used, the publisher does not bother with galley proofs and goes straight to page proof. Follow the advice in Chapter 10 about reading proof; it works equally well for electronic manuscripts. Always proofread hard copy. Proofreading on a screen does not work.

Revised Editions

As noted in Chapter 10, an electronic manuscript is extremely easy to revise. The publisher can send the author a disk of the manuscript as it was typeset, in whatever word-processing program the author originally used. The manuscript will contain all the codes, as well as the text. Revisions will be just as easy to make as they were before it was typeset. The author and publisher can agree on who will insert the codes, just as was done the first time around. The only problem is the one that makes on-screen editing difficult: to make sure that the editor can see the author's revisions, and the author can see the editor's subsequent editing. This is easily solved by using a typographic symbol to note the beginning and end of changes (something like the delimiter used in coding, though obviously you cannot use the same one), and by sending hard copy back and forth, with authorial revisions and editorial changes marked with colored ink or pencil.

The revised edition will have to be proofread carefully, just as the original edition was. And both author and editor will have to be careful about adapting the table of contents; re-numbering tables, notes, and figures; and altering cross-references (this is facilitated by the search-and-replace function). Re-indexing will also be easier: Unless the text has been changed radically the same entries can be used, and the author need merely redo the page numbers. The new entries that are needed can be added to the existing index without difficulty.

Camera-ready Copy

When sales of a book are expected to be small, it is not uncommon for publishers (especially university centers, professional societies, and specialized technical publishers) to request that the author submit camera-ready copy, which is simply a typescript that can be photographed for printing as is. Sometimes this is a condition for publication. Books that would be expensive to typeset because of technical material or foreign alphabets may also have to be provided camera-ready. Teachers' manuals and other materials supplementary to textbooks are sometimes required in this form as well. Sometimes an author prefers to provide camera-ready copy to keep control over the material; this is particularly true for critical and documentary editions. And if you have decided to be your own publisher, creating camera-ready copy is usually the most economical alternative.

Preparing Copy for a Publisher

Before personal computers became common, publishers requested that camera-ready copy be typed with a carbon ribbon on special clay-coated paper. Some publishers still are willing to use material prepared this way. With the advent of computers and high-quality printers, however, it has become possible for authors to prepare camera-ready copy that is barely distinguishable from a typeset book. Compare camera-ready copy prepared using a typewriter (Figure 14) with copy prepared using a computer and laser printer (Figure 15).

The well-equipped, computer-literate author can prepare camera-ready copy that is nearly as attractive as that prepared by a publisher. In fact, once a manuscript has been prepared electronically and properly coded, it does not make much difference whether the laser printer used belongs to the publisher or the author. Most of the work has already been done. One possible difference in quality arises from the equipment you have available. Most inexpensive

13

status and various roles. Again, it was not that the state is simply the family writ large. The rulers were quite well aware that many of those on whom they relied were not lineage members and that they must rely on non-kin allies as well. The state must rely on the loyalty of unrelated allies. It is significant that often one tried to give titles to allied rulers that had a kind of familial flavor, so that the kind of effective bond that should unite lineages should also unite the king to his officers and ministers who were not of his family.

From this familial model of the Chinese socio-political order there emerged a highly significant orientation embodied in the Chinese motto "cheng-chiao ho-i," (the unity of ruling and teaching). The universal king ideally was born supreme ruler and supreme teacher. He was the source of political power and true doctrine. The political order and the order of true doctrine stemmed from the same source. The king should, both by his behavior and by his teachings, maintain the moral order of human society and be in direct communication with heaven. In fact, this notion of a monopoly of access to heaven by the king (which was not necessarily universally recognized) established the king as a kind of exclusive vice-regent of heaven in the human order. Just as heaven maintains the order of nature (and I think some notion of an abstract order of nature emerged very early in China), the king should maintain that order within the human sphere and he should even see to it, for instance, not only that the people in his realm are taken care of, but even that all the subordinate natural spirits are cared for and fed. One thus finds certain phenomena in the relationship of the political order to religion that seem very particularly Chinese when compared to other civilizations. The Chinese government had the power to sanction or reject deities and the power

Figure 14. Typed camera-ready copy.

30   MURDER IN A PEKING STUDIO

"You'll make a hundred dollars."

"Oh, no. This is an old customer. Our store shouldn't make any money off him. This is a service because he's such a good customer. Even if the head of the shop back in Tokyo loses a little on it, that will present no problem. In short, I can't make any money on this."

"Isn't that a little strange? What you're saying is that a businessman shouldn't make money."

"Perhaps, but there are all sorts of circumstances at work here. So if you would do this for us, we'd like to give you the full five hundred dollars."

"A very curious situation indeed."

"Yes, but since the arrangement with our customer has already been made . . ." Doi wiped the sweat from his brow with the tip of his index finger.

"All right, I'll do it for five hundred dollars."

"Thank you very much."

Doi was uneasy again. His intent was to engage in a little dignified bribery, but if Wen did not know that, nothing would be gained. If Wen used the most expensive materials so that his costs came just to five hundred dollars, he would not be making any money, and the aim of bribery would not be achieved.

"And," Doi added, "our customer wished that three hundred dollars or more be applied to the rubbing fee and the rest go for mounting."

Even if Wen used Chinese fan paper or antique paper, and high-grade ink such as Ch'ien-lung imperial ink, the cost of the materials surely wouldn't exceed fifty dollars. In any case, if Wen Pao-t'ai did not make money on the deal, then Doi's transaction would fail its purpose.

"Okay, I understand," Wen said. "Bring me the image any time." Wen adjusted his position in the red sandalwood chair as if to say, Let's drop any further talk about money.

"Well, Doi, today what do you say I discuss the process of tapping the rubbing paper with the *tampo?* In fact, an interesting story about the process just came to mind."

Figure 15. Camera-ready copy from a laser printer.

laser printers create output printed at 300 dots per inch (dpi). Publishers may have invested in 600 dpi printers, and typesetters use machines that print 1,200 or more dpi. The differences in resolution are noticeable: The more dots per inch, the clearer the image. But for most scholarly books, the difference in cost outweighs the difference in clarity.

Most authors who prepare camera-ready copy use page-layout or page-makeup software. These programs have three major advantages over word-processing programs. First, most of them allow you to see a complete page on the screen in what is known as WYSIWYG form: What You See Is What You Get. Especially for people with little design experience, it is helpful to see how your design decisions are going to turn out before printing. Second, once you make your design decisions (or enter those provided by your publisher), most programs follow the instructions file after file, chapter after chapter, without your having to reinstruct them. Finally, page-makeup programs allow you to incorporate graphics directly into the text. Alternatively, they permit you a variety of choices for placement of figures by allowing you to create "windows" of different sizes. It is worth noting, however, that expensive page-makeup programs are not vital to preparing camera-ready copy, or to any other variant of desktop typesetting. The book illustrated in Figure 15, for example, was prepared with one of the less sophisticated word-processing programs. Especially if the book is of simple design, a good word-processing program may be adequate – and you get to use some of the bells and whistles that are so dangerous when the book is to be printed from different software.

If you agree to prepare camera-ready copy electronically, using a laser printer, you should get very specific instructions from your publisher. These instructions may be electronic: Your publisher can select the desired options from those offered by your page-makeup or word-processing program, providing a sort of electronic style sheet. The same instructions can be provided in writing. For example, your program will ask you how many spaces to use for a paragraph indent; your publisher should tell you what to answer. If your manuscript is complex, these instructions will be complex, too, but it will be much easier to impart the publisher's decisions to your software and printer than it would be to make the design decisions yourself. The end result will be more attractive, too, if a professional designer has contributed expertise.

Also discuss with your publisher how graphics are to be handled. If you have created simple charts or maps on a computer, these can easily be incorporated into the text. Photographs or halftones can also be incorporated by using a scanner, but the quality may be poor. In most cases, you will be asked to leave a specified amount of space in the manuscript (in the form of a "window," if you are using a page-makeup program) and to provide glossy black-and-white photos. The publisher will take care of incorporating the photographs into the text.

Allow yourself enough time to experiment with your software and printer. Read the manuals for both carefully, and work through the tutorials. If you find the manual difficult to use, select one of the published guides to the program available in your bookstore. They can walk you through the process one more time, to give you some practice and confidence. It is a good idea to work through a shorter project before undertaking a book. Also, get to know what resources are available on your campus to provide assistance on your project. Some universities have desktop publishing experts on staff to provide consultation. Even if yours does not, you can probably find someone in a user's group who has been using the same program you have chosen for some time and who is willing to share the lessons learned.

There are many cheerful books about the joys of desktop publishing on the market, but I have included none of them in the bibliography. All of them make it sound as though you simply acquire the software and a printer, write the text at your keyboard (they usually allow three months for research and writing), create dramatic graphics, and produce a beautiful, highly illustrated book with no difficulty in a matter of days. It is foolish to assume that you can sit down with a new program and a book-length manuscript and work miracles.

Plan to spend a significant amount of time learning to use your page-makeup program, and assume that you will run into problems as you go along.

Alternatively, you can hire someone to turn your edited disks (with or without coding) into camera-ready copy. Someone experienced in desktop typesetting will produce pages ready for printing either according to your publisher's instructions or independently. Because they must invest in expensive software and hardware, and because their skills are much in demand, they will charge what may seem like a high hourly rate. However, they generally work quickly and efficiently and can save you both time and frustration.

If you do not have computer equipment, you can prepare acceptable camera-ready copy using nothing more elaborate than a carbon ribbon on a good office typewriter, preferably one with a ball or daisywheel to allow the use of various typefaces. The publisher either will specify the sort of paper to be used and the size of the text page (along with details about where to put page numbers, running heads, and other elements) or will supply paper with margins and positions marked in a light blue that will not be reproduced photographically. The author then types the copy carefully, and neatly corrects it, according to the guidelines. Display type, such as chapter numbers and headings, may be typeset by the publisher or be supplied by the author in the form of press-on type or simply typed copy.

Publishers must provide detailed instructions for preparing typewritten camera-ready copy, and authors must understand them and follow them. Usually, such manuscripts are typed single-spaced with an unjustified right margin. They are typed in an area larger than the anticipated book page and reduced photographically.

Books produced camera-ready on a typewriter are often not very attractive, and they may be difficult to read. However, some books cannot be published economically unless authors provide camera-ready copy, and if these authors do not have access to computers and laser printers, or do not know how to use them, there is little choice.

Self-publishing

If you are preparing camera-ready copy to produce a book without the assistance of a publisher, you will have to do everything already discussed, but without expert help. In that case, you should consult one or two authorities on book design (see the bibliography) and, especially if you are not graphically talented or experienced, select a book that you find attractive to use as a model.

The basic design principles for a beginner to keep in mind are simplicity and symmetry. Keep the book simple by using only one typeface for everything except, perhaps, the title page and chapter numbers and titles. Distinguish levels of headings by using italics and by varying placement and spacing (locating one level flush left with extra space above and below, and the second flush left with extra space only above, for example), rather than by introducing new typefaces. Set off block quotations with extra space above and below, either in a smaller size of the same typeface or indented. Keep the notes at the back.

It is also a good idea for a beginner to select a symmetrical design. For example, you may decide that your design will focus on centered elements. In that case, the title and author on the title page will be centered, as will chapter titles and major subheadings. Or you may decide to base the design on placement of such elements flush left or, less conventionally, flush right.

If you are using a program that does a good job of right-hand justification, you will probably want to justify the text; we are used to seeing books with justified right margins. But if you are using a word-processing program that requires you to make hyphenation decisions by hand and does not have fairly sophisticated interword spacing, your book will be far easier to produce, and more attractive, if you use a ragged right margin.

Once you have chosen a design that you think looks good on the screen, print out some sample pages so that you can see the results in black-and-white, with the actual type fonts that will print out. (This is especially important if you are not using a WYSIWYG program, or if you are using one that does not place an entire page on the screen.) Try the first page of a chapter, a page of text with headings, and a page with a table or other special element. You can experiment with various changes easily until you are satisfied with the appearance of the sample pages. Record your decisions in writing for future revisions.

You should decide how elaborately you wish to produce your book according to its purpose. For example, if it is just for use in your own classroom, there is little reason to spend months designing and producing a professional-looking book. If you hope for a wider market, you may wish to spend more time at it.

Camera-ready Cautions

There is no reason why a book published from an author's camera-ready copy cannot be as good a book as one published by more traditional methods. The author's research and writing are no different, and the refereeing process is the same. A manuscript editor can work equally carefully, and a designer can work within the limitations of the technology to help create an attractive, readable book. However, desktop publishing technology creates a temptation to take shortcuts that should be resisted.

If you can easily tell that a book has been prepared from the author's camera-ready copy, then the effort was not entirely successful. In some volumes of conference proceedings, for example, the papers have been produced individually by the participants, so that each article has its own typeface and layout. These books contain irregularities that publishers normally do not tolerate, such as facing pages of different lengths, or irregular spacing between text elements. All of these problems can be avoided, however, if the preparer of the copy knows the conventions of page layout and is willing to spend the time to prepare the volume carefully.

More disturbing is the quality of the editing in some camera-ready books. In some volumes, errors in grammar and spelling are frequent. (One seven-line paragraph about the virtues of spelling and grammar checkers included two grammatical errors, one spelling error, and one stylistic error.) These problems are not inherent in the technology of preparing camera-ready copy. Rather, they are indicative of procedural problems. When an author submits laser-printed copy using page-makeup software, rather than an ordinary-looking double-spaced manuscript for the publisher to edit, the editing may be cursory. In the case of conference proceedings or other books that are difficult to bring together, require reasonably rapid publication, and attract only a small audience, the temptation to cut editorial corners is apparently strong.

If you are preparing camera-ready copy and wish to keep the editorial quality of your book high, make sure to submit an ordinary double-spaced manuscript to your publisher first, and make sure that the publisher is going to edit it. If you are working without a publisher, hire an editor to do the work. Once the manuscript has been edited and revised, you can proceed with the preparation of camera-ready copy. This need not slow down the schedule very much, because you can design the layout and learn to use the program during the editing.

The use of camera-ready copy prepared by authors makes practical the publication of much good work that might otherwise not be available to scholars. With a few precautions and no illusions about the speed or ease of the task, editorial and production standards can be maintained along with economy.

Publishing without Paper

Computers are changing publishing in more dramatic ways than are evident from the use of electronic manuscripts, which after all simply save some time and money within a very traditional process of creation, manufacturing, and distribution. Computers make it possible for author and audience to communicate directly, without the intervention of publishers. They also make it possible to revise and update material instantaneously, when this is desirable. Finally, by providing sophisticated indexing and searching procedures, they make it possible to use research and teaching materials in new and exciting ways. Although all of these possibilities are in their infancy, and all have their limitations, it is worth learning how they work so that you can take advantage of them as either a user or a creator.[2] Electronic journals were discussed in Chapter 2. They are the medium most familiar and accessible to authors. Two other media – database publications and CD-ROMs – are also developing rapidly. You have probably used one or both of these media, even if you have not considered creating a publication in these forms.

Database Publishing

Electronic databases are collections of statistics, abstracts, bibliographical listings, addresses, or other data stored in a computer, along with indexing and searching programs. Users gain access to them via a computer terminal and, unless they are local databases to which terminals are connected, a modem and telephone line or the ethernet. Most databases require users to pay a fixed subscription fee plus additional charges that depend on the amount of use. Individuals subscribe to some services – for example, those that provide current information on financial markets. Others, primarily those that provide bibliographical information and abstracts, find that most of their subscribers are libraries.

When the material to be published is voluminous and rapidly changing, an electronic database is an appropriate medium. Examples of popular databases are *Chemical Abstracts* and *Lexis*. These databases give subscribers instant

---

[2] I am indebted to numerous speakers and participants at meetings of the Society for Scholarly Publishing for their insights into the possibilities and problems of electronic publishing.

access to up-to-date information. They eliminate the need for frequent publication or for replacing sheets in looseleaf binders. Many databases are bibliographic tools that provide citations and sometimes abstracts, but some full-text databases are available.

Publications that are candidates for database publication include directories, bibliographies, and reference materials (for example, *Books in Print*). Other possibilities include abstracts and, perhaps, book reviews – material composed of units that are not too long and that should be available promptly. On a less grand scale, a database can be useful for a limited audience: For example, the membership list for a professional organization can be kept current and instantly available in a database file.

Databases are most useful in fields where currency is important, and where older material is not frequently consulted. The reason for this is simple: The material to be included in a database must be entered via a computer keyboard or, less accurately, a scanner. Material currently being generated in an electronic format is easily incorporated, and it is practical to go back a few years to include, say, scientific abstracts. But it is still impractical to go back a century to add lengthy historical documents or essays in literary criticism. The scientist is generally content with recent material, but the historian or literary critic often considers material that antedates the computer age far more important than the writings of the past decade. Thus, databases have made most headway in the hard sciences, in law, and in business. In the humanities and social sciences, however, bibliographical databases are progressing.

One other bar to the development of commercial electronic databases is the cost of developing them and protecting that investment. Once material is on a national network, it is almost impossible to control its distribution. This gives publishers little incentive to invest. With subscription services, cost may also be an issue for users. On-line searching is generally charged by the amount of time that the user spends in the search. Unless users have a large budget for such searches, this prevents the kind of browsing and exploring that many researchers like to do. Only those who are comfortable with computer searches, and familiar with the relevant databases, are likely to consult them regularly. These considerations give some advantages to CD-ROM technology, which among other things is an alternative to on-line databases.

CD-ROM

CD-ROM stands for "compact disc – read only memory." (Compact disc is conventionally spelled with a *c* to distinguish it from the computer disk or diskette.) The product is a 4.72-inch disc similar in appearance to the ones you play music from. The material on the disc cannot be altered by the user ("read only"). It is used on a special reader, in conjunction with a computer. It can be used for any purpose that an on-line database can be used for, although instantaneous updates are not possible without including an on-line attachment of some kind. But CD-ROM can also be used in ways that on-line databases cannot.

CD-ROM discs have enormous capacity. One disc can hold 275,000 typed pages of text (roughly 45 shelf feet of books) or the equivalent of 1,500 magnetic diskettes. In addition to text and data, it can carry graphics, sound, and video images (although these take up more room than text or data). Because of their enormous capacity, CD-ROM discs can be equipped with highly sophisticated searching and indexing programs (sometimes called "hypertext") that make all sorts of creative applications possible and make the discs flexible and responsive to use, even though users cannot "write" on them. Because a library or individual user buys or rents the disc, there is no cost for browsing and exploring time, which makes them less intimidating to infrequent or first-time users. And because they are more difficult to copy, publishers feel safer investing in them.

CD-ROM suffers from many of the ills of a new technology – most of all, a lack of accepted technical standards – so that some publishers are fearful of investing in products that may be limited in usefulness (this is like the BETAMAX/VHS problem). Nevertheless, a number of CD-ROM publications are available or being developed that give a sense of the technology's possibilities. Several encyclopedias are available on CD-ROM, and as players become common household equipment, certainly other encyclopedias will be published in this form. In England, the Domesday Project – a multimedia, interdisciplinary study of contemporary life in the United Kingdom – was published in this format. Yale University Press has published *Perseus*, which provides on a single disc all the classical Greek texts in Greek and in English, with variants; dictionaries, grammars, and glosses; bibliographies; maps that can be overlaid on the screen; illustrations; other material for research and teaching; and sophisticated hypertext. You can view the art collection of the British National Gallery on a CD-ROM published by Microsoft. CD-ROM is also being used for training programs and has many other potential educational applications.

CD-ROM technology has become sufficiently established that technologically sophisticated scholars are beginning to develop discs for their own use. For example, a slide collection on CD-ROM can be used easily and flexibly in the classroom and can be annotated as well. Some of these creations may prove to be publishable more generally. If you are interested in developing a CD-ROM, *Literary Market Place* contains a list of electronic publishers. A more thorough and specific guide is *CD-ROM Market Place: An International Guide to the CD-ROM, CD-I, CDTV and Electronic Book Industry*, published annually.

The Book of the Future

I am not brave enough, or foolish enough, to try to forecast what publishing will be like in ten years. It is reasonable to suppose that books and journals as we know them will still be around, but it is also reasonable to suppose that many alternative forms of scholarly communication will be flourishing. Certainly the new technological sirens are very appealing, and there is every reason to hope that they will contribute to the advancement and dissemination of knowledge. Despite their newness and the uncertainty of their economic future, they can already offer far more speed and flexibility than traditional publication, and they require less space and destroy fewer forests. And regardless of the physical form in which knowledge is distributed, the crucial elements will continue to be the thoughtful scholar and a publishing process with editorial integrity.

Chapter 12

Costs and Prices

I always used to think that publishers had to be devilish intelligent fellows, loaded down with the grey matter; but I've got their number now. All a publisher has to do is to write cheques at intervals, while a lot of deserving and industrious chappies rally round and do the real work.

Bertie Wooster, in P. G. Wodehouse, *Carry On, Jeeves*

One of the questions publishers are asked most often is "Why are books so expensive?" The answer is not simple: It involves the interacting elements of production costs and overhead, pricing and discount policies, and markets. This chapter presents a simplified explanation of these topics that should console authors and book buyers – or at least quell their suspicions.[1]

Costs

In publishing a book, a publisher incurs *direct costs* and *indirect costs*. Direct costs are those clearly attributable to publication of a specific title, such as the cost of having the book

[1] For an extensive, detailed discussion of the economics of scholarly publishing, see Herbert S. Bailey, Jr., *The Art and Science of Book Publishing* (Austin: University of Texas Press, 1970). The costs in this chapter are estimates based on figures provided by university press directors and production managers, book manufacturers, chambers of commerce, commercial-space realtors, and utility companies.

typeset. Indirect costs are overhead items, including rent, utilities, salaries, and supplies. They are the publisher's general operating costs: costs that must be incurred to publish any books at all but that cannot readily be assigned to a particular title in a way that is not arbitrary. For example, how much office space and air conditioning are needed to publish a particular book? Or consider the time of an acquiring editor, who may review several hundred proposals and dozens of manuscripts in a year, in addition to traveling to conventions, calling prospective authors, attending meetings, reviewing budgets, and attending to administrative duties such as hiring and planning. Very little of this time can be shown to contribute to the publication of a given book, yet all of it is in some sense necessary to producing all of the titles in the fields for which the editor is responsible.

Some costs may be either direct or indirect, depending on the circumstances. For example, if a publisher has a book copyedited and designed by freelancers (professionals who are not employees and are paid an hourly or per job rate), the freelance fees can easily be assigned to the book and are thus direct costs. However, if this work is done in-house, the costs can be assigned accurately only if the editor and designer keep track of the time they spend on the book, something they rarely do. Copy editors may be doing a preliminary reading of one manuscript, copyediting a second, dealing with author's revisions on a third, checking proof of a fourth, writing summaries of books for the marketing department, helping an author with permissions problems, and attending to general administrative details – all in one week. It would be possible to record all this activity and assign most of the time to the relevant titles, but little useful information would be derived from the exercise. Keeping track of time in this way does not get books published faster, better, or cheaper, so no one bothers. Therefore, in-house copy editing and design are normally included in the publisher's indirect costs.

It is sometimes useful to *allocate* indirect costs to specific titles. To do this, a publisher takes the total of such items for some period, usually a year, and then, according to some formula, assigns a portion of the total to each book published during that period. The result is a somewhat artificial, but nevertheless illuminating, attribution of general operating costs to specific titles. For our purposes, this exercise helps to show what it *really* costs, taking everything into account, to publish a book. Accountants generally allocate overhead costs in proportion to revenue. In our example, however, I will simplify the technique and divide annual overhead costs by the number of books published in a year.[2]

Direct Costs

The most significant direct costs are *production costs*. They are also the easiest to estimate. Production costs divide into two types: plant costs and manufacturing costs. Plant costs include typesetting, the preparation of artwork for printing, and the preparation of printing plates; manufacturing costs (or "running" costs) include paper, printing, and binding. They differ in that plant costs remain constant no matter how many copies of a book you print, while manufacturing costs do not.

You might compare plant and manufacturing costs to the costs of typing a paper and having it photocopied. You will pay a typist perhaps $1.00 per page, no matter how many copies of a paper you eventually make; but you will have to multiply the photocopying charge, say 5 cents per page, by the number of pages *and* the number of copies. For a thirty-page paper, thus, the typing will cost $30.00, whether you eventually make one photocopy or one hundred. The photo-

[2] Harald Bohne and Harry van Ierssel provide accounting guidelines and sample balance sheets, profit-and-loss statements, and the like in *Publishing: The Creative Business* (Toronto: University of Toronto Press, 1973). *One Book/Five Ways: The Publishing Procedures of Five University Presses* (Los Altos, Calif.: Kaufmann, 1978; rept. ed, Chicago: University of Chicago Press, 1994) illustrates a variety of cost-estimating procedures and other worksheets that university presses employ. Chapter 7 in John Dessauer's *Book Publishing: A Basic Introduction* (New York: Continuum, 1989) also details accounting practices.

copying cost, by contrast, will be $1.50 for one copy but $150 for one hundred. To carry this analysis a few steps further, as we will do shortly for publishing costs, the *total production cost* for the original plus one copy will be $31.50; if you make one hundred copies it will be $180. Now, suppose that you keep the original in a drawer and distribute the photocopies to your colleagues. Your total production cost per distributed copy, or *unit production cost,* is then $31.50 in the former case ($31.50 divided by 1) and $1.80 in the latter ($180 divided by 100). Clearly, the more copies you print, the lower the unit cost.

Let's return now to book publishing and consider an imaginary scholarly monograph of 300 finished book pages with no tables, illustrations, or other complications. The plant costs will be typesetting and plate preparation. A reasonable estimate for typesetting is $12.00 per page, for a total of $3,600. Plate making, changes in proof, and other one-time costs might total $1,500. Thus, total plant costs will be $5,100.

These costs can vary, of course, and we will later examine the effects of production costs on prices and profits. Suppose, for example, that the publisher decides to use a less expensive typesetter (perhaps an on-campus computer system) who charges $10.00 per page, with correspondingly lower charges for author's alterations and page makeup. That might reduce typesetting to $3,000 and other costs to $1,000, for a total of $4,000. An even larger reduction might be achieved by setting the book from the author's computer disks. If the author supplies camera-ready copy, typesetting costs are eliminated altogether, although plates must still be made. (In the cases where the author supplies either disks or camera-ready copy, however, costs are really being transferred from the publisher to the author, not necessarily reduced.) At the other extreme, the publisher might decide to use a more expensive typesetter (e.g., for reasons of quality or speed), raising typesetting costs to $15.00 or more per page, with higher prices for other services as well. This could take the total plant cost up to $7,500 or more. A book that has a lot of tables, mathematical copy, or material in foreign languages would of course cost significantly more to set. For our purposes, we will use a middle estimate, $5,100.

To estimate manufacturing cost (paper, printing, and binding), we have to know how many copies of the book will be printed. Let's assume a print run of 1,000, which is probably typical for the average monograph. Paper would cost about $1,000 (obviously the quality and price of paper vary enormously) and printing about $1,000. For simplicity, suppose that we are publishing a clothbound book with a jacket and no paperback edition. On that assumption, binding would cost about $1.00 per copy, for a total in this case of $1,000, and jackets (depending on how elaborate they are) about 35 cents apiece, for a total of $350. Our total cost for paper, printing, and binding, then, is $3,350. To this we must add the cost of shipping finished books to the warehouse, say $500. (Freight costs, too, vary enormously. Sometimes printed pages must be shipped to a bindery, as well as the bound books to the warehouse. Distances also vary. If the printing and binding are done locally, there may be no shipping cost.) This brings our total manufacturing cost to $3,850 and our total production cost – plant cost plus manufacturing cost – to $8,950 ($5,100 plus $3,850). To simplify the calculations to follow, we'll call it $9,000.

We can now determine the unit, or per copy, production cost of each book sold. Of the 1,000 copies printed, 100 will be given away – to the author, potential reviewers, and the Register of Copyrights. We will therefore divide the total production cost ($9,000) by the number of copies available for sale (900), yielding a unit production cost of $10.00. This is an important figure, because many publishers take the unit cost, multiply it by some fixed number – anywhere from 4 to 8 – and use the product as a rough guide to determine how much to charge for the book. This calculation is supposed to allow, in an approximate way, for overhead and marketing costs, bookseller discounts, royalties, and profits – or, in other words, for all the factors that might bear numerically on the pricing decision.

Having determined the total and unit production costs of

our imaginary monograph, we may now consider *nonproduction direct costs* – those costs for activities other than production that are easily assigned to a single title. Returning
to that typed and photocopied paper, let us assume that
you are selling the copies rather than giving them away. As
you will recall, if you made one photocopy, the unit production cost was $31.50. This means that, if you wanted to
break even on production costs, you would have to sell the
copy for $31.50. If you made 100 copies to sell to your stu-
dents and wanted only to break even on your $180 produc-
tion cost, you would price them at $1.80. But suppose that
you also wanted to cover your nonproduction direct costs:
the costs of researching and writing that particular paper. If
you are a philosopher or a theoretical physicist, you may
have incurred no travel or equipment expenses (your time
and office space we will consider as overhead or indirect
costs). If you are a historian, your research for this paper
may have included a trip to China that was devoted to
nothing else. If you are a nuclear physicist or a radiologist,
you may have to charge for, say, a week's use of a cyclotron
or a CAT scanner. In other words, the nonproduction direct
costs may be very small – or astronomical.

The range of nonproduction direct costs in scholarly publishing is not nearly so great, but the costs exist and must be
calculated. We must include the costs of acquiring, editing,
designing, and marketing a particular book. Suppose that
the press paid two specialist readers $100 each to read the
manuscript and that, after a careful consideration of editing
requirements, it gave this work to a freelance copy editor. If
our 300-page monograph (about 450 manuscript pages) requires an average amount of editing, this might cost about
$800, or $15.00 per hour for about 55 hours of the freelancer's
time. (The freelancer's work will have to be reviewed, of
course, and the manuscript finally readied for production,
but we will treat in-house editorial time as part of overhead.)
An equally common use of freelancers is for book design,
that is, for the design of the text itself (what the pages look

like), the binding, and the dust jacket. If the book is not unusually difficult to design, a freelance designer will probably charge about $400. (In-house design and production time are considered part of overhead.)

Marketing costs are another category of nonproduction costs. Under this heading, the costs of particular actions like running an ad in a journal are direct; the time of the marketing staff that designs and places the ad is part of overhead. Direct marketing costs can range from next to nothing to sky-high. We will assume that our imaginary book is displayed at conventions (sharing the cost of the booth with the other titles being shown), included in the publisher's catalogue (bearing a small portion of the cost of its production and distribution), advertised in two or three inexpensive journal ads, and sold through direct mail. The marketing budget for this book will then be about $3,000. (As a point of reference, note that a full-page ad in the *New York Times Book Review* costs about $15,000.) Our nonproduction direct costs thus total $4,400.

Indirect Costs

We must now estimate the indirect costs of publishing our imaginary monograph. Let's return again to your typed and photocopied paper. Suppose that you want to cover not only your direct costs (production and nonproduction) but also your indirect costs: the relevant portions of rent and utilities for your office, of your research assistant's salary and tuition waiver, of your salary and fringe benefits, and so forth. It is clear that these costs would vary from author to author (compare the salary of a full professor of law to that of an assistant professor of philosophy) and paper to paper (depending, for example, on how much of your time was devoted to it). It is also clear that you would have a hard time coming up with an accurate figure (how much office space was used to write the paper, as opposed to teaching your courses?). Similarly, indirect costs in scholarly publishing vary from book to book and publisher to publisher, and they are difficult to compute accurately.

The simplest way to calculate indirect costs is to estimate the total cost of operating the publishing house and allocate an appropriate portion of it to this book. The simplest way to allocate is to take the total operating cost for the year of publication and divide it by the number of titles published that year. This method is adequate for our purposes, but it is obviously oversimplified. Some manuscripts need more work than others, and both acquisition and copy editors distribute their time accordingly. Similarly, publishers may spend more time marketing one book than another. An elaborately designed book with many illustrations will take more time in the design and production departments than a simple monograph. Also, if the press uses freelancers for some books and not others, this will further skew the distribution of in-house efforts. To cope with these factors, accountants employ a formula that allocates indirect costs in proportion to actual or projected revenues from book sales. We may evade these complications by supposing that our imaginary monograph is a representative product of the press, so that a crude per book averaging of indirect costs will do.

Let us assume that our book is being published by a medium-sized press located in a middle-sized city in the center of the United States. It has 16 employees and publishes 40 titles a year. The salaries for the 16 employees, ranging from the director's $45,000 to the secretary's $12,000, total $350,000 per year. Fringe benefits amount to 25 percent of salaries, or $87,500. The press's total annual personnel cost is thus $437,500. Because of size, the press does not employ its own sales force or have many administrators (such as a personnel director, lawyer, or treasurer) that a larger house would need.

The press has adequate but not spacious quarters: It has office space of 3,000 square feet and warehouse space of 10,000. Office space in the city rents for $15.00 per square foot on average, with warehouse space going for $3.00. Using these figures, we can estimate that the press will pay $45,000 per year for office space and $30,000 for warehouse space, for a total of $75,000. Annual telephone expenses are $8,000, we shall assume, and other utilities total $12,000. Supplies and equipment cost $6,000. Postage and shipping (excluding shipping of books to customers, which customers traditionally pay, and mailing of advertising material, which is covered in our marketing estimate) run $4,000. The travel budget is $8,000. Association memberships, subscriptions, and book purchases add up to $4,000. (This includes membership in the Association of American University Presses.) If we add $5,000 for miscellaneous expenses (such as readers' fees for books not eventually published) and the inevitable unexpected expenses, the press's nonsalary overhead comes to $122,000.

We can now total these figures and allocate them to the 40 titles published annually:

Salaries and benefits	$437,500
Rent	75,000
Utilities	20,000
Supplies	6,000
Postage	4,000
Travel	8,000
Subscriptions, etc.	4,000
Miscellaneous	5,000
Total	$559,500

Dividing by 40 yields $13,987.50, which we may then allocate to each title. The indirect cost of publishing our imaginary monograph can be rounded to $14,000.

How much, then, will it cost to publish 1,000 copies of our 300-page monograph? A total of $27,400, summarized as follows:

Production costs	$9,000
Nonproduction direct costs	4,400
Allocated indirect costs	14,000
Total	$27,400

Dividing by 900 copies, this comes to $30.44 per copy, which we may call the *unit publication cost* (as distinguished from the unit production cost of $10.00). Unfortunately, this does not mean that the publisher can price the book at $30.44. If all costs had been figured accurately, and if all copies were sold, this price would enable the publisher to break even. However, it would not cover the author's royalty, bookseller discounts, publisher's profit, or margin for error. All these elements must be figured into the retail price.

From Costs to Prices

All the costs discussed so far are incurred by the publisher before publication; we may call them publication costs. But the sale of each copy of a book must repay not only the publisher but also others with an investment in it. These include the author and, in many cases, booksellers, both wholesale and retail.

The author's investment is repaid through royalties. As explained in Chapter 5, royalties are calculated as a percentage of either retail price or revenue. The publisher collects royalties when books are sold and pays them out annually.

Bookseller discounts are based on selling price. They represent a portion of the list price (what the customer pays for the book) that the publisher never receives. Publishers allow retail stores and book wholesalers (often called jobbers) to buy books at a discount. The jobbers and bookstores then charge customers more for the book (in the case of bookstores, the recommended *retail* price); that is how they pay their costs and make a profit. Each book publisher has a different discount schedule, and most offer a complicated variety of discounts, depending on the number of books ordered and the type of purchaser. For example, jobbers generally receive higher discounts than retailers, and large orders command higher discounts than do small ones. Some publishers vary their discounts according to the type of book in question, with "trade" titles that will be sold in retail stores offered at a higher discount (usually 40 percent) than those expected to sell mainly to libraries and individuals (a short discount, usually 20 percent). Textbooks commonly sell at a 20 percent discount. In addition, some publishers hire commissioned salespeople who charge a fee of 5 to 10 percent of the list price. On the other hand, when copies of a book are sold directly to readers or libraries, generally through mail order, no discount is given. Rather than try to guess how many books will be sold at each discount, we will use an average discount of 30 percent.

Because royalties and discounts are calculated as a percentage of the book's price, we cannot estimate them without pricing our imaginary monograph. To do that, let us go back to our calculation of unit production cost ($10.00) and take the simplest pricing formula (which requires that we use an arbitrary multiplier, say, 5) to give us a first shot at a price. This yields a retail price of $50.00. Let us see whether that will allow us to cover our costs.

Now we can calculate the royalties and discounts. The author is receiving a royalty of 10 percent of the list (retail) price, or $5.00 per copy. We will figure an average discount of 30 percent, or $15.00 per copy.

At $50.00, each sale would produce the following results:

Unit publication cost	$30.44
Royalty	5.00
Bookseller discount	15.00
	50.44
Price	50.00
Publisher's profit (or loss)	($ .44)

If the publisher is to make a profit, then, our monograph must sell for more than $50.00. If the publisher decided to price the book at $55.00, the figures would be:

Unit publication cost	$30.44
Royalty	5.50
Bookseller discount	16.50
	52.44
Price	55.00
Publisher's profit	$ 2.56

Note that increasing the price by $5.00 increases the publisher's net revenue by only $3.00; that is, the publisher gets slightly more than half of the increase.

In fact, the "profit" may prove to be simply a margin for error. Suppose, for example, that the publisher can actually sell only 800 copies of the book at $55.00. This small miscalculation will create a loss of $1,000 ($27,400 in publication costs against $26,400 in revenue, net discounts, and royalties). Or, if the publisher underestimates costs even slightly, this can cut into the profit. For example, if typesetting costs $13.00 per page instead of $12.00, and an unusual number of alterations is required in proof, the typesetting cost per book could be 40 or 50 cents more; if the book runs a few pages longer than expected, requiring the printing of another signature (8, 16, or 32 pages), the per copy printing bill might be 25 cents higher, and so forth. This may sound like nickels and dimes, but remember that the potential profit at $55.00 is only $2.56. It is clear that our imaginary monograph is not going to produce impressive profits. In the absence of reliable ways to forecast the market, publishers must leave themselves some room for error, and prices must reflect that uncertainty.

Prices

Despite its crudeness, the method of setting the price by multiplying the unit production cost by 5 or 6 brings us surprisingly close to what a university press like the one we have imagined should charge. Many publishers do in fact use an arbitrary multiplier; those who must make a profit use

6, 7, or 8, while nonprofit houses use 4 or 5. Usually, however, the multiplier method is just a starting point, with other considerations coming into play.

Prices and Markets

Deciding to publish a book is one thing; deciding how to publish it is another. In scholarly publishing, the initial decision to publish is based mostly on the quality of the book, with costs and markets as subsidiary considerations. Once that decision is made, however, most of what a publishing house does turns on its perception of the market. In deciding how to proceed, a wise publisher looks carefully at who is likely to buy the book and at how prospective buyers will be influenced by such things as the book's appearance, price, and promotion.

Publishers who expect a title to sell almost entirely to libraries know a number of things. The first is the number of standing orders they have – that is, how many libraries automatically order everything they publish. They also know how many other libraries are likely to buy a book from them on this subject. They believe, with some evidence, that libraries will pay up to $40.00 or $50.00 for a monograph without protest. Finally, they know that libraries almost universally discard dust jackets and are not overly concerned with the design of the scholarly books they purchase. Publishers also know that certain prepublication reviews, particularly those in *Library Journal* and *Choice*, strongly affect library sales. If these reviews come out in time, publishers may alter their print run somewhat. For some titles with small print runs, library purchases account for more than half the sales, so this is an important market to understand.

Publishers who anticipate significant sales to individuals are somewhat more concerned about keeping prices down. If they believe that most such sales will be achieved through direct mail, they may not worry too much about design and dust jackets and spend money instead on attractive flyers. If, however, they expect to sell mostly through retail book-stores, they will want the books to be as attractive as possible, so that prospective buyers will take them off the shelves to look at them. In setting the print run, publishers will also try to estimate the number of individual buyers. Such estimates are based on past sales of similar books or on the size of available mailing lists. The more specialized a book, the smaller the audience.

One of the things that makes publishing interesting is that predicting the market is so difficult. Most editors are confident of their ability to recognize good scholarship and good writing, but if a fairy godmother offered them a single (professional) wish, it would probably be the ability to predict sales. The prediction is both difficult and vital, because it determines how a book will be published. A prediction of poor sales is often a self-fulfilling prophecy, and it is impossible to know how many books have not been sold because a publisher underestimated the market. A prediction of high sales can in fact increase sales because it may result in a more extensive advertising campaign and more attractive design – though an upper limit is imposed by the book itself. For example, if you have written a monograph on the nematodes, a good marketing campaign can ensure that every nematologist hears about it. But no amount of advertising will increase the number of nematologists or create interest among purchasers of bodice-rippers. Underestimating the market means losing money that one might have made; over-estimating it means losing money, period. An accurate estimate is needed to establish both the print run and a price at which publication is financially worthwhile.[3]

To some extent, then, price is a marketing decision: Regardless of what it costs to produce this book, here is what we can sell it for. Some books – almost always those with higher print runs and, consequently, lower unit costs – can be priced significantly in excess of what costs would require. Using similar

[3] Bailey, *Art and Science,* and *One Book/Five Ways* provide other examples of such calculations.

reasoning, publishers sometimes raise prices for backlist titles (those published in earlier years that are still in print). A publisher may have issued a monograph several years ago, when both costs and book prices were lower, and priced it at $14.95. The book is still selling reasonably well and would continue to do so even at $19.95. Why not, then, raise the price? The only danger is miscalculation: By raising the price you may reduce sales to the point where you make less money overall, even while making more per copy. Another reason for raising prices on backlist books has to do with the costs of running a publishing house. Publishers must pay current costs out of revenues from books already for sale. Publishers that rely on backlist titles for much of their income must ensure that those revenues keep up with current costs. Thus, raising prices on backlist titles increases their profitability and enables the publisher to keep the books in print longer.

By contrast, marketing considerations sometimes require a lower price than would costs alone. Recall our example of the typed article. If we include in its price the cost of a well-paid full professor's trip to China, then even if we are distributing 100 copies, it might take a price of several hundred dollars per copy to break even. Although this price would be rational in the light of costs, no one would pay it. For a publisher, this kind of situation would mean that the book should not be published, that it must be published at a loss (a loss which must, in turn, be offset by greater profits from other books), or that costs must be reduced or underwritten.

If we are dealing with a nonprofit publisher, our imaginary monograph should, in theory, break even. It would be extremely difficult to make each book come out exactly with neither profit nor loss, and publishers do not try to do this. Instead, they set prices to make at least a small profit on each title. Some books will lose money despite careful projections; others may make more than expected. If a nonprofit publisher makes a lot of money on one title, that profit will simply offset the losses on others. What the publisher hopes for is to break even overall. This flexibility also allows the press to publish some titles that do not make economic sense, that cannot possibly sell enough copies at a reasonable price to break even. Similarly, profit-making publishers must make a profit overall. There is probably not a single publisher that has not lost money on at least one title. Publishers stay in business not by being right every time but by being right most of the time. Given the choice, any publisher would rather make money on a title than lose it. But for scholarly publishers, profit is not necessarily the only – or even the strongest – motive.

In setting prices, most publishers consider some combination of costs, what competing titles sell for, and what the market will bear. The notion of "competing titles" is not very useful in pricing monographs, which are generally not considered to compete with one another. (Each is, after all, unique.) For trade-oriented books and textbooks, however, this is an important concept. If, for example, you have a choice of three textbooks of roughly equal quality for a large undergraduate class, you will choose the $19.95 text over those priced at $29.95 and $34.95. Scholarly publishers do concern themselves, however, with what the market will bear. For small editions, libraries represent a large percentage of buyers. Publishers have a pretty good idea of what price will raise a librarian's eyebrows, and they may raise the price of a book to something just short of that figure. Similarly, they will think twice before setting the price any higher: If this is the sort of book that no university library can afford to pass up, the price can be higher; if it is likely to be considered an optional purchase, pricing it lower will produce more sales and greater revenue.

When publishers order a larger printing, they are anticipating sales to individuals through direct mail and bookstores. Individuals raise their eyebrows sooner than do librarians, so such books may be priced lower. This is partly a marketing decision, but it can be justified by the lower unit cost of books generated by printing more.

To see how this works, let's suppose that the press prints 3,000 copies of our imaginary monograph instead of 1,000.

Its manufacturing (paper, printing, and binding) and shipping costs will increase; the other expenditures (plant costs, nonproduction direct costs, and overhead) are constant regardless of how many copies are printed. At 3,000 copies, the publisher is printing a sufficient number of copies to realize some economies of scale in manufacturing costs; they will increase from $3,850 to $7,800, for a (rounded) total production cost of $13,000 rather than $9,000. Since all other costs remain constant (with the possible exception of marketing costs), total publication cost will increase far less dramatically, from $27,400 to $31,400. This means that our unit publication cost will be much lower: Dividing $31,400 by 2,850 (we'll give away 150 copies) yields a unit publication cost of $11.02 – considerably less than the unit cost of 900 copies, which was $30.44. Also, with a printing of 3,000 the unit production cost will decrease from $10.00 to $4.56 and the price suggested by the arbitrary multiplier of 5 will drop to $22.80, which would probably end up as $25.00. If the multiplier of 6 were used, the book would be priced at $30.00.

Table 1 summarizes the relationships among print run, costs, prices, and profit. To show these relationships clearly, I have not used the arbitrary multiplier or rounded off the prices. Instead, I have added in a return to the publisher of a percentage of the unit publication cost. The price, then, is the unit publication cost plus the author's royalty, the discount, and the publisher's return. In most cases the return is 10 percent, but for the larger print runs I have given a second example of a higher per copy return with, in consequence, a higher price. The publisher is taking greater risks on larger quantities and will expect higher returns.

This table illustrates the rapid reduction in unit cost produced by increasing the print run, and the way that reduction can be reflected in price. It also shows the interrelationships of market size, price, and costs. More prospective buyers mean larger print runs, lower unit costs, and the possibility of lower prices. The increased printings and lower prices are practical, however, only if the market estimate is accurate. If a

Table 1. *Print run, costs, prices, and publisher's profit*

Print run	Unit production cost	Unit publication cost	Profit per copy	Price
500	$16.67	$57.56	$5.76	$90.46
1,000	10.00	30.44	3.04	47.83
1,500	7.14	20.28	2.03	37.18
3,000	4.56	11.02	1.10	20.20
3,000	4.56	11.02	2.00	21.70
5,000	3.64	7.81	.78	17.18
5,000	3.64	7.81	2.00	19.62

Note: On each book sold, the author's royalty is 10% of the retail price. The average discount is 20% for 500 and 1,000 copies; 30% for 1,500 and 3,000; and 40% for 5,000.

publishing house prints 3,000 copies, lowers the price, and then sells only 1,500 copies, it will lose money – despite the lower unit cost. At a price of $25.00, for example, the loss would be $8,900 (net revenues of $22,500 against costs of $31,400). Not only does the publishing house lose money, but it has invested more scarce cash in production and is left with an inventory of unsold books to store. Table 2 shows how quickly a publisher's return shrinks (or turns into a loss) if sales are overestimated even slightly. Because the risk of over-estimating the market increases with larger print runs, the difference between expected and actual sales in the table is higher for the larger print runs.

Why Prices Vary

With this understanding of costs, prices, and markets, let's look at the mystery of why some books that seem compara-ble are priced very differently. Everyone has had the experi-ence of seeing two monographs on similar subjects and of

Table 2. *Expected sales, actual sales, and publisher's profit*

Print run	Price	Expected sales	Expected profit	Actual sales	Actual profit (or loss)
500	$90.46	450	$2,592	400	($ 574)
1,000	47.83	950	2,888	850	(355)
1,500	37.18	1,400	2,842	1,100	(3,851)
3,000	20.20	2,850	3,155	2,350	(2,905)
3,000	21.70	2,850	5,720	2,350	(790)
5,000	17.18	4,800	3,744	3,500	(7,423)
5,000	19.62	4,800	9,600	3,500	(3,153)

Note: In all cases, the author receives a 10% royalty. Average discounts are 20% for 500 and 1,000 copies; 30% for 1,500 and 3,000; and 40% for 5,000. Actual profit and loss are calculated by comparing publication cost and revenues net of royalties and discounts.

the same length published by two different presses at astoundingly disparate prices – say, $19.95 and $49.95. That does not happen in the soft-drink business or in men's socks. But in publishing, there are many possible explanations.

The most obvious is that the two monographs are not, in fact, comparable. The examples in this chapter have been based on an imaginary 300-page monograph with no illustrations, no tables, no equations, and no foreign language material. Typesetting becomes much more expensive when tables, mathematics, or foreign alphabets are introduced. Costs for page makeup, or layout, are increased by the use of tables and illustrations of any kind. The use of photographs will increase printing costs and may require the use of more expensive paper. Color plates are extremely costly. In addition, two books that both end up at 300 pages may not really be the same length. One may have been set in a narrow typeface and smaller type, with wider lines of type, less white space, and more lines per page, while the other has larger type, more space between lines, wider margins, and so forth.

Table 3. *Costs and prices*

Typesetting cost per page	Unit production cost	Unit publication cost	Likely price
$ 8.00	$6.02	$19.16	$35.00
12.00	6.87	20.01	40.00
17.00	8.16	21.30	45.00
25.00	9.66	22.80	50.00

Note: Based on 1,500 copies printed, 1,400 sold.

Typesetting costs for the first book will be considerably higher because there are more characters per page, thus more labor per page. Table 3 shows the impact of differences in typesetting costs on price.

Another reason for the difference in price may be that the two presses estimated the market differently. This can happen because one publisher is more optimistic than the other for very good reasons. For example, the publisher with a series of books in the field, and a large number of standing library orders, can reasonably expect to sell more copies than the publisher that is new to the field. Or the more expensive monograph may be the revised dissertation of an unknown assistant professor, which is likely to sell fewer copies than the third monograph of an established scholar whose first and second books sold well. The preceding discussion of costs and prices illustrated the differences in price that would result from a variety of print runs. As you recall, the total cost of producing greater quantities is not much higher than the cost of producing fewer. It is the cost per book (the unit cost) that affects the price most dramatically. For this reason, the publisher's estimate of the market – a factor that is invisible to the book buyer – is crucial.

The nature of the market, as well as its size, affects price. Publishers who expect to sell most books directly to consumers

Table 4. *Bookseller discounts and prices*

Unit pub. cost	Average discount	Price needed to break even
$30.44	0%	$30.44
30.44	10%	33.82
30.44	20%	38.05
30.44	30%	43.49
30.44	40%	50.73

Note: Based on 1,000 copies printed, 900 sold; no royalty.

at full price (publishers of professional books are a good example) may be able to price their books lower because they do not have to allow for the bookseller's 40 percent; that leaves $22.00 worth of maneuvering space on our $55.00 book. (However, they may also have a smaller market, which keeps the price high.) By contrast, the publisher who anticipates mostly library sales through jobbers must price the book high enough to cover that discount. Table 4 illustrates the impact of discounts on the likely price of our imaginary monograph.

The publisher who anticipates selling few books at a discount, then, can afford to price books significantly lower. The $55.00 book could be sold profitably at $40.00; the $25.00 book, for $20.00. Even if the average discount turned out to be 20 percent, prices could be lowered several dollars. However, to sell large numbers of books, the publisher needs the help of jobbers and booksellers. Only a very small edition could be sold without discounts.

Another factor that affects price is the rate at which royalties are paid. Obviously, if an author is earning 10 percent of the retail price on every copy sold, then 10 percent of the price (and a greater percentage of the actual revenues) is not coming back to the publisher. The less the author earns, the lower the price can be. To illustrate these differences, Table 5 shows how royalties affect prices.

Table 5. *Author's royalties and prices*

Unit pub. cost	Royalty rate	Price needed to break even
$30.44	0%	$50.73
30.44	5% of retail	55.34
30.44	10% of retail	60.88
30.44	5% of net	53.40
30.44	10% of net	56.37

Note: All copies are sold at a 40% discount; 1,000 are printed, 900 sold.

Clearly, if the author will give up royalties, or receive them at a reduced rate, the price of the book can be lowered.

Even if there are no differences in production costs, anticipated sales, discounts, or royalties, the two presses may have very different overhead costs. The one in Manhattan, New York, that is paying higher rent, utilities, and salaries may have to charge more for its books than the one in Manhattan, Kansas. Presses in desirable locations where there is a lot of competition for jobs may underpay employees. One press may do a more thorough – and costly – job of manuscript evaluation and copy editing. One press may have its costs more extensively underwritten by its sponsoring institution. Indeed, one monograph may have been underwritten by a foundation or a government agency. For our 1,000-copy edition, a $10,000 foundation grant would reduce the unit publication cost to $19.33, allowing the book to be priced at $40.00 or $45.00 instead of $55.00.

Perhaps one press is more efficient than the other, with efficiency measured by the number of titles published per dollar of overhead expense. The more books you publish, the fewer overhead dollars you need to allocate to each title. To illustrate the possibilities, take one press with 16 people and 3,000 square feet of office space that is producing 25 books per year and another that produces 45; the latter is more efficient and can apportion its overhead among more books. Using the total overhead figure from our example, the allocation in these two cases would be roughly $22,400 and $12,400 per title – a difference of $10.00 *per copy* if 1,000 copies are printed. This does not necessarily mean that one press is staffed by slow-moving incompetents. It may mean that the more efficient press includes reprints among its annual output, along with titles copublished with a British house that require almost no staff time. It may also mean that the less efficient publisher does not have the operating capital – the cash to spend on typesetting and printing – to utilize its staff and facilities efficiently.

Another explanation is that one press may publish a few trade-oriented titles that earn more money and can be used to offset the costs of less profitable monographs. Some university press catalogues include cookbooks, reference books, novels, anthologies that are used as texts, and other fast-selling items along with their monographs. (This strategy doesn't always work, however. One press published an unexpected best-seller only to have the university administration decrease its subsidy the following year by the amount of its "windfall profits.")

One possible explanation is that one press thinks – or has learned by experience – that buyers will pay higher prices for its books and therefore routinely charges more. This publisher can publish marginally profitable books that might be impossible for another press, and it can use its profits on some titles to subsidize others.

The $30.00 difference between $19.95 and $49.95, then, is no longer such a mystery. Look at the possibilities we have seen: a print run of 3,000 rather than 1,500 will let us reduce the price by $15.00 to $20.00; an average discount of 20 percent rather than 40 percent will reduce it another $5.00 to $10.00 (although these two strategies are probably not compatible); a lower royalty rate will save from $2.00 to $7.00; a subsidy from a foundation can reduce the price by $10.00 or $15.00; and even slightly greater efficiency on the publisher's part (or simply lower overhead) can be worth up to $5.00. Elementary.

Paperback and Reprint Editions

Most monographs are published originally in a hardcover edition. Sometimes a paperback edition is manufactured simultaneously, to be issued at the same time or after six months or a year. Sometimes the decision to publish a paperback edition is made later, and the book is then reprinted. Occasionally, a monograph is published only in paperback from the outset.

Paperback books are almost always priced significantly lower than casebound books. If you recall the manufacturing costs of our imaginary monograph, you will see immediately that this difference cannot be explained by the lower cost of paperback binding. We estimated casebound binding at $1.00 per copy, plus 35 cents for each jacket. The paper cover will cost about as much as the jacket, and paperback binding will cost anywhere from 10 to 25 cents depending on the quality and quantity. In other words, we are cutting costs by only 75 to 90 cents per copy. The lower price is made possible by a larger print run, which is in turn made possible by confidence in a larger market.

Publishers who manufacture cloth and paper editions simultaneously, increase the print run, and reduce unit costs generally maintain a higher casebound price and use the extra profit to reduce the price of the paperback, which may then be more attractive as a textbook. The decisions on how to price the editions are interrelated and are dependent on the view of the market.

When a publisher decides to issue a paperback edition after the casebound edition is out, the book will have to be reprinted. The cost of the edition will be lower than that of the first edition (excluding differences attributable to size), because plant costs (typesetting and plates) and such non-production costs as editing and design have been covered by the first edition. In addition, although our method of allocating indirect costs would require us to add the book's share in again, it will in fact require very little in the way of salaries and other expenses. These facts, plus the larger sales that the publisher presumably is counting on to justify a paperback edition, make a lower price possible.

A reprint of a successful book need not be a paperback, of course. If a first printing sells more rapidly than anticipated and the publisher thinks that the estimate of the market was too low, a second casebound printing can be issued. In this case, too, the publisher's costs will be reduced because the plant and other one-time costs have been absorbed and real overhead costs are small, but the manufacturing costs will be the same (again, disregarding differences attributable to the size of the print run). For practical reasons (including the need to avoid infuriating customers who paid the original price), the price will be the same or slightly higher. This means that the publisher must reprint a large enough number to make a profit at something close to the original price. It would make no sense to reprint 500 copies of our $55.00 monograph six months later and try to charge $75.00.

Sometimes the demand for a small reprint edition arises years after original publication. The book is out of print, but some libraries and a few individuals would like to have it. Then the original publisher or a reprint house that has bought the rights may bring out a small casebound edition (a few hundred copies) at a relatively high price.

Another sort of reprint edition is justified by dramatically increased demand of the sort that occurs when a book is adopted for textbook use. This results in a large paperback edition with a price low enough to make it attractive as a text.

The publisher's decision to issue a paperback or reprint edition is based on demand. In the case of paperbacks printed at the same time as the original casebound edition, the publisher is relying on an estimate of anticipated demand. For reprints, no matter what their timing or binding, the publisher will want demonstrated demand: back orders, planned text adoptions, inquiries from prospective buyers of out-of-print books, and so forth. If you have evidence that a reprint or paperback edition of your book would sell, take it to your publisher, who can then do some market research and make a decision.

Your contract will spell out a royalty schedule for any paperback edition. A reprint edition that occurs while the book is in print or soon after it sells out is governed by the original rate unless the contract specifies a change. When a book has been out of print for years, however, the publisher may want to renegotiate the royalty rate before deciding to reprint. The nature of the edition is likely to be quite different – small and high-priced – and a lower royalty rate is appropriate.

Textbooks

The same principles that we have examined for scholarly monographs apply to the costs and pricing of textbooks. Just as in scholarly publishing, text houses must price books to cover direct costs, indirect costs, royalties, and discounts – plus a profit. And prices must be comparable to those of competing titles. The main differences between the two kinds of publishing are in the scale: Textbook publishers spend much more money on each title and take far greater risks; they publish more elaborately and in much larger editions; if they do well, they and their authors make much more money.

Text publishers incur large developmental costs. They pay more readers higher fees for more detailed evaluations, and they spend much more of their acquisition editors' time and developmental editors' time working on each manuscript. Because the books are longer and more complicated, much more manuscript editorial time is required. It would not be surprising for a copy editor to spend five or six hundred hours on a major textbook. Design and production are much more elaborate, and artwork – whether original or borrowed – is expensive. Print runs are much higher, and the books must be available for faculty examination long before the publisher can expect to sell a single copy. Teachers' guides and other aids must be produced and given away. In other words, the text publisher not only must spend much more money on typesetting and printing (because of the more elaborate format, greater length, and larger print runs) but must spend it well in advance of revenue. That means borrowing money and paying interest – a cost that scholarly publishers generally avoid. Textbook publishers also maintain large sales staffs and distribute large numbers of examination copies. It is common for a textbook publisher to spend $250,000 on a single text before selling a copy, and $500,000 is not unheard of.

Textbooks are sold at a short discount (20 percent) because the bookseller takes little risk and makes only a small investment. The retailer knows that the books will be sold because they are required for courses, and although textbooks take up a lot of space, they do not require elaborate display. This helps keep prices down somewhat. Real pressure comes from the sale of used textbooks, which provides no income to publisher or author. (Perhaps the availability of this source of revenue is some consolation to the bookstores for the short discount.) For a textbook to continue making money, the publisher must develop revised editions every few years. Costs are somewhat lower on the revised editions, and they prevent the sale of used books from cutting into profits – at least for one semester.

Trade Books

The same equations that apply to monographs and textbooks also apply to trade books. However, the various costs assume different proportions, and a high print run is the key to pricing and profitability. Marketing is extremely important, because it creates the demand that justifies the high print run. Finally, income from sources other than book sales can be an important source of revenue.

When a book is published in a small edition, plant costs and overhead represent a large part of the costs. That is why, for example, an author's preparation of camera-ready copy can make a book financially viable. When a publisher expects to sell many thousands of copies of a book, by contrast, plant costs and overhead are divided among so many units that their significance decreases. The importance of spending in other areas increases, however.

Trade books must be more attractive than scholarly monographs because they must appeal to retail consumers. (Some scholarly monographs are extremely attractive and elegantly produced, but that is not their major selling point.) Trade publishers therefore invest heavily in design and production, sometimes commissioning more than one potential jacket design, for example. Four-color jackets are almost universal, and interior design may be more lavish. Paperback covers may feature metallic foil, die-cuts, and embossing.

The most important investment trade publishers make is in marketing. Trade publishers send out large numbers of complimentary copies to potential reviewers and to influential booksellers. Often they manufacture specially bound copies of page proofs for this purpose, to generate early enthusiasm and encourage advance orders. They advertise in trade and consumer magazines, which is far more expensive than advertising in scholarly journals. They may share the cost of advertising in local newspapers with an area's booksellers. The marketing department will also seek free publicity on radio and television, most often by booking authors onto interview programs. They may also sponsor regional or national author tours, or feature authors at booksellers' conventions. All of these efforts are time-consuming, and many of them are expensive. The $3,000 allotted (rather generously) to marketing our typical monograph would be totally inadequate for a trade title; ten times that much is usual.

Much of the marketing done by trade publishers is directed at retail booksellers, because they are essential to the success of trade titles. The relationship with the bookseller influences design decisions, as we have seen, and it also affects pricing. Booksellers receive a discount of at least 40 percent on trade titles, so publishers must be able to make a profit (and pay royalties) on revenues of 60 percent or less of the retail price. Logically, that would push toward higher prices, but bookstore customers will not pay the prices that are acceptable to libraries or purchasers of professional books. So the publisher must price trade books at around $20 to $25, charge the retailer $12 to $15 for them, and still make money. The only way to do this is by printing and selling a lot of copies.

Another book industry practice creates pressure for high print runs but generally reduces the publisher's profits. Retailers are permitted to return unsold books to publishers for credit. This gives the retailer little incentive to order prudently or even realistically. As a result, returns on trade titles can run as high as 50 percent, leaving publishers with large numbers of unsold books in the warehouse after demand has peaked. These books end up on remainder tables and in discount catalogues. Although publishers have complained about the returns system for decades, it seems to be the best way to get booksellers to risk shelf space and sales efforts on new authors and risky titles. So publishers must factor returns into their financial projections.

Another significant expense for trade publishers is authors' advances. Although most trade authors receive modest advances of $10,000 to $25,000, a few authors with good track records or highly desirable manuscripts can demand advances of $100,000 or more. (Celebrity authors may receive advances in the millions.) Proceeds from the book must pay for these advances, and that means very high print runs and sales, and intense marketing efforts. Also, advances are paid well ahead of sales revenue, so publishers must either give up current income from the cash, or borrow and pay interest.

In most cases, revenues from clothbound books are not adequate to pay off multimillion-dollar investments, so trade publishers seek income from other sources. Even for books with more modest prospects, sales of rights can increase publishers' and authors' incomes significantly.

The most common additional source of income is paperback sales. The publisher may issue the paperback, thus realizing income from additional sales. But some trade publishers prefer to sell paperback rights to mass-market houses like Ballantine, Vintage, or Penguin. In this case, the paperback house pays a cash advance, sometimes even before the casebound book is published. The advance, shared between author and publisher, helps to offset the publisher's expenses, or adds to profits.

Trade publishers also try very hard to sell book club rights. Book clubs do not usually pay enormous sums to publishers, but they make their decisions on the basis of the manuscript, pay early in the publication process, and allow publishers to increase their print runs by thousands of copies, further reducing unit costs. Book clubs also help advertise their selections and, through their endorsements, increase bookstore sales.

Sale of serial rights can also boost income and provide additional publicity. Consumer magazines pay significant amounts for excerpts and bring books to the attention of thousands of potential readers. They may also generate television and radio publicity.

Foreign rights can also provide impressive revenues. There is a large market for American nonfiction – especially popular science – in the United Kingdom, western Europe, and Japan. Foreign publishers are willing to pay for rights and, when necessary, to invest in translations. For the most part, however, sales of foreign rights do not affect the costs of the American edition (as book club sales do) or increase U.S. sales (as serial rights sales do); they simply bring in additional revenue.

Trade publishing is far riskier than scholarly publishing, but the potential profits are far greater. Trade publishers must put their efforts into marketing both the books and the rights attached to them. Their financial success depends on producing and selling large quantities, rather than on cutting costs or precisely targeting small audiences.

Financial Partnership

I began this book by describing publishing as a partnership between author and publisher. The financial analysis in this chapter demonstrates that the partnership is more than an intellectual one. If authors are to make money, publishers must, too.

As the author of a scholarly book, your job (beyond writing a book that people will want to buy) is to help the publisher find the real market for your book by alerting your editor or the marketing manager to organizations, review media, and other outlets that the publisher might not know. You should also help your publisher to locate possible sources of grants. If your publisher is trying to cut costs, you should cooperate by giving up a dust jacket, resisting the urge to make changes in proof, and being realistic about royalties. If you are curious about how well your book is doing (and you certainly should be), you can find out what you need to know from your royalty statements, which often list the print run and current sales figures. Royalty statements are generally issued annually, so you might want to ask for interim sales figures at six months. Don't call every week, though. The market for scholarly books doesn't move as fast as pork-belly futures.

Sometimes, the nature of the book is such that neither author nor publisher will make any money. Usually, at least for scholarly books, they both will profit modestly. Sometimes they both will do very well. But unless a publisher has offered an unconscionable contract, and the author has accepted it, it is unlikely that one will profit at the expense of the other. Publishing cannot be played as a zero-sum game.

Appendix: Sources of Grants for Publication

The following government agencies, foundations, and other programs provide grants to cover publication costs. I have provided the name and address of each group along with a brief description. For more information about these programs and about some more specialized ones, you can write to the grantors. In addition, you may wish to consult *Publication Grants for Writers and Publishers*, a book by this author and Karin Park (Phoenix: Oryx, 1991). In it we provide detailed program profiles, including typical grant amounts and titles of recent successful applications; describe decision-making procedures; explain how to apply for these grants (including instructions for application forms); discuss how to estimate costs; describe how to administer the grant if you are successful; and explain how to research other grant possibilities.

U.S. Government Programs

National Endowment for the Humanities, Division of Research
  Programs – Texts
Room 318
1100 Pennsylvania Avenue, N.W.
Washington, D.C. 20506
This program supports preparation of scholarly and annotated editions of works and documents in all humanities fields as well as translations. In the publication subvention category, application must be made by the publisher for books that have been accepted for publication.

Appendix

National Endowment for the Humanities, Division of Research
  Programs – Reference Materials
Room 318
1100 Pennsylvania Avenue, N.W.
Washington, D.C. 20506
This program supports the creation of dictionaries, historical or linguistic atlases, encyclopedias, concordances, catalogues raisonnés,
linguistic grammars, descriptive catalogues, databases, and other
reference materials in the humanities.

National Endowment for the Arts, Literature Program
Small Press Assistance
Nancy Hanks Center
Room 723
1100 Pennsylvania Avenue, N.W.
Washington, D.C. 20506
Unlike the NEH programs, the NEA supports the publication of
fiction, including translations. This program offers assistance to
nonprofit literary small presses and university presses with a his-
tory of publishing contemporary creative literature.

National Endowment for the Arts, Literature Programs
Distribution Projects
Nancy Hanks Center
Room 723
1100 Pennsylvania Avenue, N.W.
Washington, D.C. 20506
This division of the Literature Program supports the distribution
component of publication.

National Historical Publications and Records Commission,
  Publications Program
Room 300
National Archives Building
Washington, D.C. 20408
The NHPRC supports preparation of editions of U.S. historical
documents in book form or microform. This program supports
editorial projects; the following one supports publication.

National Historical Publications and Records Commission,
  Publication Subvention Grants
National Archives Building

Room 300
Washington, D.C. 20408
These grants, available to university and other nonprofit presses, underwrite the costs of manufacturing and distributing documentary editions formally endorsed by the NHPRC. Application must be made by the publisher.

National Library of Medicine, Publication Grant Program
International Programs Branch
Extramural Programs
8600 Rockville Pike
Bethesda, Maryland 20894
The NLM supports not-for-profit publication projects in biomedical science, health, health care delivery, history of medicine and the life sciences, medical librarianship, health information science, biomedical communications, and medical informatics. Projects eligible for support include monographs, translations, reference works, and conference proceedings.

Canadian Government Programs

Natural Sciences and Engineering Research Council of Canada
Scientific Publication Grants
200 Kent Street, 9th floor
Ottawa, Ontario K1A 1H5
Grants are given to Canadian publishers to assist in the provision and maintenance of high-quality Canadian publications for the dissemination of original resarch results in the natural sciences and engineering.

Social Science Federation of Canada / Canadian Federation for the Humanities
Aid to Scholarly Publications Programme
151 Slater Street, Suite 410
Ottawa, Ontario K1P 5H3
Grants are given to Canadian citizens, landed immigrants, or their Canadian publishers to assist the publication of book-length manuscripts of advanced scholarly research that require financial assistance.

Appendix

Nongovernment Programs

Calvin K. Kazanjian Economics Foundation, Inc.
R.D. 4, Box C8B
Oneonta, New York 13820
The Kazanjian Foundation supports publication and distribution of books and other printed matter in economics and related social sciences.

The Carl and Lily Pforzheimer Foundation, Inc.
Publication Grants
650 Madison Avenue, 23d floor
New York, New York 10022
The foundation supports publication of scholarly material directly related to the collection "Shelley and His Circle," which the foundation previously owned, and those dealing with subjects in which its library continues to have a major interest.

Commission of the European Communities
Printing Grants for University Theses
University Information Service
200, rue de la Loi
1049 Brussels, Belgium
Authors of dissertations on European integration may apply to this program for grants to help defray printing costs. Successful applicants must find a publisher by a deadline set by the commission.

The Dr. M. Aylwin Cotton Foundation
Publication Grants
P.O. Box 232, Pollet House
The Pollet, St. Peter Port
Guernsey, Channel Islands
Grants are available for publication costs of books in archaeology, architecture, history, language, and art of the Mediterranean area.

The Japan Foundation
Publication Assistance Program
152 West 57th Street, 39th floor
New York, New York 10019
The foundation provides financial assistance to publishers for the publication of books on or relating to Japan in the humanities, social sciences, and fine arts in languages other than Japanese.

Appendix

The Numata Center for Buddhist Translation and Research
2620 Warring Street
Berkeley, California 94704
Grants are given for Buddhist studies and scholarly Buddhist publications.

Pacific Cultural Foundation
Suite 807, Palace Office Building
346 Nanking East Road, Sec. 3
Taipei, Taiwan
Grants are available to support publication of books on Chinese culture, history, and contemporary problems.

The Translation Center
Columbia University
Room 307A, Mathematics Building
New York, New York 10027
Awards are given both to translators and to publishers for literary translations into English.

Bibliography

Basic References

Association of American University Presses, *Directory*. Annual. Distributed by the University of Chicago Press.
 Names, addresses, and descriptions of the publishing programs of the member presses.
Butcher, Judith. *Copy-Editing: The Cambridge Handbook*. 3d ed. New York: Cambridge University Press, 1991.
 The British equivalent of Chicago, but more clearly organized and concise.
The Chicago Manual of Style. 14th ed., rev. and expanded. Chicago: University of Chicago Press, 1993.
 The bible of scholarly editors.
Dessauer, John P. *Book Publishing: A Basic Introduction*. New York: Continuum, 1989.
 The third edition of a classic description of publishing, from acquisition through sales, that focuses on trade, textbook, and small press publishing.
Journal of Scholarly Publishing. Toronto: University of Toronto Press, quarterly. (Formerly *Scholarly Publishing*.)
 An excellent source of information on current problems, trends, and ideas in scholarly publishing, along with useful advice from editors on practical topics.
Literary Market Place (LMP). New York: Bowker, annual.
 A directory of U.S. and foreign publishers that provides names, addresses, and other useful information. Also includes listings for translators, literary agents, awards, and review media.
Publishers' Trade List Annual. New York: Bowker, annual.

Catalogues of current books and older books still in print of most publishers, arranged alphabetically by publisher.

Publishing Research Quarterly. New Brunswick, N.J.: Transaction Publishers. (Formerly *Book Research Quarterly*.)
This journal covers trade and textbook publishing, as well as scholarly journals and books.

Dictionaries

American Heritage Dictionary of the English Language. 3d ed. Boston: Houghton Mifflin, 1992.
An authoritative dictionary with helpful usage notes and illustrations.

Chambers English Dictionary. Rev. ed. New York: Cambridge University Press, 1990.
Excellent for British spelling and usage and for archaic words. This dictionary is organized around root words and is the best of the lot for browsing.

Merriam-Webster's Collegiate Dictionary. 10th ed. Springfield, Mass.: Merriam-Webster, 1993.
The most generally accepted desk dictionary.

Morton, Herbert C. "On the Differences of Dictionaries." *Scholarly Publishing* 20, no. 1 (October 1988): 23–34.
This article includes a lengthy review of the second edition, unabridged, of the *Random House Dictionary*, comparing it with the *Oxford English Dictionary* and *Webster's Third New International Dictionary*.

Oxford American Dictionary. New York: Oxford University Press, 1980. Paperback ed., New York: Avon, 1980.
A convenient dictionary with helpful usage notes.

The Random House Dictionary. 2d ed., unabridged. New York: Random House, 1987.
A larger, more thorough version than the earlier dictionary.

Stainton, Elsie Myers. "The Uses of Dictionaries." *Scholarly Publishing* 11, no. 3 (April 1980): 229–41.
Brief reviews of general and specialized dictionaries.

Webster's Third New International Dictionary of the English Language, Unabridged. Springfield, Mass.: Merriam-Webster, 1986.
The most generally accepted unabridged dictionary, but it does not give advice on grammar and usage.

Bibliography

Writing and Usage: General Guides

I have listed only a few of the many such guides available. If you find another that is both authoritative and helpful to you, use it.

Bernstein, Theodore M. *The Careful Writer: A Modern Guide to English Usage*. New York: Atheneum, 1965.
More detailed than Strunk and White, less difficult than Fowler.

Fowler, H. W. *A Dictionary of Modern English Usage*. 2d ed., rev. by Sir Ernest Gowers. New York: Oxford University Press, 1965.

Maggio, Rosalie. *The Dictionary of Bias-Free Usage: A Guide to Nondiscriminatory Language*. Phoenix: Oryx Press, 1991.
Although you may occasionally disagree with the author's characterization of a word as biased, this book provides sensible guidance and alternatives.

Markland, Murray T. "Taking Criticism – and Using It." *Scholarly Publishing* 14, no. 2 (February 1983): 139–47.
How to benefit from criticism by colleagues and referees, including translations of standard cryptic referees' and editors' comments.

Miller, Casey, and Kate Swift. *The Handbook of Nonsexist Writing for Writers, Editors and Speakers*. New York: Lippincott & Crowell, 1980.
A guide to spotting, avoiding, and correcting sexist language, with memorable examples.

Newman, Edwin. *A Civil Tongue*. New York: Bobbs-Merrill, 1976.
Witty, reasonable, and memorable comments on the way academics, journalists, bureaucrats, politicians, and others misuse English.

——— *Strictly Speaking: Will America Be the Death of English?* New York: Bobbs-Merrill, 1974.
More of the same.

Nicholson, Margaret. *A Dictionary of American-English Usage*. Based on Fowler's *Modern English Usage*. New York: New American Library, 1957.
For the writer interested in fine points of grammar and usage who has a fairly sophisticated grasp of the subject. Both books make for great browsing.

Stainton, Elsie Myers. "Some Pointers on Style." *Scholarly Publishing* 12, no. 1 (October 1980): 75–88.

Brief reviews of books on language and of writing manuals.

———. "Writing and Rewriting." *Scholarly Publishing* 10, no. 1 (October 1978): 75–83.

Sound advice on writing and revising.

Strunk, W., Jr., and E. B. White. *The Elements of Style*. 3d ed. New York: Macmillan, 1979.

The one writing manual you must own.

van Leunen, Mary-Claire. *A Handbook for Scholars*. New York: Knopf, 1978.

Especially useful on citation, quotations, and the usage problems most common among academic writers.

Writing and Usage: Subject-related Guides

Barnet, Sylvan. *A Short Guide to Writing About Art*. 3d ed. New York: HarperCollins, 1989.

Bellquist, John Eric. *A Guide to Grammar and Usage for Psychology and Related Fields*. Hillsdale, N.J.: Erlbaum, 1993.

Day, Robert A. *How to Write and Publish a Scientific Paper*. 4th ed. Phoenix: Oryx Press, 1992.

———. *Scientific English: A Guide for Scientists and Other Professionals*. Phoenix: Oryx Press, 1992.

Fondiller, Shirley H. *The Writer's Workbook: Health Professionals' Guide to Getting Published*. New York: National League for Nursing Press, 1992.

Fondiller, Shirley H., and Barbara J. Nerone. *Health Professionals' Stylebook: Putting Your Language to Work*. New York: National League for Nursing Press, 1993.

Gandolfo, Anita. *The Nurse's Writing Handbook*. Norwalk, Conn.: Appleton-Century-Crofts, 1984.

Huth, Edward J., M.D. *How to Write and Publish Papers in the Medical Sciences*. 2d ed. Baltimore: Williams & Wilkins, 1990.

———. *Medical Style and Format: An International Manual for Authors, Editors, and Publishers*. Philadelphia: ISI Press, 1987.

Marius, Richard. *A Short Guide to Writing About History*. Glenview, Ill.: Scott, Foresman, 1989.

Michaelson, Herbert B. *How to Write and Publish Engineering Papers and Reports*. 3d ed. Phoenix: Oryx Press, 1990.

Morgan, Peter. *An Insider's Guide for Medical Authors and Editors*. Philadelphia: ISI Press, 1986.

Bibliography

Mullins, Carolyn J. *A Guide to Writing and Publishing in the Social and Behavioral Sciences.* New York: Wiley, 1977. Reprint ed. Malabar, Fla: R. E. Krieger, 1983.

Pechenik, Jan A. *A Short Guide to Writing About Biology.* Boston: Little, Brown, 1987.

Sheen, Anita Peebles. *Breathing Life Into Medical Writing: A Handbook.* St. Louis: Mosby, 1982.
   Excellent advice on writing clearly and precisely. Although the examples are medical, the book is useful to all academic writers.

Silverman, Robert J. *Getting Published in Education Journals.* Springfield, Ill.: Thomas, 1982.

Watson, Richard A. *Writing Philosophy: A Guide to Professional Writing and Publishing.* Carbondale: Southern Illinois University Press, 1992.

Wingell, Richard J. *Writing About Music: An Introductory Guide.* Englewood Cliffs, N.J.: Prentice Hall, 1990.

Zeiger, Mimi. *Essentials of Writing Biomedical Research Papers.* New York: McGraw-Hill, 1991.

Style Manuals

The Chicago Manual of Style, 14th ed., is the standard manual for most book publishers and some journals. You should own it if you plan to write a book or to work in a field that uses it.

Most journals, however, rely on a more specialized style manual, and some have their own style sheets. This list includes only official style manuals issued by professional associations or government agencies in the United States.

For British, Canadian, and other English-language guides, see John Bruce Howell, *Style Manuals of the English-Speaking World: A Guide* (Phoenix: Oryx Press, 1983). This useful volume also includes government style manuals and manuals published by university presses and commercial publishers for their authors. It should be in your university library.

American Chemical Society. *The ACS Style Guide: A Manual for Authors and Editors.* Janet S. Dodd, ed. Washington, D.C.: ACS, 1986.

American Institute of Physics. *AIP Style Manual.* 4th ed. New York: AIP, 1990.

Bibliography

American Mathematical Society. *A Manual for Authors of Mathematical Papers*. 7th ed. Providence: AMS, 1980.

American Medical Association. *American Medical Association Manual of Style*. 8th ed. Baltimore: Williams & Wilkins, 1989.

American Psychological Association. *Publication Manual of the American Psychological Association*. 4th ed. Washington, D.C.: APA, 1994.

American Society for Microbiology. *ASM Style Manual for Journals and Books*. Washington, D.C.: ASM, 1991.

American Society of Agronomy. *Publications Handbook and Style Manual*. Madison, Wis.: ASA, 1984.

Council of Biology Editors. *Scientific Style and Format: The CBE Manual for Authors, Editors, and Publishers*. 6th ed. Edward J. Huth, ed. New York: Cambridge University Press, 1994.

International Committee of Medical Journal Editors. "Uniform Requirements for Manuscripts Submitted to Biomedical Journals." *Annals of Internal Medicine* 96 (1982): 766–70.

Modern Language Association. *MLA Handbook for Writers of Research Papers, Theses, and Dissertations*. By Joseph Gibaldi and Walter S. Achtert. 3d ed. New York: MLA, 1988.

A Uniform System of Citation. 15th ed. Cambridge, Mass.: Harvard Law Review Association, 1991.

U.S. Geological Survey. *Suggestions to Authors of the Reports of the United States Geological Survey*. 6th ed. Washington, D.C.: Government Printing Office, 1978.

Journals: General Information

Budd, Louis J. "On Writing Scholarly Articles," in *The Academic's Handbook*, A. Leigh DeNeef, Craufurd D. Goodwin, and Ellen Stern McCrate, eds., pp. 201–15. Durham, N.C.: Duke University Press, 1988.
A well-written essay on working with editors of humanities journals, with much practical advice.

DeBakey, Lois. *The Scientific Journal: Editorial Policies and Practices: Guidelines for Editors, Reviewers, and Authors*. St. Louis: Mosby, 1976.
Indispensable for new journal editors and very helpful for referees and authors in the sciences and humanities.

Bibliography

Irizarry, Estelle. "Redundant and Incremental Publication." *Journal of Scholarly Publishing* 25, no. 4 (July 1994): 212–220.
A discussion of the ethical issues and suggestions for editors and authors.

Maddox, Robert C. "We Still Have Quite a Backlog of Articles." *Scholarly Publishing* 6, no. 2 (January 1975): 127–35.
An example of how badly journal submissions can be handled.

Manten, A. A. "Scientific Review Literature." *Scholarly Publishing* 5, no. 1 (October 1973): 74–89.
An analysis of the genre, with advice to authors and editors.

Page, Gillian, Robert Campbell, and Jack Meadows. *Journal Publishing: Principles and Practice*. Boston: Butterworth, 1987.
A thorough introduction to journal publishing that is concerned with nuts and bolts.

Penaskovic, Richard. "Facing Up to the Publication Gun." *Scholarly Publishing* 16, no. 2 (January 1985): 136–40.
Good advice on finding ideas and publishers for journal articles.

Ridley, Jack B. "Vicissitudes of an Obscure Scholar." *AHA Perspectives* 21, no. 6 (September 1983): 8–9.
Further adventures in journal land.

Rodman, Hyman. "Some Practical Advice for Journal Contributors." *Scholarly Publishing* 9, no. 3 (April 1978): 235–42.
Exactly what the title says.

Scal, Marjorie. "The Page Charge." *Scholarly Publishing* 3, no. 1 (October 1971): 62–69.
An explanation of journal financing and the role of page charges. Includes a discussion of rates and policies on waivers.

Strain, Boyd R. "Publishing in Science," in *The Academic's Handbook*, A. Leigh DeNeef, Craufurd D. Goodwin, and Ellen Stern McCrate, eds., pp. 216–25.
A concise summary of considerations for authors of scientific articles.

Thyer, Bruce A. *Successful Publishing in Scholarly Journals*. Thousand Oaks, Calif.: Sage, 1994.
A brief guide to submitting and revising articles.

Zink, Steven D. "Journal Publishing in the Field of U.S. History." *Scholarly Publishing* 11, no. 4 (July 1980): 343–59.
Suggestions for improving communication between authors and editors of scholarly journals.

Bibliography

Guides to Journals

Each of these guides provides information on the subjects covered, refereeing policy, submission requirements, page fee policy, and editor's address. Some provide advice on writing and manuscript preparation. Most also give length of time for refereeing and other details. Remember, though, that these guides date very quickly. Always consult the current issue of the journal, especially for the editor's name and address.

Many of these guides are reviewed briefly in two articles by Stanley P. Lyle, "Authors' Guides to Scholarly Periodicals," *Scholarly Publishing* 10, no. 3 (April 1979): 255–61; 15, no. 3 (April 1984): 273–79.

General Guides

Directory of Electronic Journals, Newsletters, and Academic Discussion Lists. Washington, D.C.: Association of Research Libraries, annual.

This guide is published on 3½-inch disks, IBM compatible, in DOS Wordperfect format. Part 1 is a directory of electronic journals and newsletters. Part 2 is a directory of academic discussion lists.

Directory of Publishing Opportunities in Journals and Periodicals. 5th ed. Chicago: Marquis Academic Media, 1981.

This extensive and thorough volume should be in your university library.

Subject Area Guides

BUSINESS AND ECONOMICS

Cabell, David W. E., ed. *Cabell's Directory of Publishing Opportunities in Business and Economics.* 5th ed. Beaumont, Tex.: Cabell, 1990.

Miller, A. Carolyn, and Victoria J. Punsalan. *Refereed and Nonrefereed Economic Journals: A Guide to Publishing Opportunities.* New York: Greenwood, 1988.

Vargo, Richard J. *The Author's Guide to Accounting and Financial Reporting Publications.* Rev. ed. New York: Harper & Row, 1981.

Bibliography

EARTH SCIENCES

Papa, Gail, and Sharon Marsh, eds. *Writer's Guide to Periodicals in Earth Sciences.* 2d ed. Alexandria, Va.: American Geological Institute, 1986.

EDUCATION

Cabell, David W. E. *Directory of Publishing Opportunities in Education.* 3d ed. Beaumont, Tex.: Cabell, 1992.

Collins, Mary Ellen. *Education Journals and Serials: An Analytical Guide.* New York: Greenwood, 1988.

Dyer, Thomas G., and Margaret Davis. *Higher Education Periodicals: A Directory.* Athens: Institute of Higher Education, University of Georgia, 1981.

Judy, Stephen N., ed. *Publishing in English Education.* Montclair, N.J.: Boynton/Cook, 1982.

Katz, Sidney B., Jerome T. Kapes, and Peggy A. Zirkel. *Resources for Writing for Publication in Education.* New York: Teachers College Press, 1980.

Levin, Joel. *Getting Published: The Educators' Resource Book.* New York: ARCO, 1983.

Loke, Wing Hong. *A Guide to Journals in Psychology and Education.* Metuchen, N.J.: Scarecrow Press, 1990.

Parker, Barbara A. *Journal Instructions to Authors: A Compilation of Manuscript Guidelines from Education Periodicals.* Annapolis: PSI, 1985.

ENGINEERING

Balachandran, Sarojini. *Directory of Publishing Sources: The Researcher's Guide to Journals in Engineering and Technology.* New York: Wiley-Interscience, 1982.

Miller, Richard K. *Directory of Technical Magazines and Directories.* Atlanta, Ga.: Fairmont Press, 1982.

Scull, Roberta A. *Publishing Opportunities for Energy Research: A Descriptive Guide to Selective Serials in the Social and Technical Sciences.* New York: Greenwood, 1986.

HEALTH SCIENCES AND MEDICINE

Ardell, Donald B., and John Y. James, eds. *Author's Guide to Journals in the Health Field.* Author's Guide to Journals Series. New York: Haworth Press, 1980.

The Author's Guide to Biomedical Journals. New York: Mary Ann Liebert, 1994.

Binger, Jane L., and Lydia M. Jensen. *Lippincott's Guide to Nursing Literature: A Handbook for Students, Writers, and Researchers.* Philadelphia: Lippincott, 1980.

Meiss, H. R., and D. A. Jaeger, comps. *Information to Authors, 1980– 1981: Editorial Guidelines Reprinted from 246 Medical Journals.* Baltimore: Urban & Schwarzenberg, 1980.

Mirin, Susan K. *The Nurse's Guide to Writing for Publication.* Wakefield, Mass.: Nursing Resources, 1981.

National Cancer Institute. *A Compilation of Journal Instructions to Authors.* Publication 80–1991. Bethesda, Md.: U.S. Department of Health, Education, and Welfare, Public Health Service, National Institutes of Health, National Cancer Institute, 1979.

Warner, Steven D., and Kathryn D. Schweer. *Author's Guide to Journals in Nursing and Related Fields.* Author's Guide to Journals Series. New York: Haworth Press, 1982.

HISTORY

Steiner, Dale R., and Casey R. Phillips. *Historical Journals: A Handbook for Writers and Reviewers.* 2d ed. Jefferson, N.C.: McFarland & Co., 1993.

LANGUAGES AND LITERATURE

Mackesy, Eileen M., and Karen Mateyak, comps. *MLA Directory of Periodicals: A Guide to Journals and Series in Languages and Literatures.* New York: Modern Language Association of America, biennial.

LAW

Mersky, Roy M., Robert C. Berring, and James K. McCue, eds. *Author's Guide to Journals in Law, Criminal Justice, and Criminology.* Author's Guide to Journals Series. New York: Haworth Press, 1979.

LIBRARY AND INFORMATION SCIENCE

Alley, Brian, and Jennifer Cargill. *Librarian in Search of a Publisher: How to Get Published.* Phoenix: Oryx Press, 1986.

Stevens, Norman D., and Nora B. Stevens, eds. *Author's Guide to Journals in Library and Information Science.* Author's Guide to Journals Series. New York: Haworth Press, 1982.

Bibliography

MUSIC

Basart, Ann Phillips. *Writing About Music: A Guide to Publishing Opportunities for Authors and Reviewers*. Berkeley: Fallen Leaf Press, 1989.

PHILOSOPHY AND RELIGION

American Philosophical Association. *Guidebook for Publishing Philosophy*. Newark, Del.: APA, 1986.
Dawsey, James M. *A Scholar's Guide to Academic Journals in Religion*. Metuchen, N.J.: Scarecrow Press, 1988.

POLITICAL SCIENCE

Political and Social Science Journals: A Handbook for Writers and Reviewers. Clio Guides to Publishing Opportunities, no. 2. Santa Barbara, Calif.: ABC-Clio, 1983.

PSYCHOLOGY

Loke, Wing Hong. *A Guide to Journals in Psychology and Education*. Metuchen, N.J.: Scarecrow Press, 1990.
Mullins, Carolyn J. *A Guide to Writing and Publishing in the Social and Behavioral Sciences*. New York: Wiley, 1977. Reprint ed., Malabar, Fla.: R. E. Krieger, 1983.
Wang, Alvin Y. *Author's Guide to Journals in the Behavioral Sciences*. Hillsdale, N.J.: Erlbaum, 1989.

SOCIAL SCIENCES

Mullins, Carolyn J. *A Guide to Writing and Publishing in the Social and Behavioral Sciences*. New York: Wiley, 1977. Reprint ed., Malabar, Fla.: R. E. Krieger, 1983.
Political and Social Science Journals: A Handbook for Writers and Reviewers. Clio Guides to Publishing Opportunities, no. 2. Santa Barbara, Calif.: ABC-Clio, 1983.

SOCIAL WORK

Mendelsohn, Henry N. *An Author's Guide to Social Work Journals*. 3d ed. Washington, D.C.: NASW Press, 1992.

Refereeing

Banner, James M., Jr. "Preserving the Integrity of Peer Review." *Scholarly Publishing* 19, no. 2 (January 1988): 109–15; "Guide-

lines for Peer Review of Sponsored Book Manuscripts." *Scholarly Publishing* 20, no. 2 (January 1989): 116–22.
Banner offers suggestions to improve the peer review process, including the provision of a description of the process for authors. The second article includes the description provided by Banner's own press.

DeGeorge, Richard T., and Fred Woodward. "Ethics and Manuscript Reviewing." *Journal of Scholarly Publishing* 25, no. 3 (April 1994): 133–45.
A good review and discussion of the obligations of authors, editors, and publishers.

Forscher, Bernard K. "The Role of the Referee." *Scholarly Publishing* 11, no. 2 (January 1980): 165–69.
What journal editors expect from referees.

Harman, Eleanor, and R. M. Schoeffel. "Our Readers Report." *Scholarly Publishing* 6, no. 4 (July 1975): 333–40.
Suggestions for referees of scholarly manuscripts.

James, M. R. "Casting the Runes." In *The Ghost Stories of M. R. James.* 2d ed. London: Arnold, 1974.
A memorable argument for referees' anonymity.

Stieg, Margaret F. "Refereeing and the Editorial Process: The AHR and Webb." *Scholarly Publishing* 14, no. 2 (February 1983): 99–122.
A case study of how refereeing and editorial evaluation actually work.

Ward, Norman. "The Not So Gentle Reader." *Scholarly Publishing* 9, no. 2 (January 1978): 139–42.
A pleasant essay on the joys and hazards of reading manuscripts.

Zuckerman, Harriet, and Robert K. Merton. "Patterns of Evaluation in Science: Institutionalization, Structure, and Functions of the Referee System." *Minerva* 9 (1971): 66–100.
A study of the history of refereeing, a case study of *The Physical Review,* and conclusions about the system.

Reviewing Books

Budd, John. "Book Reviewing Practices of Journals in the Humanities." *Scholarly Publishing* 13, no. 4 (July 1982): 363–71.
How journals select reviewers.

Bibliography

Hoge, James O., ed. *Literary Reviewing*. Charlottesville: University Press of Virginia, 1987.
This thoughtful volume discusses the duties, problems, and ethics of literary reviewing. Topics covered include reviewing criticism, literary history, literary biography, bibliographies, and editions of letters, journals, and diaries.

Hoge, James O., and James L. W. West III. "Academic Book Reviewing: Some Problems and Suggestions." *Scholarly Publishing* 11, no. 1 (October 1979): 35–41.
Good suggestions for book reviewers and what editors look for in a review.

Klemp, P. J. "Reviewing Academic Books: Some Ideas for Beginners." *Scholarly Publishing* 12, no. 2 (January 1981): 135–39.
Suggestions on reviewing books for journals.

Walford, A. J. *Reviews and Reviewing: A Guide*. Phoenix: Oryx Press, 1986.
A discussion of the art of reviewing and a guide to review media in various fields.

Dissertations

Fox, Mary Frank. "The Transition from Dissertation Student to Publishing Scholar and Professional," in *Scholarly Writing and Publishing: Issues, Problems, and Solutions*, Mary Frank Fox, ed. Boulder, Colo.: Westview Press, 1985.
A very short essay on developing habits of work and of thought that will contribute to scholarly productivity.

Harman, Eleanor, and Ian Montagnes, eds. *The Thesis and the Book*. Toronto: University of Toronto Press, 1976.
An indispensable guide for revisers of dissertations, helpful for referees and, particularly, for those who are not sure how writing for book publication is distinguished from other writing.

Finding a Publisher

General Information

Day, Colin. "The University Press: An Organic Part of the Institution." *Scholarly Publishing* 23, no. 1 (October 1991): 27–44.
An excellent review of the current state of university presses.

Denham, Alice, and Wendell Broom. "The Role of the Author." *Scholarly Publishing* 12, no. 3 (April 1981): 249–58.
Basic advice on preparing a manuscript, finding a publisher, and working with your publisher.

Funk, Robert W. "Issues in Scholarly Publishing." *Scholarly Publishing* 9, no. 1 (October 1977): 3–16; 9, no. 2 (January 1978): 115–29.
Publishing by learned societies.

Halpenny, Francess G. "Of Time and the Editor." *Scholarly Publishing* 1, no. 2 (January 1970): 159–69.
A cogent explanation of why university press reviewing and editing take so long and some suggestions for authors.

Hartman, Joan E., and Ellen Messer-Davidow, eds. *Women in Print II: Opportunities for Women's Studies Publication in Language and Literature.* New York: MLA, 1982.
A collection of essays on finding a publisher for feminist scholarship, divided into sections on establishment and alternative publishing.

Hawes, Gene R. *To Advance Knowledge: A Handbook on American University Press Publishing.* New York: American University Press Services, 1967.
Although written in a period of rapid university press expansion and optimism, this book remains an articulate exposition of the purpose and workings of university presses.

Johnson, William Bruce. "Ethical Procedures for Authors and Publishers." *Scholarly Publishing* 7, no. 3 (April 1976): 253–60.
A discussion of multiple submissions, rejections, refereeing, objectivity, and reviews.

Kerr, Chester. "One More Time: American University Presses Revisited." *Scholarly Publishing* 18, no. 4 (July 1987): 211–35.
Kerr reports on the state of university press publishing, a task he performed in 1949 and 1969 as well.

One Book/Five Ways: The Publishing Procedures of Five University Presses. Los Altos, Calif.: Kaufmann, 1978. Reprint ed. Chicago: University of Chicago Press, 1994.
An illustration of how five university presses would have handled the same manuscript, including sample contracts. Note, however, that the financial estimates and technology all date to the 1970s.

Parsons, Paul. *Getting Published: The Acquisitions Process at University Presses.* Knoxville: University of Tennessee Press, 1989.
A study of decision making at a university press.

Bibliography

Working with Your Editor

Mansbridge, Ronald. " 'My Publishers Are Terrible. . . .' " *Scholarly Publishing* 11, no. 2 (January 1980): 133–40.
Authors' complaints about copy editing, unanswered letters, and unkept promises, and advice on how to avoid the problems.
Stainton, Elsie Myers. "A Mixed Bag: Getting Along Together." *Scholarly Publishing* 9, no. 2 (January 1978): 149–58.
Further information on editor-author relations.
———— "Another Mixed Bag." *Scholarly Publishing* 9, no. 3 (April 1978): 219–30.
More advice on getting along with editors, with clues to their mysterious ways.

Legal Issues Generally

Goldfarb, Ronald L., and Gail E. Ross. *The Writer's Lawyer: Essential Legal Advice for Writers and Editors in All Media.* New York: Times Books, 1989.
A guide to First Amendment rights, copyright, libel, contracts, privacy, and other legal matters, with clear discussions of recent cases. It also includes a chapter on obtaining research material under the Freedom of Information Act.
Norwick, Kenneth P., and Jerry Simon Chasen. *The Rights of Authors, Artists, and Other Creative People: The Basic ACLU Guide to Author and Artist Rights.* 2d ed. Carbondale: Southern Illinois University Press, 1992.
Polking, Kirk, ed. *The Writer's Friendly Legal Guide: An Easy-to-Use, Accessible Guide to Copyright, Libel, Contracts, Taxes – Everything Writers Need to Know to Avoid Legal Hassles.* Cincinnati: Writer's Digest Books, 1989.

Contracts

Harvey, William B. "The Publishing Contract." *Scholarly Publishing* 8, no. 4 (July 1977): 299–314.
The standard contract's provisions, with comments.
Wincor, Richard. *Rights Contracts in the Communications Media.* New York: Law and Business, 1982.

Bibliography

An explanation of contracts directed at publishers but useful for authors.

Libel

Ashley, Paul P. *Say It Safely: Legal Limits in Publishing, Radio, and Television*. Seattle: University of Washington Press, 1976.
A readable and comprehensible explanation of libel law.
Sanford, Bruce W. *Libel and Privacy*. 2d ed. Englewood Cliffs, N.J.: Prentice Hall Law & Business, 1991.

Subventions

Ervin, John, Jr. "When a University Has No Press." *Scholarly Publishing* 8, no. 1 (October 1976): 17–21.
Possibilities for publishing assistance from the author's home university.
Germano, William P. "Helping the Local Faculty with Publication Support." *Scholarly Publishing* 15, no. 1 (October 1983): 11–16.
A survey of subsidy practice.
Smith, Datus C. "An Anatomy of Subsidies." *Scholarly Publishing* 6, no. 3 (April 1975): 197–206.
Explains the variety and importance of subsidies to publishers, as well as the problems they raise.
Smith, John Hazel. "Subvention of Scholarly Publishing." *Scholarly Publishing* 9, no. 1 (October 1977): 19–29.
A survey of university press subvention policies and practices.

Multiauthor Books

Black, Cyril E., and Carol Orr. " 'E Pluribus Unum': Symposia and Publishers." *Scholarly Publishing* 5, no. 2 (January 1974): 145–52.
Shortcomings of symposia, criteria for good ones, and publication thereof.
Horowitz, Irving Louis. "The Place of the Festschrift." *Scholarly Publishing* 21, no. 2 (January 1990): 77–83.
Useful ideas to improve the genre.

Bibliography

James, Rowena G. "Et Alia." *Scholarly Publishing* 2, no. 1 (October 1970): 59–65.
Helpful suggestions for early planning of multiauthor books.
Meyers, Jeffrey. "On Editing Collections of Original Essays." *Scholarly Publishing* 17, no. 2 (January 1986): 99–108.
A first-person account by the editor of three such volumes.

Textbooks

Arnold, David L. "Faculty Perceptions of the Scholarship and Utility of Writing College-Level Textbooks." *Publishing Research Quarterly* 9, no. 2 (Summer 1993): 42–54.
A study that surveyed faculty and department chairs to determine their evaluation of the scholarship required to write a textbook and the likelihood that such work will be rewarded.
Heilenman, L. Kathy. "Of Cultures and Compromises." *Publishing Research Quarterly* 9, no. 2 (Summer 1993): 55–67.
A discussion of the conflicts between the culture of academe and that of textbook publishers, with suggestions for resolving them.

Trade Books

Callenbach, Ernest. *Publisher's Lunch: A Dialogue Concerning the Secrets of How Publishers Think and What Authors Can Do About It.* Berkeley: Ten Speed Press, 1989.
A series of conversations between an acquiring editor and a prospective author in which each sets out typical concerns and attitudes.
Knauer, Joyce. "Scholarly Books in General Bookstores." *Scholarly Publishing* 19, no. 2 (January 1988): 79–85.
Although directed toward university press staff, this article is a useful description of the lay audience and the bookseller's role in reaching it.
Luey, Beth. "University Press Trade Books in the Review Media." *Scholarly Publishing* 25, no. 2 (January 1994): 84–92.
An evaluation of presses' effectiveness in getting their books reviewed in the popular media.

Bibliography

Agents

Dorn, Fred J. "Do Scholarly Authors Need Literary Agents?" *Scholarly Publishing* 14, no. 1 (October 1982): 79–86.
> Sometimes, and if so, how to find one and what to expect.

Literary Agents of North America. New York: The Associates, annual.
> A detailed guide.

Mechanics

Illustrations

Brouwer, Onno. "The Cartographer's Role and Requirements." *Scholarly Publishing* 14, no. 3 (April 1983): 231–42.
> How to work with a professional cartographer.

Council of Biology Editors. *Illustrating Science: Standards for Publication.* Bethesda, Md.: CBE, 1988.
> An excellent guide to preparing, submitting, and producing high-quality illustrations of all kinds. Despite its title, it is useful for authors in all disciplines.

Eakins, Rosemary, and Elizabeth Loving, eds. *Picture Sources U.K.* London: Macdonald, 1985.
> A subject guide to picture collections in the United Kingdom, including addresses, coverage, and procedures. It also contains a brief introduction to doing picture research.

Evans, Hilary and Mary. *Picture Researcher's Handbook: An International Guide to Picture Sources and How to Use Them.* 5th ed. New York: Van Nostrand Reinhold, 1992.

MacGregor, A. J. *Graphics Simplified: How to Plan and Prepare Effective Charts, Graphs, Illustrations, and Other Visual Aids.* Toronto: University of Toronto Press, 1979.
> A brief, clear book that delivers fully on its subtitle's promise.

Robl, Ernest H., ed. *Picture Sources.* 4th ed. New York: Special Libraries Association, 1983.
> Provides descriptions of 980 picture collections, including subject coverage, people to contact, and procedures.

Tufte, Edward R. *The Visual Display of Quantitative Information.* Cheshire, Conn.: Graphics Press, 1983.
> An elegant, detailed book about the use and abuse of graphs. More extensive than MacGregor; vital for the writer in statistical fields and fascinating for others.

———. *Envisioning Information.* Cheshire, Conn.: Graphics Press, 1990.
Another superb volume, this time with more color and discussions of electronic media.

Copyright and Permissions

Harman, Eleanor. "On Seeking Permission." *Scholarly Publishing* 1, no. 2 (January 1970): 188–92. Practical advice that emphasizes an early start.
Mesrobian, Arpena. "Banditry, Charity, or Equity." *Scholarly Publishing* 1, no. 2 (January 1970): 179–87.
An excellent, balanced explanation of publishers' permissions policies, with examples of requests granted and denied.
Patterson, L. Ray, and Stanley W. Lindberg. *The Nature of Copyright: A Law of Users' Rights.* Athens: University of Georgia Press, 1991.
Scarles, Christopher. *Copyright.* New York: Cambridge University Press, 1980.
A clear, brief guide to U.S. and British copyright.
Strong, William S. *The Copyright Book: A Practical Guide.* 4th ed. Cambridge: MIT Press, 1993.
The classic in the field.
Thatcher, Sanford G. "A Publisher's Guide to the New U.S. Copyright Law." *Scholarly Publishing* 8, no. 4 (July 1977): 315–33.
A useful, readable summary.
U.S. Library of Congress. Copyright Office. "How to Investigate the Copyright Status of a Work." Washington, D.C.: U.S. Government Printing Office, 1977.
An explanation of how to determine whether a work is still protected by copyright and who holds the rights.
———. "The Nuts and Bolts of Copyright." Washington, D.C.: U.S. Government Printing Office, 1978.
An official summary of the law.

Proofreading

Butcher, Judith. *Typescripts, Proofs and Indexes.* New York: Cambridge University Press, 1980.
A good, brief handbook.

Bibliography

Harman, Eleanor. "Hints on Proofreading." *Scholarly Publishing* 6, no. 2 (January 1975): 150–57.
Very practical, detailed suggestions.

Indexing

Butcher, Judith. *Typescripts, Proofs and Indexes*. New York: Cambridge University Press, 1980.
A good, brief handbook.
Mulvany, Nancy C. *Indexing Books*. Chicago: University of Chicago Press, 1994.
For the author who wants to learn more about the theory and practice of indexing.
Spiker, Sina. *Indexing Your Book: A Practical Guide for Authors*. Madison: University of Wisconsin Press, 1987.
Very helpful advice on how to compile an index.

Electronic Manuscripts and Electronic Publishing

Electronic Manuscripts

Association of American Publishers. *An Author's Primer to Word Processing*. New York, 1983.
A brief introduction to producing an electronic manuscript.
The University of Chicago Press. *Chicago Guide to Preparing Electronic Manuscripts for Authors and Publishers*. Chicago, 1987.
A guide to the practices of the University of Chicago Press that offers one possible procedure and typesetting code.

CD-ROM

Benford, Tom. *Welcome to CD-ROM*. New York: MIS Press, 1993.
Botto, Francis. *Multimedia, CD-ROM, and Compact Disc: A Guide for Users and Developers*. Wilmslow, Eng.: Sigma, 1992.
CD-ROM Market Place. Westport, Conn.: Meckler, annual.
Crane, Gregory. "'Hypermedia' and Scholarly Publishing." *Scholarly Publishing* 21, no. 3 (April 1990): 131–55.
A description of the conception and development of the Perseus Project, a CD-ROM for the study of classic Greek texts.

Bibliography

Helgerson, Linda W. *CD-ROM: Facilitating Electronic Publishing.* New York: Van Nostrand Reinhold, 1992.

Myers, Patti. *Publishing with CD-ROM.* Arlington, Va.: Meckler Publishing Corp. and the National Composition Association, 1986. A useful and accessible introduction to CD-ROM.

Nagy, Joel. *Apple CD-ROM Handbook: A Guide to Planning, Creating, and Producing a CD-ROM.* Reading, Mass.: Addison-Wesley, 1992.

Raimes, James. "Developing a CD-ROM." *Journal of Scholarly Publishing* 25, no. 2 (January 1994): 107–13.

Sherman, Chris, ed. *The CD-ROM Handbook.* New York: Intertext/ McGraw-Hill, 1994.

Internet

Braun, Eric. *The Internet Directory.* New York: Fawcett Columbine, 1994.

Directory of Electronic Journals, Newsletters, and Academic Discussion Lists. Washington, D.C.: Association of Research Libraries, annual.
This guide is published on 3½-inch disks, IBM compatible, in DOS Wordperfect format. Part 1 is a directory of electronic journals and newsletters. Part 2 is a directory of academic discussion lists.

Hahn, Harley, and Rick Stout. *The Internet Yellow Pages.* Berkeley: Osborne McGraw-Hill, 1994.

Maxwell, Christine, and Czeslaw Jan Grycz. *New Riders' Official Internet Yellow Pages.* Indianapolis: New Riders, 1994.

Newby, Gregory B. *Directory of Directories on the Internet: A Guide to Information Sources.* Westport, Conn.: Meckler, 1994.

Robbins, Robert J. "Biological Databases: A New Scientific Literature." *Publishing Research Quarterly* 10, 1 (Spring 1994): 5–27. A thorough, thoughtful analysis of the impact, advantages, and problems of scholarly database publishing.

Desktop Publishing, Design, and Camera-ready Copy

Lee, Marshall. *Bookmaking : The Illustrated Guide to Design, Production, Editing.* 2d ed. New York: Bowker, 1979.

Although this book provides more detail than an amateur designer needs, it is easy to follow.

Stokoe, William C. "Publishing from a Very Small Desk Top." *Scholarly Publishing* 20, no. 2 (January 1989): 67–71.
A brief account of the author's desktop publication of symposium proceedings.

Tibbo, Helen R. "Specifications for Camera-Ready Copy: Helping Authors Be More Productive." *Journal of Scholarly Publishing* 25, no. 4 (July 1994): 221–32.
What publishers need to tell authors so that they can produce camera-ready copy efficiently.

Williamson, Hugh. *Methods of Book Design: The Practice of an Industrial Craft*. 3d ed. New Haven: Yale University Press, 1983.
This book is meant for professional designers, but it does provide an introduction to the principles of book design.

Economics

Bailey, Herbert S., Jr. *The Art and Science of Book Publishing*. Austin: University of Texas Press, 1970.
A detailed analysis of the business side of publishing.

Broderick, John C. "The Cost of a Bad Book." *Scholarly Publishing* 18, no. 2 (January 1987): 83–88.
Broderick computes the costs of researching, writing, publishing, cataloguing, and storing a monograph.

Potter, Clarkson N. *Who Does What and Why in Book Publishing: Writers, Editors and Money Men*. Secaucus, N.J.: Birch Lane Press, 1990.
The last chapter is a very clear explanation of some publishing business practices.

Index

Index

T
?
12